Advance Praise for India's Financial Markets

"*India's Financial Markets* presents a clear and concise overview of the current climate in Indian financial markets. From the discussions of specific products and markets to the explanations of sensitive cultural issues and practices, it is a must read for anyone planning to do business in India. Furthermore, for those who are involved in international financial markets ex India, it is imperative that you have at least a basic understanding of how Indian markets will intersect with the global financial landscape. This book provides that insight."

  —**Patrick Catania**, Chairman, Asia West Group, Chicago, United States

"This detailed and insightful examination of the numerous facets of the financial services industry in one of the world's most promising emerging markets is a must-read for anyone with a serious interest in Indian finance. Drawing on their long years of experience, the authors also make a number of recommendations for improvements in the regulation and structure of Indian financial markets which both government and private sector participants would do well to consider."

  —**John P. Davidson**, Managing Director, Risk Governance Group, Citigroup, United States

"Knowledge and understanding of the Indian financial markets is vital to any financial services firm with global aspirations. Shah, Thomas and Gorham have provided an overview of these markets that is sure to become a standard reference for practitioners. Written with a clarity and pace that is to be applauded, *India's Financial Markets* tells you the how and why of investing in India and provides essential information on the markets, institutions and instruments that are integral to Indian financial services. By focusing on the markets themselves, it avoids extraneous detail and provides practical insights regarding trading, clearing and settlement, as well as the legal and regulatory framework of Indian finance. It will be an invaluable guide for practitioners and students alike."

  —**Richard G. DuFour**, Executive Vice President, Chicago Board Options Exchange, United States

"This is a great introductory book to Indian finance. It provides good and interesting insights into the Indian capital markets and a comprehensive understanding of the complexities involved in Indian finance. It will serve as a useful reference tool and you will find yourself coming back to the book time and again."

  —**Nimesh Kampani**, Chairman, JM Financial Group, United States

"*India's Financial Markets* is equally impressive in depth, content, simplicity and lucidity of writing style, and its treatment of critical core and emerging issues that influence Indian financial markets.

....a must-have for any financial analyst or economist located anywhere, who has a professional or personal interest in surveying, understanding, or investing in, the Indian economic and financial-market scene."
—**Percy S Mistry**, Chairman & CEO, Oxford International Group, India, from the *Foreword*

"For the reader looking for a high quality over-view of the Indian Financial System through the eyes of observers who have been intimately involved with the evolution of the modern Indian financial system, this is the perfect book. For each market it succinctly presents the current state of affairs using carefully researched datasets and also discusses problems and potential future directions in which the market may evolve."
—**Nachiket Mor**, President, ICICI Foundation, United States

"What I love most about this book is the insight the authors provide regarding how these markets really work. This is truly an insider's guide. There is no other work as current, complete and insightful. I really enjoyed this book."
—**Ravi Narain**, Managing Director, National Stock Exchange, India

"This book is the definitive introduction to Indian financial markets. It caters to the practitioner's interest in just the right amount of detail, while also providing insights based on analysis that will make this a delight for the discerning reader. It is a "must read" for anyone seeking to enter the financial sector in India, one of the fastest growing economies of the world. It is also a very useful introduction to Indian finance for anyone interested in understanding India."
—**Raghuram Rajan**, Eric Gleacher Distinguished Service Professor of Finance, Graduate School of Business, University of Chicago, United States

"*India's Financial Markets* is a compact treasury of practical insights on how India's financial economy really works. Anyone seeking to understand Indian financial and derivative markets will find no better source."
—**Nick Ronalds**, Executive Director, Futures Industry Association, Asia

"The investment world has been captivated by the phenomenal growth and returns from the Indian markets. What this book points out very eloquently is that this is just the beginning of the India story. Outside the equity markets, there are huge opportunities waiting to be tapped in currency, fixed income, commodities, and real estate. The authors have been thought leaders in the ongoing liberalization of the regulatory framework in the country and continue to play a key role in the transformation of the institutional landscape. This book lets you hear them relate the story. While such books typically tend to be marketed to foreign readers, I think this is a must read for every Indian banker."
—**Sayee Srinivasan**, Director, Asian Product & Market Development, CME Group Inc., India

India's Financial Markets

ELSEVIER

The Elsevier and IIT Stuart
Center for Financial
Markets Press

Stuart School of Business
ILLINOIS INSTITUTE OF TECHNOLOGY

Center for Financial Markets

Series Editor: Michael Gorham

The Elsevier and IIT Stuart Center for Financial Markets Press is a partnership between Elsevier Inc. and the IIT Stuart Center for Financial Markets at the Illinois Institute of Technology's Stuart School of Business. The partnership was created to publish a series of books pertaining to developments in global financial markets. The books explore the markets, institutions, and instruments that are integral to the global financial system. The titles in the series can take a country-specific approach as in *India's Financial Markets,* or an institutional approach across countries as in *The Dramatic, Global Transformation of the Modern Exchange* (forthcoming 2009). The goal of the Elsevier and IIT Stuart Center for Financial Markets Press is to publish books that provide a deep understanding of the workings of these wonderful and mysterious things called financial markets.

Series Editor Michael Gorham is Industry Professor and Director of the IIT Stuart Center for Financial Markets at Illinois Institute of Technology in Chicago. Mike serves on the board of directors for two exchanges—the CBOE Futures Exchange and the National Commodity and Derivatives Exchange of India. He serves on the Business Conduct Committees of the Chicago Mercantile Exchange and the National Futures Association, the editorial boards of the GARP Risk Review and of Futures Industry magazine. He is also regional director of the Global Association of Risk Professionals for Chicago. He served as the first director of the Commodity Futures Trading Commission's new Division of Market Oversight, a division of 100 economists, lawyers, futures trading specialists and others dedicated to the oversight of the nation's 12 futures exchanges. Earlier, he worked for 4 years as an economist at the Federal Reserve Bank of San Francisco and 18 years in various capacities at the Chicago Mercantile Exchange. He holds a BA in English literature from the University of Notre Dame, an MS in food and resource economics from the University of Florida and a Ph.D. in agricultural economics from the University of Wisconsin. He served for two years in the Peace Corps in Malawi, Africa.

India's
Financial
Markets

An Insider's Guide
to How the Markets Work

Ajay Shah
Susan Thomas
Michael Gorham

AMSTERDAM • BOSTON • HEIDELBERG
LONDON • NEW YORK • OXFORD
PARIS • SAN DIEGO • SAN FRANCISCO
SINGAPORE • SYDNEY • TOKYO

Stuart School of Business
ILLINOIS INSTITUTE OF TECHNOLOGY

Center for Financial Markets

7/16
LAD 2/16
tv 5

Elsevier
30 Corporate Drive, Suite 400, Burlington, MA 01803, USA
Linacre House, Jordan Hill, Oxford OX2 8DP, UK

Library of Congress Cataloging-in-Publication Data
Shah, Ajay.
    India's financial markets/Ajay Shah, Susan Thomas, Michael Gorham.
        p. cm.
    Includes bibliographical references and indexes.
    ISBN 978-0-12-374251-3 (hardcover)
1. Finance–India. 2. Financial institutions–India. 3. India–Economic conditions–1991-
I. Thomas, Susan, Dr. II. Gorham, Michael. III. Title.
    HG187.I4S53 2008
    332.10954–dc22

                                            2008012458

British Library Cataloguing-in-Publication Data
A catalogue record for this book is available from the British Library.

ISBN: 978-0-12-374251-3

For information on all Elsevier publications,
visit our Web site at *www.books.elsevier.com*

Printed in the United States of America
08 09 10 11 12   10 9 8 7 6 5 4 3 2 1

DEDICATIONS

This is dedicated to our parents.

—Ajay Shah and Susan Thomas

This is dedicated to Patti, Rachel, and David, three incredible human beings from whom I have derived much joy and wisdom, and to my old friend Bharat Jhunjhunwala who first introduced me to this mysterious and wonderful place called India.

—Michael Gorham

CONTENTS

FOREWORD

This book by Michael Gorham, Ajay Shah and Susan Thomas (the latter two being the foremost independent financial economists in India today) is INDISPENSABLE! No bookshelf that pretends to be sufficiently knowledgeable about Indian economics or finance at the beginning of the 21st century can afford to be without it. It is a must for any financial analyst or economist located anywhere who has a professional or personal interest in surveying, understanding, or investing in the Indian economic and financial-market scene.

It is of import for bankers (commercial and investment), capital market specialists, asset managers, investment operatives in sovereign wealth funds, drivers of mergers and acquisitions, portfolio managers, institutional portfolio as well as corporate direct foreign investors, private bankers, emerging market specialists, brokers in the global securities industry, exchange executives; *indeed for anyone with a professional or investment interest in knowing what makes Indian markets tick.*

I would recommend it for knowledgeable individuals (providing of course that they are sufficiently literate/numerate to have acquired post-graduate qualifications) wanting to acquire Indian assets to account for a part of their net worth. With India well on the way to becoming one of the world's four largest economic blocs (after EU, US/NAFTA and China) there can be few people in the world of finance without such an interest, whether established or nascent. That automatically implies a very large market for this book.

This volume is an equally important read for policy and decision-makers in the public or private domains with an institutional interest in investing in India now or in the near future. It is essential reading for senior officialdom (whether in national governments, multilateral agencies or foresight-focused policy institutes) and for accomplished academics in any top university with an India-focused program.

The canvas this book covers is breathtakingly ambitious in width and scope. It is equally impressive in depth, content, simplicity and lucidity of writing style, and its treatment of critical core and emerging issues that influence Indian financial markets. It is exhaustive in detailing how Indian financial markets have evolved, and how far they have come since 1992–1993. But it is equally honest and lucid about how much remains to be done before Indian finance can be equated fully with markets, instruments, institutions, regulation (in terms of policy, practice and architecture) standards and practices that apply in the best of the rest of the world. Astute readers would gain an immediate and definitive sense of exactly where Indian finance now lies—between being among the more developed emerging markets (way ahead of China but behind Brazil and Chile) but lagging much too far behind globally significant markets like Singapore.

Its contents cover the economic backdrop and context for India's financial markets; the evolution of its debt and equity markets for both public and privately issued securities; the role and emergence of Indian securities exchanges that are now among the most technologically proficient in the world; the belated emergence of its derivatives market and their subsequent lopsided development; the increasing role of realty and property investment in Indian financial markets; and a discussion of routes of entry into India (e.g., via Mauritius) for both portfolio and direct investors.

That far-from-exhaustive list is one indication (there are many others) why this book has to be bought (and quickly) by anyone with an interest in "financial India." It is likely to be useful both as an operating manual for practitioners with an India-focused interest as well as a reference work that will remain valuable for some time to come.

The only hope one can express after reading it is that the authors will be sufficiently diligent and mindful of the needs of their readership to update it every so often (at least every five years) to keep them (and their successors) abreast of how Indian finance continues to evolve and progress a pace.

Percy S. Mistry
Chairman, Oxford International Group
March, 2008

About Percy Mistry

Mr. Percy Mistry is Chairman of the Oxford International (OI) Group, comprising companies engaged in investment banking, asset management, private equity investment and corporate finance services in emerging markets. OI operates in Europe, North America, South and Southeast Asia, the Indian Ocean islands and Eastern & Southern Africa. Mr. Mistry is also an Advisor to the Executive Secretary of UN-ECA and has consulted for a number of international organizations (the UN, various multilateral development banks and the Commonwealth Secretariat) on work in Asia, Africa and the Caribbean. He helped the Commonwealth Secretariat establish the first Commonwealth Equity Fund; directed a study on Privatization in Commonwealth countries; assisted with its work on international finance; and evaluated the Secretariat's assistance to member countries with various international negotiations.

PREFACE

In early 2008, the top 3,000 firms in the Indian equity market had a market capitalization of $1.8 trillion. Thousands of foreign financial firms were invested in this market. In addition, there were substantial FDI, private equity and debt investments by foreigners in India. India had made the transition from being a peripheral issue to being part of the strategic thinking of all global financial firms. A sea change has taken place in a decade: for many international financial firms, India did not matter in 1998, but by 2008 it was essential to plan and execute an India strategy.

The individuals who would plan and execute an India strategy for a global financial firm are the prime target audience of this book.

We take a certain familiarity with stock, bond, currency and derivatives markets as a given. This is not an introductory finance textbook. From this foundation, we describe Indian finance, and offer insights into it. The attempt is to help a practitioner rapidly obtain a working familiarity, and genuine insight, into Indian finance.

Indian finance is cluttered with detail. A full and comprehensive description of Indian finance involves enormously more detail, particularly because the landscape is littered with detritus from decades of obsolete government policy. We have exercised judgment in focusing on the few issues that matter and will matter. Our hope is that this yields a compact book that conveys the essence of how Indian finance works, while not being burdened by extraneous facts. One key element of this effort has been to place key financial *markets* at the center of examination. This gives greater insight when compared with describing Indian finance through a classification scheme of classes of financial firms.

To add to the texture of the book, we have included a short photo essay on the "Architects of Indian Financial Markets." While time and space prevented us from including everyone who ought to be in such an essay, we hope that our effort will give readers a greater appreciation of the public and private sector players who have contributed significantly to the building of modern financial markets in India.

While the book is primarily aimed at practitioners, it can also be used in teaching in two ways. For courses on emerging market finance worldwide, it can support a segment on India. Courses on finance being taught in India could use a combination of mainstream finance textbooks coupled with this book to provide a treatment of India.

In writing this book, we benefited from extensive help from CMIE in terms of access to databases about firms and financial markets. We are grateful to Golaka Nath of CCIL for help on the currency and fixed income markets, and to Suprabhat Lala of NSE for help on the equity market. The real estate chapter greatly benefited from inputs from Rajesh Dokwal of Sampada Consultancy India; Manoj Motta of K. Raheja Corp, who promoted Inorbit Malls; Hemant Shah of Akruti Nirman; Professor K.N. Vaid of the Akruti Real Estate Institute of Research and Management and Madhu Khandelia of M2K Group, New Delhi. Thanks also to IIT Stuart student Jinesh Sutaria for research assistance.

CHAPTER 1

The Economy

1.1 OVERALL GROWTH EXPERIENCE

There is a new global interest in India's growth acceleration. What is perhaps well known is that from independence in 1947 up to 1979, GDP growth averaged 3.5%, which lagged behind many other economies. This was particularly disappointing given that the population was growing at 2.2% a year in that period. A per capita GDP growth of just 1.3% per year implied that the Indian GDP would double only once every 53 years. That in turn meant that mass poverty would get eliminated at a glacial pace in India.

However, from 1979 onward, GDP growth started accelerating, to a point in 2006 where trend GDP stood at 7%, with the previous few years having seen growth of more than 7%. Table 1.1 summarizes the experience with acceleration of growth over the decades.

This acceleration of GDP growth was accompanied by a deceleration of population growth. At the time of writing, it appeared that India had a trend GDP growth rate of 7.5% with a population growth rate of 1.5%, giving a per capita GDP growth rate of 6% a year, which induces a doubling every 11.5 years. This constitutes a dramatic improvement when compared with the starting point of a doubling every 53 years.

Table 1.2 shows the change in the structure of GDP.[1] The share of agriculture in GDP dropped sharply from 55.1% in 1950–1951 to 18.5% in 2006–2007. Industry has grown modestly from 15% to 26.6% over this same period. Services has grown dramatically from 29.6% to 54.9%; India appears to be "leapfrogging" to the structure of rich countries where services dominates.

---

[1] While India as a free nation was born in 1947, the statistical system for most major time-series has been in operation from 1951–1952 onward. The Indian fiscal year runs from April to March. As an example, the year 2003–2004 runs from 1 April 2003 through 31 March 2004.

Figure 1.1 shows quarterly GDP growth data for the recent five years. When compared with the information in Table 1.1, it is clear that GDP growth has dramatically increased in the period after 2002. On average, GDP growth after 2000 was 7.31%. From 2003 there has been a powerful rise in the growth rate to around 8%. One of the most interesting puzzles about India lies in deciphering this growth acceleration. Will India revert to lower growth rates of the order of

TABLE 1.1   How GDP Growth Accelerated After the 1970s

Decade	GDP growth
1950s	3.91
1960s	3.70
1970s	3.08
1980s	5.38
1990s	5.58
2000s	7.31

TABLE 1.2   Composition of Output (in %)

Year	Agriculture	Industry	Services
1950–51	55.1	15.0	29.6
1960–61	50.6	18.9	30.3
1970–71	44.3	22.1	33.6
1980–81	37.9	24.0	38.0
1990–91	31.4	25.6	42.7
2000–01	23.9	25.8	50.3
2006–07	18.5	26.6	54.9

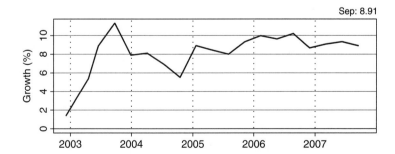

FIGURE 1.1   GDP Growth in Recent Years (quarterly data)

7%? Or have deeper changes taken place so that a growth of 8% and above will be sustained?

In this chapter, we seek to look behind the well-known facts about GDP growth, and obtain a better understanding of the strengths and weaknesses of India at the level of growth and macroeconomics. This forms a vital foundation for thinking about the role of Indian financial products and markets in a global strategy.[2]

1.2   UNDERSTANDING INDIA'S POST-INDEPENDENCE TRAJECTORY

The most important element of India's post-independence trajectory is the withdrawal into autarky and socialism, and the gradual recovery from this policy framework. Evolution of the merchandise trade to GDP ratio stood at 16.63%. From that point on, for many decades, economic policies emphasized autarky and government controls. This led to a decline in the trade to GDP ratio. Historically, some of the lowest values of this ratio were found in the 1969–1977 period (see Figure 1.2 and Table 1.3).

In parallel, from 1960 onward, evidence started appearing about how superior growth resulted in other economies when they started using outward-oriented and market-oriented growth strategies. A particularly outstanding example is South Korea, which started out behind India in 1960. There was

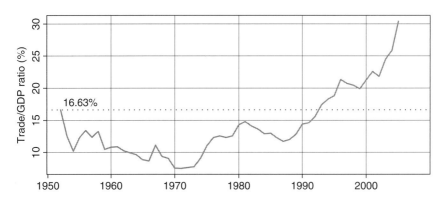

FIGURE 1.2   Evolution of the Merchandise Trade to GDP Ratio

[2]An excellent pair of big-picture lectures about India are Kelkar (2004b), which offers insights into the GDP growth acceleration in India after 2002, and Kelkar (2005) which looks forward at the policy challenges of India.

TABLE 1.3   Eight Political Regimes, 1947–2008

Administration	Period
I. Prime Ministers Nehru and Shastri: incipient socialism; severe adverse shocks in 1962, 1964, 1965 and 1966.	1947–1966
II. Prime Minister Indira Gandhi: sharp retreat toward autarky and socialism; breakdown of democracy for 20 months in 1976	1966–1977
III. Janata Party: first efforts in dismantling socialism	1977–1980
IV. Indira Gandhi and Rajiv Gandhi: domestic-focused liberalization	1980–1989
V. Confusion and currency crisis	1989–1991
VI. Prime Minister Narasimha Rao (Congress)—second liberalization—continued by Prime Ministers I. K. Gujral and Deve Gowda	1991–1998
VII. Prime Minister A. B. Vajpayee (NDA): strong progress on economic reforms	1998–2004
VIII. Prime Minister Manmohan Singh (UPA): difficulties in reform	2004–

an increasing awareness among intellectuals and policymakers in India by the late 1970s that mistakes in economic policy strategy had been made, particularly the accentuation of government control of the economy that came about under Prime Minister Indira Gandhi from 1966 to 1977. Scholars such as Jagdish Bhagwati, T. N. Srinivasan and Anne Krueger played a significant role in deciphering the difficulties of the prevailing policy framework, and arguing that a fundamental change of course was required.

GDP growth started accelerating from 1979 onward, reflecting the economic reforms introduced by the Janata Party which won the general elections in 1977. These reforms were greatly broadened in the 1980s by Prime Ministers Indira Gandhi and Rajiv Gandhi, assisted by an IMF program in 1981. The reforms of the late 1970s and 1980s were very important in terms of easing entry barriers in the domestic market, and in reducing price controls. These elements of liberalization helped accelerate growth, which gave confidence in market-oriented policies and paved the way for further progress in economic policy thinking. However, the reforms of this period did not emphasize globalization: the trade to GDP ratio actually fell for much of the 1980s.

From the viewpoint of an acceleration in the trend of GDP growth, 1979 is the break date: the trend in GDP growth averaged 3.5% prior to 1979 and steadily accelerated thereafter. However, on the critical issue of when economic globalization started in India, the break date is 1991, when far-reaching reforms took place in the aftermath of a currency crisis and an IMF program (Bhagwati, 1993). The distinguishing feature of the 1991 reforms, and the stance of economic policy after that, has been integration into world economy. India got back to its 1952 levels of the trade to GDP ratio (16.63%) in 1993. China had that level of trade to GDP ratio (16.63%) by 1980, which suggests that the Indian reform effort lagged the Chinese effort by 13 years. It is ironic that, in many respects, communist China was able to break free of autarkic and socialist policies earlier and more effectively than democratic India.

Two key facts about the trade to GDP time-series are: (1) The lowest value of trade to GDP was 7.5%, and (2) in 1952, the ratio was more than twice as high at 16.63%. The most recent value was four times bigger at 30.41%. Thus, the trade to GDP ratio plunged by a factor of 2.2 times in the period of socialism. But it has recovered by a factor of 4 times thereafter.

The economy rapidly responded to the reforms of the early 1990s, with sharp growth in manufacturing exports and an impressive investment boom with the construction of factories. For the first time, growth above 7% was observed for three consecutive years.

The National Democratic Alliance (NDA) coalition, which ruled from 1999–2004, made important progress on economic policy. The NDA started out in a very difficult period, with the recession of 1998–2001. However, after that, the economy responded well to these reforms by bouncing back to the highest-ever rates of growth. There was an emphasis on privatization, creation of infrastructure, equity market reforms, considerable reduction of trade barriers (Panagariya, 2005), a steady pace of easing capital controls, and long-term structural reform on issues such as the fiscal system and the replacement of the civil service pension by the New Pension System. The clarity and pace of reforms slowed down with the UPA which came to power in 2004. Despite weak progress on reforms, the energies unleashed by economic reforms have so far remained effective at delivering excellent growth rates.

1.3   INTERPRETING THE GROWTH EXPERIENCE

As is well known in growth economics, changes in GDP respond to changes in labor, changes in capital and changes in productivity.[3] On all three counts, India has fared well in the post–1980 period. Private final consumption was above 90% of GDP until 1970, and the savings rate only started creeping up to impressive numbers after 1980. The fraction of the working population (ages 15–60) also started improving from the late 1970s onward. Finally, from 1977 onward, economic policy has been shifting away from socialist positions, which

---

[3] There is a considerable literature which engages in "growth accounting" with Indian data seeking to obtain estimates of total factor productivity (TFP) growth. Such calculations are plagued by difficulties of measurement both of manhours of labor and capital stock adjusted for inflation and depreciation. The Indian statistical system is particularly weak on both these issues. Our effort here consists of obtaining limited insights using the two data elements—GDP and the number of workers—which are relatively trustworthy.

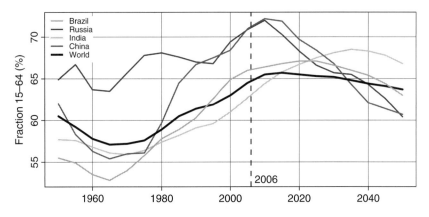

FIGURE 1.3   Fraction of Population, Ages 15–64

has helped in increasing productivity. All three factors combine in explaining the acceleration of growth from the late 1970s onward.

1.3.1   Drivers of Growth

This section discusses the few most important factors that will drive growth in the coming decade. The major factors at work can be classified into "pre-existing strengths" as opposed to "new factors."

The pre-existing strengths include political stability, quality and quantity of labor, a common law tradition, strong institutions such as the judiciary and the election commission, and strong domestic consumption. These strengths were always present, but a deficient policy environment led to a poor translation of these strengths into growth. The new factors at work are a less restrictive State, a high quality and quantity of capital, strong private corporations, improvements in infrastructure, and globalization.

Labor

It is conventional to focus on citizens between ages 15 and 64 as "the working population," and to define the proportion of the population in this age range as a workforce ratio. As Figure 1.3 shows, India will be the last large country in the world to experience the demographic transition.[4] Within a few years, the Chinese workforce ratio will peak, and from there on, the process of ageing will

---

[4]The numerical values for the graph are sourced from *World Population Prospects Database: The 2004 Revision* by the United Nations Population Division. In all cases, the "Medium" scenario is used.

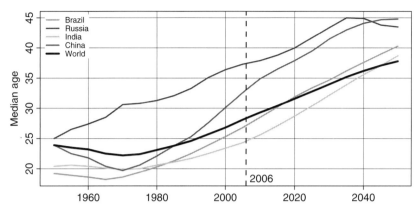

FIGURE 1.4   Median Age

act against Chinese GDP growth. In India's case, the outlook for a few decades involves a rising workforce ratio and thus accelerating GDP growth. A related story is visible in the median age (see Figure 1.4).

The second change taking place in the labor force is equally significant for economic growth. This concerns the *quality* of the labor force. Every year, the human capital of the stock of labor goes up, through gains in education and (more important) gains in experience. Every year, a cohort at age 60 leaves the labor force, while everyone at younger ages adds one year of experience. The loss of human capital of the retiring cohort is smaller given the relative obsolescence of their knowledge.

While the formal educational system suffers from numerous weaknesses, there is an active process of learning by doing in the context of a globalized and competitive economy. As an example, IT is a highly skill-intensive area where Indian universities are very weak. Yet, India has become an IT superpower with over 1.5 million IT professionals. This has been achieved through a combination of private sector education companies, such as NIIT or Aptech, and on-the-job learning. This is likely to be the mechanism through which human capital is created in the future also.

While the formal education system is weak, significant progress on certain basics is taking place. High school examinations are difficult by world standards. There is an increasing shift toward private schools, where market forces exert pressure on schools for performance.

A self-reported knowledge of English serves as an interesting measure. English is spreading through improvements in schools, and through the world of work. An analysis of a household survey database named IRES, released by the Ministry of Finance and ADB, shows that nearly 40% of the young earners—in the age group 20 to 30—have at least a rudimentary ability to read English.[5]

Incremental workers, incremental education and incremental experience of the existing stock of workers: these add up to a powerful fundamental driver for high economic growth.

Alongside these remarkable features of the labor force, there is a parallel phenomenon of slow growth of organized sector employment, which roughly corresponds to employment in large firms. In the period from 1994 to 2001, even though output by large firms rose dramatically, employment actually dropped slightly. This appears to be partly a response to restrictive labor laws, which gives firms a strong incentive to stay small, and thus avoid the strictures of labor law. Production is often organized in complex ways where a large firm contracts out parts of production to numerous small firms, each of which is efficient in labor contracting by avoiding labor laws. This tends to exert an upward bias on the size of the "informal sector."

1.3.2 CAPITAL

The evidence points to a continually positive growth in both the quantity as well as the quality of capital available in the domestic economy.

Quantity of Capital

The quantity of capital is determined by domestic household saving, public sector saving and the current account deficit. Recent trends suggest that in the years to come, the savings rate will go up; substantially larger amounts of capital are likely to be deployed into the growth process. The factors at work in their evolution are

Indian demographic factors will increase the savings rate: Children and the elderly tend to save less; saving is the highest in the working years. Using NCAER survey data, we find that in 1994–1995, when the overall savings rate was 20.3%, the savings rate dropped to 16.9% when the head of household was under age 30 (Pradhan *et al.*, 2003). The highest savings rate, at 23%, was found in households where the head of household was 50 to 60 years old. In the case of urban households, these effects were more pronounced, with a savings rate of just 7.8% when the head of household was under age 30.

---

[5]A note of caution must be added: all measurement of literacy is weak. A man who "claims to read English" can probably slowly read one letter at a time. The Pratham database shows that in 2007, 20% of *rural* children between grade 3 and grade 5 had a minimal ability to read English.

Hence, the demographic projections which lead us to believe that India will have a bigger fraction of the population in the age group from 15 to 64 also lead us to expect higher savings rates in the future. Further, keeping household characteristics the same, a larger number of children would induce higher consumption, so declining fertility is likely to induce higher saving.

Higher income will increase the savings rate: A second factor that is at work is the sheer GDP growth. NCAER data shows that low income households have extremely low savings rates. Remarkably enough, only 1.9% of all saving (as of 1994–1995) was done by households with below-median income, which had 21.9% of all income. We see that the poorest 80% of the population account for half the income, and that this group accounts for 23.9% of total savings. As a rough approximation, we may say that significant savings behavior only took place in the top quartile of the income distribution of 1994–1995. Households in the top decile have a much higher savings rate (35.8%) compared with the general population.

Economic growth steadily pushes households above the absolute income threshold required to be in the top quartile by income distribution as of 1994–1995. Every year, a larger number of households graduates into the income group where saving will commence. The bottom 30% of the 1994–1995 income distribution has near-zero or negative saving. GDP growth would shrink this set of zero-savings households. The top quartile of the 1994–1995 income distribution has high savings rates. GDP growth pushes more households into this set of high-savings households. Through this process, holding other aspects of the environment of the household constant, high GDP growth rates are likely to generate a steady escalation of the savings rate.

A bigger current account deficit would help: India has made progress on the easing of capital controls, and in the future it is likely that there will be greater capital account convertibility. This further eases constraints on the quantity of capital: firms with good projects are readily able to finance them using global capital also.

Public sector saving may improve: The Fiscal Responsibility and Budgetary Management (FRBM) Act obligates the central government to eliminate the revenue deficit by 2008–2009, and to contain the fiscal deficit below 3% of GDP by this date. Similar fiscal responsibility efforts are also underway at state governments. These are likely to yield further improvement in public sector saving, though in the immediate future there are important risks to achieving the FRBM targets.

The sheer numbers involved above are larger than has ever been seen in the past. A 30% savings rate applied to a $1 trillion GDP implies that there is a flow of annual saving of $300 billion, a certain fraction of which flows into the financial system.

Quality of Capital Allocation

The financial sector controls the efficiency with which incremental capital formation is converted into incremental GDP. India has fared unusually well, when compared with other emerging markets, in fostering a well functioning financial sector.

Many countries all over the world have experienced problems with banking. Difficulties in banking escalate into major macroeconomic problems when the banking system is itself large, when compared with GDP. In India today, bank deposits are just 48% of GDP, and net nonperforming assets are just 2.3% of assets. Indian banking has many problems (Hanson, 2003; Mor and Chandharaseker, 2005). However, the key feature is that banking is small enough that difficulties in banking cannot derail the economy. India has not solved the problems of banking; rather, the problems of banking have been bypassed by shifting into a stock market dominated financial system. India differs from most developing countries by having the Anglo-Saxon framework with large and liquid public securities markets, and by having bank deposits which are relatively small when compared with GDP (Thomas, 2006a). This is illustrated in Table 1.4 (from Sheng, 2006), which shows international data for bank deposits as a percent of GDP. The Indian value of bank deposits to

TABLE 1.4 Bank Deposits to GDP – An International Comparison

Country	Deposits/GDP	
	1990	2004
China	75.6	177.8
India	31.4	51.1
Indonesia	29.8	38.9
Korea	32.6	68.8
Malaysia	52.1	88.7
Singapore	74.3	104.4
Thailand	56.8	79.7
Japan	100.0	120.5
Germany	53.8	96.7
UK	87.8	115.0
US	59.6	58.8
Europe	42.1	86.8

GDP—of 51%—is the lowest in the table apart from Indonesia. However, India is unlike the Anglo-Saxon model in that firms have low leverage. Firms in India thus find it difficult to source debt either from the banks or from the bond market.

The specialization appears to be one in which banks focus on payments services and debt financing for households (such as home loans) while securities markets service the needs of large firms where equity financing dominates. Banks have retooled themselves, shifting away from a corporate loans focus to a personal loans focus. Personal loans have risen dramatically from 1% of GDP in 1999–2000 to 5.98% of GDP in 2004–2005 (an annual growth rate of 58.34% over this period). The bulk of this growth has been in housing and in "other loans" which includes credit cards.

This distinction has been made possible by a remarkable revolution in the stock exchanges in terms of a completely new design replacing traditional notions about how the market should be organized. In 2005, India's National Stock Exchange (NSE) and Bombay Stock Exchange (BSE) were the third largest and fifth largest exchanges in the world, measured by the number of trades.

The competitive speculative process on the stock market is now the dominant force shaping access to capital for a firm or an industry, which has taken over the decisions of how capital is allocated in the country. The total turnover on the equity spot market plus the equity derivatives market adds up to roughly twice that of GDP. Trading is dominated by small local economic agents. See Tables 1.5 and 1.6 for turnover and market capitalization.

Other parts of the traditional financial sector have been opening up as well. The insurance sector, which used to be a monopoly of public sector companies, has been opened up, albeit with a cap on foreign ownership at 26%. A new frontier in financial sector development lies in pension sector reforms (Dave, 2006; Shah, 2006). From 1998 to 2003, an intensive effort took place to brainstorm alternative strategies in pension reforms, and to design an institutional architecture that would be uniquely well suited to solve the unique problems of the Indian setting. This led to important cabinet decisions in 2003 which are now being implemented.

The basic thrust of these reforms is to build a defined contribution pension system, where workers would get a range of investment choices and fund managers. Centralized recordkeeping infrastructure is envisaged, which gives scale economies, keeps down transactions costs, and maximizes the contestability of the market for fund management services. This new pension system has been mandatory for all new recruits to the central government from January 1, 2004, onward. For one generation, this will involve transition costs because the government will be paying contributions to new recruits while paying pensions to older workers.

TABLE 1.5   A Statistical Picture of the Equity Market (December 2006)

Parameter	Units	Value
The CMIE Cospi Index		
Number of firms		2,563
Market capitalization	Billion USD	797
P/E		20.20
Spot + Derivatives turnover	Billion USD (2005)	1,294
Share of institutional investors in turnover	% (2005)	10.3
Average trade size on NSE spot (2005)	USD	522
Correlation between Nifty and S&P 500	(2005 and 2006)	0.3804

TABLE 1.6   Trends in CMIE Cospi Market Capitalization

	CMIE Cospi Market Capitalization		
Date	Trillion INR	Billion USD	% to GDP
March 2000	9.56	219	53.35
March 2001	5.30	113	27.46
March 2002	7.05	144	33.62
March 2003	5.51	116	24.42
March 2004	11.87	274	46.68
March 2005	16.82	386	59.14
March 2006	30.27	680	
March 2007	35.36	803	

1.3.3   STRONG PRIVATE CORPORATIONS

When compared with other emerging markets, India is unusual in having burgeoning entrepreneurship and vibrant corporations. Firms are more likely to be publicly traded and tend to have relatively good corporate governance. Since India is a developing country, opportunities for entrepreneurship are found in most industries. This is unlike the pattern seen in mature market economies, where an industry is characterized by steep entry barriers unless a technological or other dislocation takes place. There is a continuous flow of projects where entrepreneurs are doing new things in mundane areas such as food processing, retail, restaurants, etc. A new private equity industry is in place, with fairly substantial investments being deployed at incubating these projects.

The popular indexes focus on the most actively traded 30–50 firms. (see Figure 1.5). A much broader view is taken by the CMIE Cospi[6] index. This index defines the "broad market" as firms where trading takes place on at least 66% of trading days, and reflects the set of firms who have access to equity financing from the public market. The access to a robust equity market for financing has shaped up as the most important source of financing for invest-ment. The CMIE Cospi club seems to have grown in number a great deal, and now has roughly 2,800 firms. The dips in the graph reflect fluctuations of market liquidity, where some firms fail to achieve trading on 66% of trading days.

In Figure 1.6, the black line shows the market capitalization of the "broad market" (as defined above). The gray line shows non-food credit of banks to

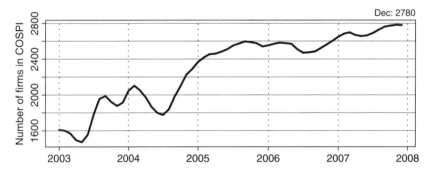

FIGURE 1.5   Number of Firms in the "Broad Market"

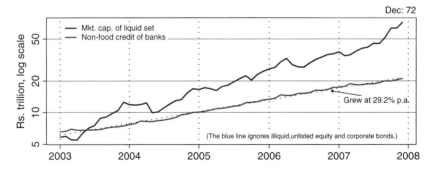

FIGURE 1.6   Banks and Markets as Sources of Funding for Firms

[6] CMIE is the Centre for Monitoring Indian Economy, a private firm that has collected, standardized and sells a database on Indian firms which goes back to 1987.

individuals and firms. It highlights the domination of equity financing. While non-food credit has grown very strongly in the recent period, such growth is not sustainable because it has to ultimately grow in line with (a) bank deposits and (b) equity capital raised by banks.

In December 2005, Credit Lyonnais and Asian Corporate Governance Association put out a scorecard with their subjective assessment about the quality of corporate governance in Asia based on five areas: rules and regulations, enforcement, political and regulatory environment, international accounting and auditing standards, and "a nation's corporate governance culture." Out of a maximum of 100, the scores were Singapore (70), Hong Kong (69), India (61), Malaysia (56), Taiwan (52), South Korea (50), Thailand (50), Philippines (46), China (44), Indonesia (37). This shows India lagging behind Singapore and Hong Kong, but doing better than many other Asian countries.

Another ranking for corporate governance in Asia is drawn from McGee (2008), who reports the following scores (out of 100): India (83.6%), Malaysia (77.3%), Korea (76.4%), Pakistan (75.5%), Thailand (72.7%), Philippines (64.5%), Indonesia (60%) and Vietnam (50.1%). In the class of these eight country case studies, India was rated as having the best corporate governance.[7]

1.3.4   INFRASTRUCTURE AND THE INDIAN SERVICES STORY

India has traditionally had weaknesses in the physical infrastructure of transportation. This has had a considerable impact on manufacturing.[8] As the World Bank's 2006 *Development Policy Review* remarks, "In a desert, one should find camels not hippopotamuses. If rain is scarce, one should find animals adapted to the scarcity of water." With the "infrastructure deficit," the successful industries and firms are likely to be infrastructure camels. Due to these limitations, manufacturing growth has been weak. Manufacturing exports growth, with growth rates ranging between 20% and 30%, has substantially lagged behind Chinese exports growth rates. On the other hand, export of services, which is parsimonious in terms of infrastructure requirements, has been a natural area for India to succeed in.

In the early 1990s, problems of transportation and communications were high on the minds of policymakers, particularly in the light of heightened competition local firms faced, owing to reduced protectionism. The path chosen involved competitive markets in infrastructure, with private sector production,

---

[7] On the subject of corporate governance in India, see Sarkar and Sarkar (2000).

[8] A second factor, which has strongly influenced manufacturing, has been the taxes paid for moving goods within the country.

under a framework of sound regulation. This has been a difficult path to take, an observation that has been found in numerous other countries. There are subtle difficulties in finding the right policy mix, the right "rules of the game" which provide sound incentives to private firms to produce adequate quantities of these goods, while at the same time avoiding monopolistic profit rates. As an example, electricity generation in California has been bedeviled by problems, lurching between blackouts on the one hand and supernormal profits by utilities on the other.

For many years, there was universal pessimism about Indian infrastructure. From 1991 onward, State investment in infrastructure slowed down considerably, but the new policy framework had not fallen into place. However, by 2007, important progress was being made on telecom, roads, ports, railways and aviation. The weakest links are now electricity and urban infrastructure.

In *telecom*, revolutionary gains have been obtained by injection of competition from foreign and private vendors, under the framework of an independent regulator. Growth rates in excess of 30% per year have been observed for over a decade. India is a rare country where the two major technologies for mobile telephony—GSM and CDMA—are locked in competitive battle, with customers reaping the rewards of this competition. Some kinds of telephony services are now the cheapest in the world.

By the late 1990s, revolutionary progress was visible in telecom, which helped to ignite exports of IT services and IT-enabled services. These involved firms which could expend modest coping costs, such as installation of generators, in order to overcome gaps in other infrastructure, such as electricity distribution, and achieve global sales by harnessing Indian labor. The decisive input required for these "infrastructure camels" was telecom, where policies fell into place from the late 1990s onward.

In the area of *roads*, the National Democratic Alliance (NDA) initiated a project to build new highways, which increased the sustained mean velocity from 30 kph to 80 kph. These new highways are built under the aegis of a new agency called National Highway Authority of India (NHAI). The new highways typically involve tolling and private developers. Highway construction has involved learning new institutions, revenue sources, and contracting mechanisms.[9]

In the area of *ports*, port operations have been increasingly contracted out to international firms who have specialized expertise in this subject. The state of Gujarat stands out as having created a competitive environment in ports, with 41 ports studding its coastline.

The impact of improved infrastructure upon growth works through two channels. Reduced transactions costs help increase international trade, and thus

---

[9]See http://ajayshahblog.blogspot.com/2005/12/indias-new-highways.html.

deliver gains from trade. But equally important, improvements in infrastructure help growth by harnessing "internal gains from trade" within the country. The classical gains-from-trade story is being repeated *within* the country, when firms 1,000 km apart are able to trade for the first time, thanks to the low transactions costs.[10]

To take a concrete example, it is now possible for a factory to be located 400 km away from the port of Jawaharlal Nehru Port Trust (JNPT)[11] where it is able to recruit extremely inexpensive labor. Raw materials and finished goods can be moved to JNPT within five to six hours using the new NHAI roads. The services of an international port management company like P&O can be utilized at JNPT. The entire movement of raw materials and finished goods can be managed through a global IT system, using broadband connectivity at the factory and connectivity all the way along the road with CDMA/GSM communication coupled with GPS location tracking. These developments have induced an entirely new phase: it is now possible to produce in India while being integrated into global production chains. This makes possible the labor arbitrage of buying labor at the low wages of a location 400 km away from JNPT while selling goods in the world market.

Progress through institutional transformation is taking place in all aspects of infrastructure. The pace of progress is heterogeneous, but there is pressure from the electorate demanding better infrastructure and a new willingness on the part of the political class to utilize institutional innovations. At the same time, important problems continue to afflict infrastructure. User charges continue to be inadequate, and resource constraints have hence often slowed down the pace at which infrastructure projects are done, even in areas where institutional problems have been resolved. As an example, in telecom, there is no issue with user charges, and enormous investments have been financed through debt and equity issuance of telecom companies. But in an area like roads, inadequate user charges continue to induce slower investment than is required and is now feasible thanks to institutional innovations. The present system of road user charges will only generate around Rs.1.6 trillion or $34.5 billion (totally) over the next decade, leaving a funding gap of Rs.1 trillion or $21.6 billion *per year* given existing investment targets and maintenance requirements.

The electricity sector has been bedeviled by political problems in establishing sound distribution companies which are able to combat theft. In the capital city of New Delhi, more than a third of the electricity that is purchased by the distribution companies is stolen.

---

[10]See http://www.mayin.org/ajayshah/MEDIA/1997/gt-internal.html.

[11]JNPT is near Bombay.

Urban infrastructure has made negligible progress in the last twenty years, primarily owing to difficulties in the way local government is organized, and conflicts of interest between the state (i.e., province) as an administrative unit and the requirements of cities. Chinese investments in infrastructure continue to outpace those being put in by India every year. As an example, Chinese annual expenditures for highways continue to be roughly 10 times larger than India's annual expenditures.

Looking forward, the gap between India and China on labor law, on infrastructure and on the VAT regime is likely to persist. China will continue to have an important edge on industries that intensively require cheap labor coupled with top quality infrastructure (i.e., large amount of movement of low-value goods). India will continue to have an edge on infrastructure camels: industries which require smaller movement of goods, and emphasize high-skill value addition by employees. On the margin, incremental improvements in infrastructure will improve the profitability of these infrastructure camels and make it possible for them to creep into broader areas.

This reasoning is consistent with the high growth rates of manufacturing exports, particularly skill-intensive manufacturing exports such as automobile exports or diamond polishing, that have been observed in the last decade. A simple services versus manufacturing story would have implied that the growth of services would have generated a strong currency which would have held back manufacturing exports growth. But this has not happened. This suggests that strong productivity growth in manufacturing has been taking place, and has overcome the strength of the currency.

The share of manufacturing in GDP has grown modestly, to a level of 25% of GDP. A unique feature of Indian growth is the rise of a large services sector at relatively low levels of per capita GDP. Some economists believe that a manufacturing stage is an essential way station in the process of economic development. So far, India appears to be successfully contradicting this position, with high economic growth and a small manufacturing sector.[12]

1.3.5 GLOBALIZATION

One of the most important phenomena about the Indian economy in the 1990s was the growth of international trade. We see striking changes in policy in the period following 1991–1992. India has engaged in unilateral removals of barriers to trade, and this process has been assisted by WTO obligations. Capital

[12]Sometimes, concerns are expressed about reliability of statistics on services, where it is felt that services data is grossly overstated. Recent explorations of these questions (Gordon and Gupta, 2004) suggest that such fears are overstated.

controls have been eased, giving greater financial integration. At present, there is *de facto* convertibility for firms, foreign institutional investors, non-resident Indians, and inbound FDI. A complex system of capital controls inhibits global diversification by local households, transactions in the Indian market by global individuals and debt inflows.

This process of globalization has far-reaching ramifications for accelerating GDP growth, by giving gains from trade, by giving dynamic benefits in terms of improved competition and flow of knowledge into the country, and by improving the allocative functions of finance.

Table 1.7, adapted from Shah and Patnaik (2007a), summarizes India's globalization. While GDP, measured in USD, grew at a compound rate of 9.63% per year, gross flows on the current account and the capital account grew much faster. Owing to an extensive program of trade liberalization, and services exports made possible by telecommunications technology, gross flows on the current account rose at a compound rate of 15.79%. Similarly, through a more modest easing of capital controls, gross flows on the capital account grew at a slower rate of 14.57% per year. Together, gross flows across the border rose from 47.22% of GDP to 90.65% of GDP. This constitutes a substantial change in the degree of globalization of the economy.

Even though a complex combination of capital controls is in place, the capital account is fairly open for FDI, and for foreign institutional investors. In addition, there is a strong relationship between a large and open current account and capital controls. The needs of firms engaged in trade exerts increased pressure to ease many capital controls. Once there is a large current account, capital controls become increasingly porous (Patnaik and Vasudevan, 2000). The

TABLE 1.7 India's Integration with the World, 1992–93 to 2005–06

	Billion USD			Percent to GDP	
	1992–93	2005–06	Growth (%)	1992–93	2005–06
Net capital flows	5.16	24.69	12.79	2.36	3.41
Loans	0.41	4.74	20.69	0.19	0.65
Banking capital	3.83	1.37	−7.58	1.75	0.19
FDI (inbound)	0.32	7.69	27.86	0.14	1.06
FDI (outbound)	0.00	−1.96		0.00	−0.27
Portfolio equity	0.24	12.49	35.44	0.11	1.72
Rupee debt servicing	−0.88	−0.57		−0.40	−0.08
IMF	1.29	0.00		0.59	0.00
Other	−0.04	0.93		−0.02	0.13
Metric of integration	103.25	657.04	15.30	47.22	90.65
Current account	59.93	403.13	15.79	27.41	55.62
Capital account	43.32	253.91	14.57	19.81	35.03

current account can be used to implement cross-border capital flows through over or under invoicing, lags in payments and trade credit. Significant movement toward *de facto* convertibility has taken place across these elements of openness. Thus, net capital flows grew by 12.79% per year. The outstanding feature of this increase appears to be a profound change in the *composition* of capital flows. Official flows receded, replaced by a dramatic growth in FDI and portfolio equity. A major new development is the emergence of $1.96 billion of *outbound* FDI by Indian companies who are becoming multinationals.

The high growth of services exports has been based on two distinct components. In the earlier period, invisibles revenues were primarily obtained through remittances from Indian workers working abroad. Recent years of improvements in telecommunications mean that many services, which were previously non-tradeable, could now be produced as part of global production chains. Export-oriented services production ranges from high volume production of low-end services such as accounting, all the way to services that require highly specialized and high-wage staff, such as research and development. For example, research laboratories located in India by major US companies have filed for over 1,000 patents with the US Patent and Trademark Office.

The high degree of public awareness about India's success in these IT-enabled services exports has led to a widespread perception that India is faring extremely well in services exports. But this is matched by another perception that India has failed in obtaining growth in manufacturing exports. This perception is inconsistent with the high growth which is *also* seen with merchandise exports. Exports of transportation equipment (both finished goods and components, put together) serve as a useful measure of how manufacturing exports is faring. In the recent period, growth rates of consistently above 30% are visible (see Figure 1.7). These growth rates contradict the simple caricature of India being weak in manufacturing and strong in services.

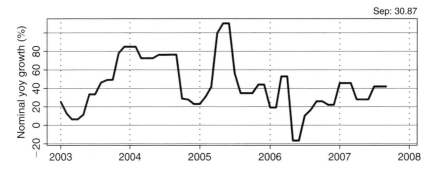

FIGURE 1.7   Transportation Equipment Exports Growth (smoothed)

1.3.6 Consumption at Domestic Households

Sound data for most kinds of consumer goods does not exist. Most retailing is done by small firms where no data is released. Large quantities of durables such as air conditioners are assembled by small workshops across the country, and substantial "gray market" sales of imported consumer durables takes place. In order to obtain evidence about growth in consumption, and the rise of the middle class, we need to look at products where imports are negligible and small workshops are not important producers.

One such industry is the automobile industry. Table 1.8 shows the evolution of two-wheelers (motorcycles and motor-scooters) and cars. "Estimated stock" is the sum of sales of the previous seven years, which makes a conservative assumption that a vehicle more than seven years old is not on the roads.[13] In both cases, the growth of units sold substantially exceeds GDP growth. They are "superior goods" with income elasticities greater than one.

The same data also gives us crude estimates about the number of middle class households. We may assume there is no more than one car or one two-wheeler per household. In this case, there were perhaps 37 million households (comprising 189 million people) who owned a motorized vehicle in 2005. This is consistent with the idea that there is a large middle class, and that it is doubling in size every five to seven years.

In an ideal world, households should be able to smooth consumption across the business cycle so that consumption is smoother than GDP. Empirical

TABLE 1.8   Motor Vehicle Sales, 1991 to 2005

	1991	2005	Growth rate (%)	Time-to-double (years)
	(million)			
Two-wheelers				
One-year sales	1.81	6.57	10.46	7.0
Estimated stock	10.10	32.50	8.71	8.3
Cars				
One-year sales	0.18	0.98	14.05	5.3
Estimated stock	1.05	4.85	12.14	6.0

[13]From 1991 to 2005, the quality of two-wheelers and cars has gone up substantially. In 1991, the Maruti 800 dominated the market. By 2005, there was a wealth of alternatives, all of which are bigger and better than the Maruti 800 model.

evidence on the cyclical properties of consumption is not available. However, we may hazard some conjectures. Consumption smoothing requires financial depth through possession of liquid wealth such as securities, and it requires credit access. At present, most households lack both kinds of tools for consumption smoothing. Hence, it is likely that consumption in India is more sensitive to the business cycle than in countries like the United States and the UK.

1.3.7   LOOKING FORWARD

From first principles, economic growth comes from changes in labor, capital and productivity. The discussion above has brought out strengths on all three fronts:

- Demographics, education and learning-by-doing are generating a process of improvements in labor.
- Capital is characterized by a rising savings rate, improved access to foreign savings, and a market-dominated financial system with information processing done through speculative markets.
- Finally, improvements in infrastructure, rationalization of the role of the State in the domestic economy, reducing barriers to trade and heightened competition between competent firms are key drivers of productivity growth.

India is hence in a remarkable situation where there is a positive outlook on all the three ingredients that go into growth: labor, capital, and productivity (Kelkar, 2004b). This suggests that the trend GDP growth rate will further accelerate in the future. However, the present state of knowledge does not permit numerical estimates of either the date or the magnitude of this acceleration.

1.4   TRENDS AND VOLATILITY IN GDP GROWTH

GDP growth seems to involve growth cycle fluctuations about a long-term trend GDP growth rate, which, in turn, has been steadily accelerating. In order to measure this phenomenon, we create a ten-year moving average of GDP growth, in order to eliminate some of the distracting noise in the growth cycle.[14]

Years of negative GDP growth were observed in the past, and were invariably associated with a drought. The reduction of the share of agriculture in GDP

---

[14]For a business cycle perspective on Indian macroeconomics, see Shah (2008).

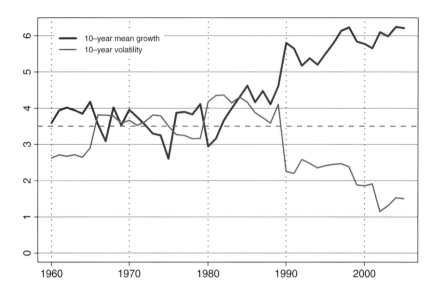

FIGURE 1.8   Ten-Year Moving Average Growth and Its Volatility

has led to a diminished importance of such issues. Fluctuations away from the trend were largely driven by agriculture in the earlier years; in recent decades the drivers have been modern phenomena like investment and inventory fluctuations of firms.

In understanding the evolution of GDP, it is particularly interesting to look at the ten-year moving average and standard deviation of annual GDP growth, to get at the underlying long-term trends (see Figure 1.8). This evidence highlights two main facts. First, from roughly 1979 onward, the trend in GDP growth has accelerated from 3.5%. Second, the volatility of GDP growth has dropped sharply. In 1980, India was a low-mean, high-variance macroeconomy. Over the years, it has increasingly become a high-mean, moderate-variance macroeconomy.

The most recent values suggest that the mean or trend GDP growth is around 6.2% with a cycle around it which has a standard deviation of roughly 1.9 percentage points. It appears fair to think that under "normal business cycle fluctuations," GDP growth will not drop below 4.5%. Growth below 4.5% would require a currency crisis or a political crisis. This reasoning suggests that while the economy will be growing at good rates, this will not be growth at a steady, unvarying rate. The economy will definitely witness cycles in growth rate. Business cycles in the Western sense of the term are unlikely to be found since the probability of negative GDP growth is negligible. The growth cycle is affected by both local factors and the global business cycle.

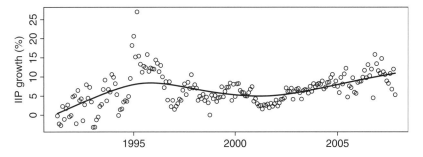

FIGURE 1.9   Growth in Indian Industrial Production after 1990

As a consequence of globalization, we should expect a greater synchronization between the Indian growth cycle and the global cycle. A foretaste of this was observed in the 2001–2002 period, when the world and India both experienced a short but synchronized dip. Figure 1.9 shows the long time-series of monthly data for growth in industrial production. Superposed on this is the business cycle. This shows the broad story of the growth cycle in the post-1990 period. High growth in 1995–1996 was followed by lower growth in 2000–2001 and then by generally higher growth thereafter.

1.4.1   RISKS to GDP GROWTH

There are four big questions that capture the risk factors to the Indian economy. They are

1. How much is the Indian economy vulnerable to the monsoons?
2. Can the high, and still increasing, levels of investment be sustained?
3. How disciplined is government fiscal expenditure?
4. How vulnerable is the Indian economy to the global business cycle?

We deal with these four factors below.

Monsoon Risk Has Diminished

The impact of the monsoon on the Indian economy is largely through agricultural performance. There is a less significant link between the monsoon and the manufacturing sector which affects the GDP growth.

The share of agriculture in the economy is rapidly shrinking, just as it did in all advanced economies. The share of agriculture in GDP has dropped from 55% in 1950 to 33% in 1991 to 25% in 2000. At present, it is below 20%.

Furthermore, the share of agriculture has been dropping at an *accelerating* pace. From 1965–1966 to 1983–1984 (18 years), the share of agriculture dropped by 11%. In contrast, the last drop of 8 percentage points took place from 1996–1997 to 2005–2006 (9 years). We might predict that within ten years, the share of agriculture will be down to 10%. As with China, a conceivable path for India is to have a shift away from self-reliance toward imported food.

The links between agriculture and GDP arise from both the demand side and the supply side. On the demand side, rural incomes rise when agriculture does well. The rise in rural incomes leads to greater demand for industrial products. For example, consumer goods do well when rural incomes rise. In some cases the impact is immediate, in others it comes slowly. For example, the sales of shampoos, soap and bicycles might respond immediately, whereas the sales of motorcycles, fertilizer, tractors and TVs increase somewhat later.

On the supply side, an increase in agricultural production increases the supply of food and raw materials. Cereals, fruit, vegetables, milk, meat, eggs, etc. enter the consumption bundle of households. Their plentiful supply and lower prices, following a good monsoon, reduces the cost of living. Real incomes of both urban and rural populations increase. They both have more to spend on nonagricultural products. Also, there are a large number of industries that use farm products as raw materials. Products such as sugarcane, cotton and oilseeds are directly used by industry. Cheaper raw materials augur well for these industries. Further, many nonagricultural businesses may not do well when there is a bad monsoon and a fall in farm income. But today even the impact on consumption by workers and shareholders is not as sharp as it used to be. Higher financial savings and physical assets as well as access to credit allows households, especially in urban areas, to smooth consumption. At the same time, the stock of formal sector finance available to individuals is small, at 6% of GDP.

An important change that has accompanied the decline in the share of agriculture is the growth of foreign trade. This has reduced the impact of agricultural performance on nonagricultural sectors. The sharp increase in the share of manufactured goods that were exported in the last fifteen years have made manufacturing far more resilient to the ups and downs in the demand associated with changes in farm incomes.

In the period before the 1990s, a drop in agricultural growth rates was accompanied by a sharp drop in nonagricultural growth. Manufacturing and services grow slowly not only in the year of a decline, but even beyond that year into the first few months of the next year. This has changed. The last time GDP saw an actual decline was in 1979–1980—a result of a very bad monsoon—when agricultural output fell by a shocking 13%, and an oil price shock shook the world. Not surprisingly, industrial growth declined by over 3%, and GDP fell by 5.2%. But in the 1990s when agricultural output declined, though industrial growth slowed down, industrial production did not fall. Even when agricultural output fell by 7% in 2002–2003 (again, a very bad monsoon), industrial growth remained positive at 6.6% and services at 8%. Overall GDP grew at 4%. In 2004–2005 when agriculture grew at 1.15%, GDP grew at 7%.

GDP forecasting models that are used to estimate the impact of the monsoon are, in general, backward looking. Usually the elasticities that have been estimated reflect the response of the economy to the monsoon over the last 30 years. This tends to overstate the impact of the monsoon on nonagricultural growth and on overall GDP growth. Thus, while the monsoons are still important, particularly for farm incomes and for certain industries, the impact of the monsoons on the economy is often overstated. Today the economy is far more resilient to monsoons than it ever was.

Can High and Growing Investment Be Sustained?

After 2001–2002, there was a remarkable increase in the investment rate: from 23% of GDP in 2001–2002 to 30.1% in 2004–2005. This investment was financed by a rise in both the gross savings rate and net capital flow from abroad. The domestic savings rate rose over this period from 23.6% to 29.1%. Net capital flow swung from a net outflow of 0.7% of GDP to a net inflow of 0.8%.

Public savings consist of dissavings of the government and savings of public sector enterprises. This has shown a remarkable swing. In 2001–2002 the public sector as a whole was making losses of Rs.46,377 crore ($9.5 billion). In 2004–2005 the government and public sector enterprises together saved Rs.69,390 crore ($15.9 billion). This was a shift from −2.0% to +2.2% of GDP. One part of the increase in the public saving rate has been achieved by fiscal consolidation at both the state and central levels. The combined fiscal deficit of the centre and states has fallen from 9.9% of GDP to 7.7% over this period.

Corporate savings, which reflect higher retained profits of the private corporate sector, have also risen from 3.6% of GDP in 2001–2002 to 4.8% of GDP in 2004–2005. This reflects buoyant business cycle conditions and the procyclicality of profits. Profits are among the first to be hit when a business cycle turns, and should not be thought of as giving a "trend" increase in the savings rate.

Fiscal Pressure

With the implementation of the FRBM Act, India has clawed back from a fiscal disaster over the last six years (Kelkar, 2004a; Lahiri and Kannan, 2001).

But early signs suggest that fiscal difficulties could resurge by 2010. Proposed expenditures are large while revenue collections could shrink.

The UPA government has initiated large-scale spending programs such as the National Rural Employment Guarantee Act (NREGA),[15] increased the funding going into Sarva Shiksha Ahiyan (SSA),[16] initiated the 6th Pay Commission (In India, the periodic "pay commissions" decide on pay increases for civil servants.), and possibly a raft of welfare provisions including defined benefit pensions for 400 million unorganized sector workers. When implemented, these programs, in a few years, could lead up to additional spending of well over Rs.1 trillion ($21.5 billion). In addition to these spending programs, there is a populist oil price policy which could ultimately hit the budget when oil companies owned by the government cannot run losses any more. Tax buoyancy has been adversely affected by the introduction of Special Economic Zones (SEZs) with generous tax breaks.

In the worst scenario, the deficit targets under fiscal responsibility legislation will be violated and the fiscal deficit could be roughly 3 percentage points of GDP worse than is expected under the baseline case. This is not a large dent in the investment rate which is expected to exceed 30% of GDP.

Vulnerability to the Global Business Cycle

High growth in recent years has been aided by unprecedented high global GDP growth. However, world GDP growth in 2006 and 2007 has slowed, and further reductions in world GDP growth are likely. Hence, it is important to understand the extent to which high economic growth in India will be influenced by the global business cycle.

Asset prices in India have seen a growing correlation with global prices because of integration through trade, capital flows and monetary policy. While the full time-series from 1991 onward[17] shows a correlation of 0.165, the correlation coefficient has risen steadily from 1995 onward to a level of 0.535 in 2007 (see Table 1.9).

An international comparison in Table 1.10 focuses on weekly returns from January 2005 through December 2007. The order of increasing correlations with the US market appear to be: Brazil > India > Russia > China.

---

[15]The NREGA is a government program that guarantees 100 days of employment, at a low wage, to all rural adults.

[16]SSA is a government program aimed at building more schools and recruiting more teachers.

[17]Each row in the table shows the correlation coefficient of weekly returns for the calendar year.

TABLE 1.9   Growing Correlation between Nifty and S&P 500

Year	Correlation	Year	Correlation
1991	0.132	2001	0.419
1992	−0.288	2002	0.146
1993	0.220	2003	0.339
1994	0.131	2004	0.319
1995	−0.055	2005	0.413
1996	0.061	2006	0.385
1997	0.272	2007	0.535
1998	0.291		
1999	0.131		
2000	0.152		

TABLE 1.10   Correlation Matrix of Stock Market Returns of US and BRIC Countries, 2005–07

	India	US	Brazil	China	Russia
India	1.000	0.440	0.517	0.196	0.385
US	0.440	1.000	0.679	0.149	0.405
Brazil	0.517	0.679	1.000	0.206	0.561
China	0.196	0.149	0.206	1.000	0.083
Russia	0.385	0.405	0.561	0.083	1.000

There are three channels through which a downturn in the world economy, and particularly in the United States, would affect India:

1. Slowing world GDP growth will affect demand for Indian exports. Twenty percent of the Nifty index is made up of IT companies, where revenues are almost entirely exports. An analysis of commodity-level trade data shows that for commodities which make up 40% of Indian exports, over 20% of Indian exports go to the United States. These commodities are spread over a broad range in industry classification; there is no sharp focus on any one or two industries. Two examples of interesting industries with US exposure are gems and jewelry (15% of Indian exports, where 28% goes to the United States) and garments (6% of Indian exports, where 34% goes to the United States). In a downturn, US consumers are likely to slow down on purchases of jewelry to a greater extent than is the case with clothes. Indian export growth will be affected both by slowing world demand for manufactured goods and by pricing pressure from Chinese firms, who are under less pressure of earning profits and paying dividends when compared with Indian firms.

The identical issues apply to imports also. A global downturn would lead to lower prices of goods and services globally. Indian firms which compete with imported goods would face pricing pressure, particularly from Chinese firms who can more readily lower prices because they work in an environment of weak corporate governance and weak creditors' rights. This would adversely affect profits and investment in India.

2. Beyond the trade channel, US monetary policy exerts an effect on Indian monetary policy. In places across the world like China and India, which peg their exchange rates to the United States, there is a lack of monetary policy autonomy owing to the use of the pegged exchange rate (Patnaik, 2003, 2005). These countries experience tighter monetary policy also, in synchrony with tighter monetary policy in the United States. Intuitively, higher interest rates in the United States lead to capital leaving India, and could lead to a weaker rupee. But since the RBI runs an INR-USD pegged exchange rate, they will be forced to raise rates in order to defend the rupee. Thus, tight monetary policy in the United States coupled with a INR/USD pegged exchange rate will generate tight monetary policy in India.

3. With remittances, software exports and business process outsourcing, there are two conflicting possibilities. On one hand, in the event of a slowdown in the United States, India could become the front line of the US business cycle with tens of thousands of workers in India getting sacked. On the other hand, when margins in the United States come under pressure, US CEOs could choose to sack workers in the United States and send more jobs to India. It is not yet clear in which direction this factor will move the growth story.

In the existing framework of macroeconomic policy, neither fiscal policy nor monetary policy in India are organized in a way that counteracts the business cycle. When difficult scenarios arise, macroeconomic volatility is likely to be acute, owing to the lack of stabilizing macro policy that is found in mature market economies. Looking forward, the picture is one of the existing (high) levels of GDP volatility, coupled with an increased correlation with global GDP growth.

1.4.2   PERFECT STORM?

The worst scenario that could occur in the 2009–2010 period involves a coming together of some of the following elements:

- General elections are scheduled to take place in 2009. This will increase populist pressures which would adversely affect investor confidence and increase political risk.

- There would be pressure in meeting deficit targets under extant fiscal responsibility legislation in 2009, particularly with the 6th pay commission wage increases which would kick in from 2010.[18]
- There could be a global business cycle downturn in 2008–2010, which propagates into Indian firms which then reduce investment.
- There could be a global retreat of capital from emerging markets in the next global downturn. RBI could choose to zealously defend the INR/USD pegged exchange rate, which would involve higher local interest rates at the wrong time in the business cycle.

The four key risks which are important in looking into the coming years are (a) global business cycle downturn, (b) monetary policy tightening at the wrong time, (c) fiscal stress and (d) populism. There is a monsoon lottery every year, but the importance of this is now much diminished.

For an interesting comparison, the 1998–2003 period was a useful learning ground on the effects of volatility on the economy, with several negative shocks coming together:

1. There were fears of contagion into India from the East Asian financial crisis. There was sharp rupee volatility, and the short rate was raised by 200 basis points on January 16, 1998, as part of an interest-rate defense of the pegged exchange rate. This was a clear case of pegging inducing pro-cyclical monetary policy, for this interest rate hike came at an unfortunate time in the business cycle.
2. In May 1998, India tested nuclear weapons, which led to global economic sanctions.
3. In 1999, general elections were held, with a consequent increase in uncertainty for investment.
4. In 2000 the global drop in IT stocks led to sharp declines in Indian IT stock prices also. This turned into a systemic crisis with the failure of the Calcutta Stock Exchange, and the "Ketan Parekh" scandal. This led to a crisis at the Bombay Stock Exchange (the second largest exchange) where the president was forced to step down, and a crisis at the largest mutual fund, UTI.
5. The WTC attacks on 9/11/2001 led to a global economic downturn.

---

[18]Civil service wages are periodically revised through the constitution of a "pay commission." The 5th pay commission, coupled with poor political decisions, led to massive wage increases for junior staff, and hence an escalation of expenditure for both centre and states. The 6th pay commission will be constituted in a few weeks, and decisions based on its recommendations will be taken by the UPA government shortly before the 2009 elections are announced. There are, hence, widespread fears that the 6th pay commission will lead to very generous pay raises for junior staff. If this comes about, the first year with a full impact on the consolidated expenditure of centre and states will be 2009–2010.

6. In 2002–2003, there was a drought, and agriculture GDP dropped by 7%, which was the worst decline since 1979–1980.

Through this period, GDP growth slowed to 4.3%. This suggests that the range of possible outcomes for annual GDP growth in coming years perhaps lies between 4% and 10%.

1.5 CONCLUSIONS

India is a paradoxical blend of some enormous strengths and some enormous weaknesses. The most important strength appears to be a good quality labor force with a supportive demographic outlook for the coming 25 years. This labor force is being effectively harnessed by a vibrant set of private companies, operating in a genuine market economy, with resources being allocated by a genuine equity market based on speculative price discovery. The productivity of these private companies is being positively influenced by high levels of competition, by globalization, and a gradual process of improving infrastructure.

In these respects, India fares well when compared to China, which has a gloomy demographic outlook, with weak firms, a bank-dominated and State-influenced financial system, and a considerable role for State planning as opposed to market forces in shaping the fortunes of firms.

Looking forward, it is very likely that the quality and quantity of labor will go up. It is very likely that domestic savings and foreign capital inflows will go up. Putting these together, without any ambitious assumptions about improvements in productivity, it is very likely that this mere piling on of labor and capital will generate an acceleration of growth in the coming decade. A particularly attractive feature of this long-term scenario is the lack of political risk: after independence in 1947, there was only one breakdown of democracy (in 1976–1977) for a period of 19 months.

The weakest link in the Indian growth story is the State. Indian economic growth is greatly constrained by an inadequate quantity and quality of public services such as law and order, the judiciary, infrastructure, etc. The functioning of the State is bedeviled by (a) a lack of focus upon these critical services as the task worth accomplishing and (b) poor productivity and efficiency in the production of these services. The processes of democracy have, thus far, only weakly disciplined the State into focusing on public services and on delivering results. All too often, the State is seen to focus upon transfer programs, or distortionary interventions into the functioning of the market.

Under a pessimistic scenario, India will make no progress on reining in the State. In this case, in the years to come, the acceleration of growth will derive primarily from the accretion of labor and capital. If, however, in the coming years, the Indian State is able to improve its focus and the quality of execution in producing public goods, then powerful productivity growth could also come about.

CHAPTER 2

The Firms

A key feature of India's financial system today is the trading of stocks and bonds issued by firms. This is new. If we looked at the characteristics of Indian firms 25 years ago, the business landscape was dominated by a small set of family-owned and -financed companies. These family-owned business houses controlled the process of firm creation. Virtually all of the major firms were controlled by one of these families.

A fascinating new feature that has emerged in the last two decades is an entrepreneurial energy from completely new players that has resulted in some of the most successful firms ever seen within India, including firms with very visible global footprints. Many of these new firms have come about in new areas, such as software or telecom. This new entrepreneurial dynamism, which has been manifested by taking new management teams and firms into new industries, has been critically supported and financed by the equity market. So this chapter will focus on a thorough description of the companies of the new India and through the numbers we will see the new face of Indian firms.

2.1 THE CMIE DATABASE

The Centre for Monitoring Indian Economy (CMIE) maintains a comprehensive database, going back to the late 1980s, of Indian firms. This database is not a sample. It endeavors to be a census of every large firm in the country, including all kinds of firms such as listed firms, cooperatives, partnerships, public sector firms, etc. At the same time, CMIE obtains information for this database on a best-efforts basis. While the coverage of the database is extensive, there is no guarantee that every firm that existed in a certain year will be included in the database. In addition to creating a database with a history of firm data, CMIE has an elaborate methodology of normalization where concepts and definitions are standardized across firms and across time. This ensures comparability of data across firms and across time.

In this chapter, we focus on the nonfinancial firms observed in this database in two 1-year periods (1999–2000 and 2004–2005, five years apart). For 1999–2000, the CMIE database contains 5,794 firms and for 2004–2005 it contains 5,632 firms. The data that we examine is not panel data; a set of firms is observed in 1999–2000 and a different set of firms is observed in 2004–2005. These differences reflect (a) birth and death of firms and (b) inconsistent availability of financial statements at CMIE. However, we will interpret the aggregate financial statements of all firms in a given year as representing the structure of Indian nonfinancial firms.

Aggregated financial statements from the CMIE database are highly credible because it is possible to "drill down" from the aggregate numbers to individual firms, and because CMIE has thousands of users who require high quality of normalized data at the level of individual firms. The process of normalization, quality assurance and extensive utilization of firm-level information induces quality in the aggregate information.[1]

2.2   THE LARGE NONFINANCIAL FIRMS OF INDIA

In a series of tables, we show sum totals of various variables for nonfinancial firms, thus summarizing the characteristics of these firms. We will also show averages—the aggregate divided by the number of firms. These averages should be interpreted with some care because the distribution of firm size is highly skewed, with a few large firms having considerable importance. The large number of small and medium enterprises (SME) in each of these sets has relatively little importance. As a rule of thumb, the biggest 100 firms account for two-thirds of the total.

2.2.1   OUTPUT

Table 2.1 shows broad facts about the dataset. The gross sales (i.e., revenues) of the firms rose from \$235 billion to \$397 billion. In 2004–2005, the average firm had sales of \$70 million. Over this five year period, the top line growth averaged 11% (in USD).[2]

---

[1]Aggregated financial statements about firms from the CMIE database are used in quarterly GDP estimates of the Central Statistical Organisation (CSO).

[2]The CMIE definition of "gross sales" is *Sales generated from the main business activities of a firm. It excludes other income and income from non-recurring transactions, income of extraordinary nature and prior period incomes.*

TABLE 2.1 Output

	Aggregate (billion USD)		Average firm (million USD)		Growth per Year (percent)
	1999–2000	2004–2005	1999–2000	2004–2005	
Gross sales	235	397	41	70	11.03
Gross value added	47	85	8	15	12.52

TABLE 2.2 International Trade

	Aggregate (billion USD)		Average firm (million USD)		Growth per Year (percent)
	1999–2000	2004–2005	1999–2000	2004–2005	
Foreign currency earnings	21	65	4	12	26.01
Foreign currency expenditure	39	87	7	15	17.31

The contribution of these firms to GDP is the sum of the gross value added of each firm, which (in turn) is the sum of payments for land, labor, capital and enterprise. This value added rose from $47 billion to $85 billion, with a faster growth rate of 12.52% per year in USD.

2.2.2 INTERNATIONAL TRADE

Table 2.2 gives an indicator of the increasing outward orientation of Indian firms. Firms report their *direct* import or export activities in their annual reports. If a firm purchases imported goods from another (trading) firm, these are not counted in these measures. Hence, the values seen in the table are underestimates.

The aggregates show that in 2004–2005, the large nonfinancial firms had imports of $87 billion and exports of $65 billion. Over the recent five years, their import growth was 17.31% a year while their export growth was 26.01%. These high growth rates have led to large changes in two structural ratios. The exports as percent of sales grew from 8.7% in 1999–2000 to 16.5% in 2004–2005. Similarly, imported raw materials grew from 18.1% of raw material expenses to 23.7% over these five years.

TABLE 2.3   Expenditure

	Aggregate (billion USD)		Average firm (million USD)		Growth per Year (percent)
	1999–2000	2004–2005	1999–2000	2004–2005	
Raw materials	131	222	23	39	11.16
Wages	17	24	3	4	7.04
Energy	11	15	2	3	7.23
Selling costs	11	17	2	3	9.86
Administration	14	22	3	4	8.31
Interest	13	9	2	2	−5.84
Depreciation	10	16	2	3	10.02

2.2.3   EXPENDITURE

Table 2.3 gives an understanding of the expenditures of these firms. The major expenditure was on raw materials, which grew from $131 billion to $222 billion. Wages were a small component, growing at 7% a year from $17 billion to $24 billion. Wages as a fraction of net sales actually dropped over this period. The average wage bill in the dataset was just $4 million in 2004–2005.

Interest costs dropped sharply from $13 billion to $9 billion over this period, reflecting both a drop in interest rates and a substantial deleveraging of the firms. This deleveraging is discussed in greater detail later.

2.2.4   PROFITS

As the previous tables show, gross sales and raw material expenses both grew by 11% per year over these five years. However, other components of expenditure grew by less than 11%. As a consequence, profitability grew well. Table 2.4 shows information for profits, where the CMIE database consistently separates out non-recurring transactions for all firms for all years. This shows that the profit before interest, depreciation and tax (PBDIT) grew by 23.28% per year. This gave magnified gains in the profit before tax (PBT) of 34.30% per year, partly because interest payments grew slowly. Finally, the profit after tax (PAT)—the bottom line—grew by a remarkable 38.11% per year. Even for a firm where the P/E was stable over these five years, the sheer growth in earnings would generate stock market returns of 38.11% per year.

This evolution of profits has induced significant changes in profitability ratios. The PBDIT expressed as percent of gross sales rose from 13.2% to 15.5%.

TABLE 2.4   Profits (net of non-recurring transactions)

	Aggregate (billion USD)		Average firm (million USD)		Growth per Year (percent)
	1999–2000	2004–2005	1999–2000	2004–2005	
PBDIT	31	62	5	11	14.65
PBT	8	35	1	6	34.30
PAT	5	23	1	4	38.11

The PAT as percent of gross sales grew from 2% to 5.8%. Finally, the PAT expressed as percent of total assets grew from 1.7% to 5.9%. At a P/E of 20, the aggregate profit of $23 billion in 2004–2005 induced a market capitalization of roughly $460 billion for these firms. As is well known, the aggregate market capitalization of Indian firms in 2007 was $1 trillion. The explanation for the gap between these two values lies in (a) the growth in net profit from 2004–2005 to 2006–2007 and (b) the inclusion of financial firms in the overall market capitalization of $1 trillion, in contrast with Table 2.4 which deals with only non-financial firms.

2.2.5   ASSETS

Table 2.5 shows the structure of assets of the firms. While total assets grew by 8.3% per year, inventories only grew by 3.29% a year, showing increased efficiency in the operations of firms. The most important application of assets is, of course, the creation of fixed assets. Net of depreciation, the aggregate assets of the corporations amounted to $155 billion in 2004–2005.

2.2.6   LIABILITIES

Turning to the balance sheet, Table 2.6 shows the structure of liabilities. The aggregate balance sheet size of the firms grew from $277 billion to $413 billion, an average annual growth of 8.3%. The average firm grew from a balance sheet size of $48 million to $73 million.

The major feature of the structure of liabilities was the near-stagnation of debt financing. Total borrowing went from $113 billion to $123 billion, an average annual growth of just 1.77%. This greatly lagged the expansion of equity capital from $92 billion to $158 billion, a growth of 11.41% per year.

TABLE 2.5   Assets

	Aggregate (billion USD)		Average firm (million USD)		
	1999–2000	2004–2005	1999–2000	2004–2005	Growth per Year (percent)
Gross fixed assets	174	269	30	48	9.09
Net fixed assets	109	155	19	27	7.33
Investments	18	45	3	8	19.78
Inventories	42	49	7	9	3.29
Cash	14	39	2	7	22.98
Receivables	66	88	11	16	5.79
Total assets/liabilities	277	413	48	73	8.30

TABLE 2.6   Liabilities

	Aggregate (billion USD)		Average firm (million USD)		
	1999–2000	2004–2005	1999–2000	2004–2005	Growth per Year (percent)
Equity	92	158	16	28	11.41
Debt	113	123	19	22	1.77
Current liability and provisions	72	111	12	20	9.01
Total assets/liabilities	277	413	48	73	8.30

Later in this chapter, we will argue that this approach to measurement greatly *understates* the importance of equity financing.

2.2.7   SOURCES AND USES OF FUNDS

Table 2.7 interprets the difference between the balance sheet of 2004–05 and that of 1999–00 as a 'sources and uses of funds' statement. The overall balance sheet size grew by $221 billion.

On the financing side, this was made up of $78 billion of equity, $42 billion of debt and $80 billion of current liabilities. The largest component (35.22%) was equity financing. Debt financing accounted for only 18.98%.

The bulk of the incremental $78 billion of equity capital was comprised of retained earnings. On average, the dividend payout ratio is roughly 25%. As an example, of the $23 billion of profit after tax seen in Table 2.4, $6 billion was paid out as dividends and $17 billion was retained—this constituted growing total assets through equity financing.

TABLE 2.7   Sources and Uses of Funds

	Change from 99–00 to 04–05 (Billion USD)	Share in overall change (Percent)
Sources of funds		
Equity	78	35.22
Debt	42	18.98
Current liability	80	36.21
Others	21	9.50
Uses of funds		
Gross fixed assets	147	66.71
Investments	33	14.71
Others	41	18.55
Total assets/liabilities	**221**	**100.00**

TABLE 2.8   Efficiency Measures

	1999–2000	2004–2005
Gross value added per net fixed assets	0.44	0.55
Gross value added per total assets	0.17	0.21
Days of raw material	64	48
Days of finished goods	32	20
Energy expense per gross value added	0.23	0.18

Turning to the uses of the funds, the most important application was that of adding $147 billion of gross fixed assets, which accounted for 66.71% of the incremental assets.

2.2.8   EFFICIENCY MEASURES

Table 2.8 examines the aggregate accounting data from the viewpoint of arriving at metrics of efficiency. The gross value added per net fixed assets shows how effectively the firms were converting fixed assets into output. This improved from 0.44 to 0.55. More generally, the gross value added per total assets shows how effectively the firms were converting the overall assets into output. This grew from 0.17 to 0.21. Over this period, the incremental capital-output ratio for these firms worked out to 3.56. This incremental capital-output ratio is broadly in line with that seen for the Indian economy as a whole.

Inventory management improved, with raw material inventories dropping from 64 days to 48 days, and finished goods inventories dropping from 32 days to 20 days. Finally, the expenditure on energy per unit gross value added dropped from 0.23 to 0.18. Hence, all the efficiency measures show significant improvement from 1999–2000 to 2004–2005.

2.3   ROLE OF EQUITY FINANCING

There is an extensive literature that compares "bank-dominated" financial systems against "market-dominated" financial systems. In the latter, the dominant forces shaping the allocation of capital are the stock market and the bond market. In contrast, bank-dominated financial systems accord primacy to banks in shaping resource allocation. Since earlier financial sector reforms had a focus on equity market development in India, we seek to understand if the reforms made an impact on the financing decisions of Indian firms. When seeking to understand corporate financial structure, researchers have a choice between *flow* and *stock* measures.[3]

Flow measures suffer from a lack of appropriate marking to market. For example, when tariffs are reduced, a large drop in the value of many factories ought to be registered in the year of tariff reduction. This is generally not captured by accounting procedures. Stock measures at book value suffer from difficulties with treatment of inflation and depreciation. For example, old assets such as steel factories of TISCO tend to be wrongly portrayed on the balance sheet as having a low value.

We present some evidence on changes in corporate financial sources based on *market-value measurement of stocks*, which does not suffer from the difficulties of measurement of flows. We analyze the shift from debt to equity by examining patterns in the debt-equity ratios for Indian firms between 1989 and 2004.[4]

On the books of a firm, equity and debt are generally priced at historical value which leads to distorted inferences. In our analysis, we use the market value of equity.[5] At any point in time, the market value of all firms is comparable, and constitutes a superior measure of the equity capital in a firm compared with the book value of equity. One problem in using the market value is that the shares issued by some firms are highly illiquid, and the market values cannot be trusted.[6] Hence, we limit ourselves to the universe of firms in the CMIE

---

[3]Green et al. (2002) have an extensive discussion of difficulties of measurement in corporate finance.

[4]For some other research on corporate financial structure in India, see Shirai (2004), Topalova (2004), Love and Peria (2005).

[5]This is similar to the computation of Table IIIa in Rajan and Zingales (1995).

[6]For example, one firm exists, which has near-zero trading volume, and a market capitalization of Rs.1 trillion.

TABLE 2.9   Financing Patterns of Cospi Firms

Year	Net worth (Rs. Crore)	Borrowings (Rs. Crore)	Mkt. Cap. (Rs. Crore)	Debt-equity ratio	
				Book Value	Market Value
1989–1990	57,251	81,936	37,425	1.43	2.19
1990–1991	70,942	119,226	55,176	1.68	2.16
1991–1992	79,832	144,513	213,688	1.81	0.68
1992–1993	96,784	176,448	140,783	1.82	1.25
1993–1994	130,440	188,152	326,136	1.44	0.58
1994–1995	186,770	228,337	343,954	1.22	0.66
1995–1996	232,232	274,652	400,927	1.18	0.69
1996–1997	266,614	309,156	375,466	1.16	0.82
1997–1998	303,115	355,763	444,224	1.17	0.80
1998–1999	327,772	390,536	444,904	1.19	0.88
1999–2000	368,628	423,518	842,887	1.15	0.50
2000–2001	403,298	445,073	494,933	1.10	0.90
2001–2002	420,432	508,018	563,447	1.21	0.90
2002–2003	464,156	508,165	545,741	1.09	0.93
2003–2004	522,034	493,936	1,176,976	0.95	0.42
2004–2005	621,838	602,419	1,673,743	0.97	0.36

The data used is for the CMIE Cospi companies, to avoid spurious results associated with companies where negligible equity trading takes place. In 1989–1990, the book value of equity of these companies was Rs.57,251 crore and the book value of debt was Rs.81,936 crore. This implied a debt-equity ratio of 1.43. However, the market value of equity was Rs.37,425 crore. Using this more accurate value, the debt-equity ratio in 1989–1990 worked out to 2.19.

Cospi index, which consists of all firms where trading took place on at least 66% of the days in the last three months. For these firms, a reliable estimate of the market value of equity is readily available.[7]

Unlike equity, debt in India is an opaque market. Most firm debt is held in the form of loans rather than bonds. In addition, since there is no active corporate bond market in India, these bonds are not liquid and, therefore, cannot be valued using a market price. Hence, we use the book value of debt. We expect that this is likely to lead to an *overestimate* of the value of debt, since corporate debt is high yield and generally trades at a discount to book value.

The debt-equity data for Indian firms from 1989–1990 to 2004–2005 are shown in Table 2.9. The traditional debt-equity ratios, based on book value, shows that the Indian corporate sector deleveraged dramatically from 1.82 in 1992–1993 to 0.97 in 2004–2005. The story is even more dramatic when the market value of equity is used: this shows deleveraging from 2.19 times

[7]In August 2007, there were 2,727 firms in this set.

in 1989–1990 to 0.36 today. The table shows that the period of successful equity market reforms (as opposed to a relatively stagnant banking sector and debt market) has been associated with a visible rise in the importance of equity as a source of financing. For large firms, the Indian financial system is moving to an equity market dominated one, rather than a banking dominated one.

This is contrary to findings that, the world over, the use of debt financing has increased over the last decade (Mitton, 2005). The study finds that it is particularly so in emerging markets, where one of the factors driving the rise in debt financing has been higher domestic supply of funds. The other important factor is shown to be opening up to the international economy.

Another way of obtaining evidence on the alternative modes of firm financing is to examine the stock of capital associated with financing mechanisms. Intuitively, this may be viewed as the composition of the portfolio of a representative household in India at a point in time. Three key facts, as of September 2007, were:

- The market capitalization of the largest 2,727 firms added up to Rs.45.28 trillion.[8]
- The nonfood credit of the (entire) banking system was Rs.19 trillion. Of this, roughly Rs.6 trillion goes to firms.
- The market capitalization of the corporate bond market was estimated at Rs.5 trillion.[9]

These three estimates are done on a marked-to-market basis, and do not suffer from the problems of accounting notions of value. This suggests that the securities markets shaped Rs.50 trillion of resources going to firms, compared with Rs.6 trillion through the banking system. This ratio is suggestive of the increasing domination of securities markets in resource allocation. Furthermore, it points to the domination of equity financing.

These relationships are not an artifact of one point in time. Figure 2.1 shows that for most of the period after 2002—when the equity market reforms fell into place—the market value of the Cospi companies was substantially larger than the (market value) of nonfood credit. The evidence suggests that both entrepreneurs and households have most likely adapted their financing patterns in favor of the securities markets and, particularly, the equity market.

---

[8]This estimate *understates* the importance of the equity market, since it only counts the 2,727 largest firms.

[9]The stock of dematerialized corporate bonds at NSDL was a little more than Rs.4 trillion, and the stock of commercial paper was at Rs.0.5 trillion. These add up to Rs.4.5 trillion. Based on this, it is estimated that the total stock of corporate debt securities stands at Rs.5 trillion.

There is a slight double-counting here, to the extent that banks own corporate bonds.

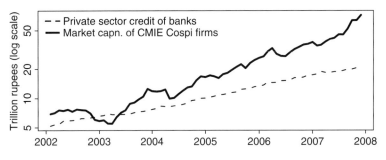

FIGURE 2.1   Banks and Markets in Firm Financing

2.4   REGULATION OF FIRMS

Firms in India are governed under the Companies Act, 1956. This is administered by the Ministry of Corporate Affairs (MCA). All firms that are registered
in India, as proprietorships, partnerships as well as limited liability firms have
to be registered with the Registrar of Companies (ROC), a department within
the MCA. In addition to maintaining the registry of firms, it plays a regulatory
function of supervising the behavior of firms and taking legal action against
violations. The primary legal framework is set by the rules in the Companies
Act of 1956. Given that the economic environment has changed dramatically
since that time, the Companies Act has seen several changes since then. In
fact, the Act has undergone amendments at nearly regular four-year intervals.
Within this Act and its amendments, the firms have to follow the rules set for
disclosure, structure, financing, etc.

The implementation of the legal framework into operational details is set
by the chartered accountants. There are three nodal bodies that oversee the
chartered accountants and that play a role in corporate affairs: the Institute of
Chartered Accountants of India (ICAI), the Institute of Company Secretaries of
India (ICSI) and the Institute of Cost and Works Accountants of India (ICWAI).
All these agencies are incorporated under the separate acts of the Companies
Act and answer to the MCA. The other material act that forms part of the
legal framework for the governance of firms in India is the Competition Act
of 2002, which sets the legal framework for action against anti-competitive
trade practices. This act of 2002 replaced the earlier anti-competitive policy
framework set as the Monopolies and Restrictive Trade Practices Act of 1969.

In addition to the MCA which supervises and monitors the registered firms
in India, the Securities and Exchanges Board of India (SEBI) has regulatory
jurisdiction over the *listed* firms. This includes a say in the regular disclosure by
firms, setting the process and procedure through which these firms can finance

new projects as well as the role of acting as compliance officer of these firms. Despite sharing the regulatory responsibility, there is no clear co-ordination between the MCA and SEBI on their regulation of listed firms. Recently, these regulatory overlaps have meant additional costs—particularly of disclosure—to listed firms that have resulted in distinct changes in financing trends. For example, the number of firms raising funds either through internal sources or through private placements have seen a dramatic increase in the last five years, despite significant improvements in market mechanisms to source public funds.

CHAPTER 3

Private Equity and the IPO Market

Traditionally, firm financing in India was obtained through (a) equity from a parent company, (b) loans from a bank or a development financial institution[1] (DFI) or (c) equity markets. These were funding sources available to the largest companies in the country; small firms typically obtained financing from family and friends. Bank/DFI funding was done based on asset-based collateral, which meant that firms with an emphasis on service provision without fixed assets could access funds only at very high rates, if at all. As in most developing economies, the most accessible source of funds was from a parent company, so much so that the ownership pattern among firms in India in the early nineties was markedly skewed toward ownership by an Indian business group.

Today, the process of financing involves a wider variety of sources: in addition to the traditional sources of income, there are foreign institutional investors, private equity funds, Qualified Institutional Placements (QIP), Global Depository Receipts/American Depository Receipts (GDR/ADR), and Foreign Currency Convertible Bonds (FCCBs).

Funding for small enterprises still remains with family and friends. Internal sources of funding are a significant source of funds for large and well-established firms. The institution of a DFI as a source of funding for large projects has become defunct—there are no longer large government-sponsored DFIs as sources of funding for new enterprises. A pool of professional private equity (PE) investors is increasingly a significant source of funding for entrepreneur-driven firms moving into the next phase of their growth. The private equity asset class includes venture capital, buyouts, and mezzanine investment activity.

---

[1] The largest government-sponsored DFIs in India were the Industrial Development Bank of India (IDBI) and the Industrial Credit and Investment Corporation of India (ICICI). Both IDBI and ICICI today are banks with widespread shareholding.

In this chapter, we first focus on the PE investors in India, the size of the sector today, and the institutions through which the development is taking place. Next, we focus on the exit strategies available. In this, our primary focus will be on the IPO process in India, where the market today is well-entrenched in size and pricing characteristics as well as participants and institutions.

3.1   PRIVATE EQUITY INVESTMENT

The professional PE fund is a relatively recent phenomenon in India. The first PE capital inflows into the country was by multilateral agencies like the World Bank in partnership with the Government of India. The entry of the first foreign PE funds was in the second half of the nineties. Their participation in the industry rode on the back of the global IT boom, where IT in India was viewed as the prominent funding opportunity. After the 2001 crash in the market, there was a temporary drop in the number of both funds as well as investments. Despite this, there was a sufficiently large number of successes among these first entrants into the PE industry in India and this drew in a larger number of funds and investments in the following period.

Table 3.1 (from Dossani, 2006a) illustrates the growth in this industry as well as the changing profile of the target funding stages. While the multilateral agencies and the government were prominent during the early focus on seed and developmental funding, the more recent period has a far larger set of participants with both Domestic PE as well as Foreign PE fund firms. The focus of the investment is also different from the early period: today's funds have a greater focus on late-stage funding, buyouts and private investment in public equity (PIPE). The focus is mainly on private equity rather than venture capital, which is a funding source that is growing at a slower pace.

Publicly available sources of collated information on the PE industry is hard to find. One such credit source of information are publications by TSJ Media Private Ltd. (TSJ). From their reports, the picture that emerges about the state of PE activity in India in 2005 and 2006 is shown in Table 3.2.

The bulk of PE funding comes from outside the country. From the viewpoint of India's capital controls, all PE investments are either classified as foreign institutional investment (FII) (for investments in listed companies) or foreign direct investment (FDI) (for investments in unlisted companies). Under the FII category, the PIPEs are large transactions contracted between the PE fund and the firm, and pure FII transactions are purchases by the PE fund on the secondary market.

In contrast, India-based funds appear to have greater dominance in VC funding. Fifty-eight percent of the deals were done by India-based funds in 2006.

TABLE 3.1   Phases of Growth of Indian Risk Capital

	Phase I Pre-1995	Phase II 1995–1997	Phase III 1998–2001	Phase IV 2002–2005
Primary Stages and Sectors	Seed, Early-Stage and Development —Diversified	Development Diversified —Telecom	Early-Stage and Development —IT	Growth/Maturity Diversified
Primary Sources of Funds	World Bank, Government	Government	Overseas Institutional	Overseas Institutional
Total Funds: ($m)	30	125	2,847	5,239
Number of Funds	8	20	50	75
Seed/Early-Stage ($m)	5	15	657	250
Number of Transactions	10	20	273	58
Development ($m)	25	110	2,168.1	3,107
Number of Transactions	20	45	273	288
Growth/Maturity ($m)			21.9	1,882
Number of Transactions			2	100
Total Number of Transactions	30	65	548	446
Average Investment ($m)	1	2	5.20	11.75

However, there are also a significant number of new technology-based VC funds as well as VC funds with Silicon Valley connections that started direct investment activity in 2006. Therefore, it is possible that global funds might have an increasingly greater dominance in the VC space going forward.

We should also note the growth in the size of the PIPE investments. The number of PIPE deals in 2005 was more than double the figure in 2004 (Table 3.2 shows only 2005 and 2006). Though PIPE growth slowed in 2006 reportedly due to a large number-pre-IPO placements, the number of PIPE deals in 2007 is placed at 400 PE deals, valued at roughly Rs.692 billion. Some of the top deals in the year included Temasek Holdings USD 1.9 billion investment in telecom and a group of FIIs, including the Deutsche Bank and Citigroup, investing USD one billion in infrastructure.

Despite the current dominance of late-stage funding and PIPEs, the outlook for the growth of this industry to include seed-funding and early-stage funding is optimistic (Dossani, 2006):

- The industry displays the ability to grow the managerial capability necessary to manage an increasing pool of funds and projects.

TABLE 3.2 Features of the PE Industry in 2005 and 2006

	2005	2006
PE investments	USD 2.25 billion	USD 7.5 billion
number of deals	302	148
VC investments	USD 268 million	USD 508 million
number of deals	44	92
Size of largest PE investment	USD 127 million	USD 996 million
By source of funds (number of deals, value of investments)		
Global PE funds		173, USD 5.2 billion
India-based PE funds		124, USD 1.7 billion
By target industry		
Largest target industry (by number and value of deals)	IT and IT-ES (44 deals, USD 474 million)	IT and IT-ES (87 deals, USD 1.5 billion)
Second largest target industry (by number and fraction of deals)	Manufacturing (26, USD 366 million)	Manufacturing (55 deals, USD 962 million)
By stage (number and value of deals)		
Early Stage	28, USD 150 million	59, USD 241 million
Growth Stage	24, USD 332 million	46, USD 551 million
Late Stage	40, USD 632 million	108, USD 3.6 billion
PIPE	49, USD 820 million	66, USD 1.6 billion
Buyouts	6, USD 375 million	14, USD 1.4 billion
By exit		
Total number of exits (number)	42	39
IPO (number)	17	19
Largest IPO (value of funds raised during IPO)	USD 342 million	USD 224 million (in an NYSE IPO)
Largest reported M&A (original investment, value at exit)	USD 292 million, USD 1.4 million	USD 134 million, USD 736 million

Further, the management, being independent and professional rather than strategic and state-dominated, bodes well for a further scale-up in managerial capability to sustain this growth.

- The source of funds are largely institutional and, therefore, has a longer-term investment perspective.
- The management structure is one that follows the structures seen more in a developed-economy setting rather than those seen typically in East Asian economies like Korea. This is likely an outcome of the global network of firms participating in the Indian PE sector, which will be important in order to source funds as well as the human capital required as the industry requirement grows.
- The domestic PE funds are spread across the large metros of Bombay, Delhi and Bangalore as opposed to being concentrated in the financial center, Bombay. The wider the spread of the PE industry, the larger the number of entrepreneurs the industry can access.

For example, the TSJ publications report the breakup of PE and VC investments by regions and cities across 2005 and 2006 in Table 3.3. The growth of the PE as well as the VC industry across the two years shows that the investments are spreading to find the growth of entrepreneurs across the country.

Therefore, even though Tables 3.1 and 3.2 bear evidence that the focus of the PE industry is more on investment in late-stage/PIPE deals rather than early stage deals, we might bear in mind that this is a relatively young and rapidly changing industry. One aspect of the early stage deals is that the average size of investments required in such deals is bound to be smaller than the average investment size required at the later stages. Therefore, the investment value is commensurately smaller. Last, it is worthwhile that investments at these stages are not stagnant: there *is* growth in investments at the early and growth stages as well.

Given these features, it is likely that the growth of the PE industry will be sustained. However, there are several features that can be bottlenecks to smooth progress. Several of the problems the industry faces start from the structures PE firms have to operate in in India, which translate into transactions costs for the firms to enter the industry. We start with a brief description of the PE industry structure.

3.1.1 STRUCTURE OF THE PE SECTOR

India has both domestic PE and foreign PE firms. Domestic PE firms are either established as trusts, or set up as a company. They have to be registered with the

TABLE 3.3   VC and PE Investments by Region in 2005 and
2006

	2005		2006	
	No.	USD Million	No.	USD Million
PE investments				
South	56	943	111	1,600
West	54	923	112	3,700
North	30	360	58	1,900
East	4	68	11	130
Bangalore	21	368	40	1,500
Bombay	37	695	69	1,800
NCR*	26	322	41	395
Chennai	15	321	22	354
Hyderabad	14	168	17	492
Pune	9	91	10	1,100
VC investments (number of deals, value of investments)				
South			52	287
West			26	132
North			13	82
East			1	1
Bangalore			33	183
Bombay			24	128
NCR*			11	75
Chennai			9	53
Hyderabad			6	36

* NCR: The National Capital Region. Numbers for NCR include Delhi, Gurgaon
and NCR.

Securities Exchanges Board of India (SEBI). SEBI is reponsible for the regulation
of the PE industry under the Venture Capital Regulations Act of 1996.

Under the Venture Capital Regulations Act, PE funds have to comply with
certain restrictions:

1. Domestic PEs can only take investors with a minimum investment of
   Rs.500,000. The total size of the domestic PE has to be above Rs.50
   million.

   There are no such restrictions on the Foreign PEs.
2. However, Foreign PE firms have restrictions on how much they can invest
   in domestic firms: not more than 25% of the funds can be invested with
   a single domestic PE fund.

   At least 75% of the investment must be invested in unlisted equity
   shares. Foreign PE firms face some sectoral and security restrictions on
   investment under SEBI rules.

In 2006, there were 80 domestic PE and 39 foreign PE funds in India. Most of the foreign PE funds (all but one) were based out of Mauritius.[2] Since Mauritius has a tax treaty with India, routing the funding of the PE means a lower tax burden on the investors in the PE fund.

In fact, the high rate of capital gains tax imposes a transaction cost on the PE firms operating in India. Further, the recent environment has become more expensive in terms of the taxation of PE firms. For example, for PE firms registered with SEBI, the income earned from investments in portfolio companies would normally not have been liable to tax. Instead, investors of the PE firm would have been liable for taxes on amounts distributed by the PE firm. The Finance Budget 2007 limits the amount of the tax exemption available to the PE firm, which would further increase the cost of running a PE firm in India.

Dossani (2006) reports that there are pros and cons to running a PE firm in India. Among the problems he lists are (a) lack of well-established domestic network of entrepreneurs, financiers, firms, and research institutions, (b) a poor operating environment including poor corporate governance at the smaller firms and an inefficient legal system and (c) the tax environment and a costly process to create a tax-efficient structure for international investors. Among the advantages of being in India are (a) cost competitiveness, which may be vanishing fast, and (b) the development of a strong capital market environment which is capable of providing capital for the next-stage growth. This latter includes a thriving IPO market for primary issues, as well as other sources of funding such as the QIP.

3.1.2   EXITS FOR A PE INVESTMENT

A top priority for a PE firm while investing in a project is to identify a plausible strategy for exit. Therefore, a PE business is more likely to thrive in an economy where it has access to choices of exit. The three useful elements for a PE industry are (a) a well-functioning IPO market which yields valuations comparable to those found on a well-functioning secondary market; (b) a large set of listed firms who might like to buy firms and (c) an incoming stream of FDI where international firms might like to buy firms. As was seen in Table 3.2, India has a benign environment containing all three aspects.

A last, upcoming venue for PE/VC exit is the international equity markets. The first Indian company to list purely outside India was rediff.com. The company was held in Kothari Pioneer's Internet Opportunities Fund and went IPO

---

[2]Mauritius has a tax treaty with India, where all firms from Mauritius running a business in India are eligible for capital gain tax exemption.

as an American Depository Receipt (ADR) at NASDAQ in June 2000. Since then, there have been a few such exits,[3] but these are not yet the norm in the PE industry.

Of the three exit mechanisms, India has a rather unique IPO market mechanism. The IPO market in India was one of the first that started using the electronic book-building mechanism to list the equity shares of a new company. We discuss this market mechanism next.

3.2   THE IPO MARKET

The Indian IPO market in the pre-reforms period was controlled by the Controller of Capital Issues (CCI)—a department at the Ministry of Finance. The firm would set the quantity of the issue to be raised. But the CCI would decide at what price the shares would be issued. Typically, the prices were set at either Rs.10 or Rs.100. In 1992, the CCI was closed down. Today, firms issue shares at market-determined prices, through a variety of market intermediaries and market mechanisms. In 2007, India was reported to be the 5th largest IPO market globally, raising $8.5 billion (or Rs.342 billion) across 101 issues. The largest IPO in 2007 was a real estate development firm (DLF) which raised about Rs.92 billion.

3.2.1   MARKET PARTICIPANTS

The participants that make this market are:

1. Issuers: An unlisted firm has to satisfy eligibility criteria before it can do an IPO, some of which are:

   a. Has net tangible assets of at least Rs.30 million in each of the preceding 3 full years.
   b. Has a net worth of at least Rs.10 million in each of the preceding 3 full years.
   c. The aggregate of the proposed issue (and all previous issues made in the same financial year) is not more than five times the present net worth.

2. Investment Banks: They can play two roles in the issue process.

   a. In a public issue, the investment banker does due diligence on the firm, decides a price and takes care of the formalities such as

---

[3]One was the largest IPO exit in 2006 of WNS Global, one of the largest BPO companies in India which listed as an IPO on the New York Stock Exchange.

       the dematerialization of the shares and filing the statement with
       SEBI.

   b. If the issue is privately placed, an investment banker, after due dili-
       gence, decides a price and places shares among a closed network of
       clients.

3. Exchange: The platform on which any trading, clearing and settlement
    take place. Both the exchanges, the National Stock Exchange as well as
    the Bombay Stock Exchange have the facility to issue an IPO using an
    electronic, book-building platform.

3.2.2 Market Mechanism

The dominant mechanism to issue an IPO for a firm in India is the book-building
process. In the book-building process, bids are received at various prices from
the investors. Each bid needs to specify a quantity as well as a price. Once the
book is complete, the price is set at that level so that the maximum number of
shares can be sold. Book building requires that the firm indicate a floor price.
The time given for the exercise is at least three working days and not more than
seven working days when bids can be submitted. On the exchanges, the bidding
is done electronically: investors can bid at any price, retail investors have the
option to bid at the cut off price. These bids are binding once the book is closed;
the bids can be modified until the close. The bidding demand is displayed at
the end of every day. The investment bank analyzes the demand generated and
determines the issue price in consultation with the issuer.

    The Indian electronic book-building exercise involves limits for different
kinds of investors. For example, at least 25% of the issue is reserved for individual investors, where the size of a retail bid is capped at a maximum of
Rs.50,000 (around USD 1,250).

    At the close of the book building, the winning bids are allotted shares pro-
portional to the quantity they bid. The shares are directly credited into their
depository accounts in dematerialized form. All shares issued in India today
are mandatorily issued in dematerialized form; physical share certificates are
no longer issued.

3.2.3 Market Outcomes

The Indian IPO market has had three different phases of market activity: pre-
liberalization in 1992, post-liberalization to 1997 when there was a crash in the
Indian equity market, and 2003 to the present. The post-liberalization period
saw a boom in IPOs coming to the market. However, with the market crash in

TABLE 3.4   Issues in the Equity Market, IPO and SEO

Issue	2004–2005		2005–2006	
	Number	Amount (Rs. billion)	Number	Amount (Rs. billion)
IPOs	23	1,238	79	1,093
Issues by Listed Companies	37	1,587	60	1,645
Public Issues	11	1,226	24	1,236
Rights Issues	26	362	36	409

1997, the spate of IPOs dropped to a trickle. It was from 2002–2003 onward that there has been a return of large IPO issues in the Indian market. Table 3.4 shows the growth of all equity issues in 2004–2006.

The underpricing in the IPO issues is positively correlated with the amount of the oversubscription. For example, Bubna and Prabhala (2007) find that IPO issues coming to the market today are oversubscribed, on average, by around eight to nine times. They find that the same period had a market-adjusted mean underpricing in IPOs of around 33%.

Gopalan and Gormley (2007) find how the IPO market liberalization changed the choice of financing among Indian firms:

- The IPO market liberalization opened up financial access more for young firms compared to large family-owned business. They found a significant decrease in the age of firms that accessed equity financing in the post-liberalization period.
- Once these firms were able to access equity markets, the reliance on alternative and more expensive sources of funding (such as trade credit) reduced.

CHAPTER 4

The Public Equity Market

In this chapter, we describe the public equity market, i.e., the universe of firms which are listed.

4.1 PRODUCTS, VENUES, MARKET DESIGN

The Indian equity market involves the following trading venues:

- The National Stock Exchange (NSE)
- The Bombay Stock Exchange (BSE)
- ADRs listed at NYSE and NASDAQ
- GDRs traded in Europe
- A globally dispersed offshore OTC equity derivatives market

4.1.1 NSE AND BSE

The public equity market within India, both spot and derivatives, takes place almost entirely at the two exchanges—NSE and BSE.[1] The exchanges have an essentially identical trading system, with the following features:

- There is an open electronic limit order book with order matching by the trading computer.
- There are no market makers.
- Both exchanges trade equity spot and equity derivatives.
- There is T+2 demateralized settlement on the equity spot market.

[1]For a treatment of the exciting story that led up to the modern structure of the Indian equity market, see Echeverri-Gent (2007) and Shah and Thomas (2000).

TABLE 4.1   Circuit Breaker Mechanism

Time	Size of movement		
	10%	15%	20%
Before 13:00	1 hour	2 hours	Halt
13:00–14:30	30 minutes	1 hour	Halt
After 14:30	None	Halt	Halt

Both exchanges trade from 9:55 A.M. to 3:30 P.M. in IST, which is five and a half hours added to GMT. India is unusual in having the din and fury of two very active exchanges doing spot and derivatives trading on equity from 9:55 A.M. to 3:30 P.M., and no equity trading at any other time of the day.

Table 4.1 describes the circuit breaker mechanism which is triggered by movements of Nifty or the BSE sensex. If large moves take place early in the day, they induce a halt of trading. If very large moves take place, and there is not enough time left, trading halts for the day. This mechanism has been triggered twice in history: on May 17, 2004, when the incoming UPA administration sent out signals of socialist economic policies, and in October 2007, when capital controls were introduced against participatory notes.

There is an upstairs market where brokerage firms search for counterparties for outsized orders. However, almost all of this institutional turnover is exposed to the public order book. The institutional counterparties locate each other by telephone, but after that, both counterparties place their large limit orders on the public order books of one of the two exchanges.[2] Both exchanges do dematerialized delivery through two competing depositories, the National Securities Depository Ltd. (NSDL) and the Central Depository Services Ltd. (CDSL).[3] NSE is a shareholder in NSDL while BSE is a shareholder in CDSL. While NSDL and CDSL compete in offering depository services, a customer is fully free to have an account with NSDL or CDSL, and then choose to trade on any of the two exchanges. The choice of exchange and the choice of depository are independent: the settlement processes on either exchange work fully with settlement on either depository.

[2]Institutional investors expose their order to the screen for two reasons. First, it gives them access to the highly efficient clearing and settlement processes of the exchanges. Further, visibility of their transactions on the exchange screens in this fashion is mandated by the regulator.

[3]NSDL commands dominant market share, with 196 billion dematerialized shares, as compared with 30 billion shares at CDSL.

TABLE 4.2 Structure of Daily Average Equity Turnover in
March 2007

	Spot	Derivatives	Sum	
		Billion USD		Share (%)
NSE	1.81	7.47	9.28	90
BSE	0.84	0.19	1.03	10
Total	2.65	7.66	10.31	100

Table 4.2 shows an example of the structure of average daily turnover
seen in March 2007 on NSE and BSE. NSE has dominant market share in
derivatives, and a 2:1 advantage when it comes to the spot market. These
market share relationships between NSE and BSE have been stable from 2002
onward. On average, the Indian equity market involves trading of $10.3 billion
a day.

In early 2007, the NSE equity spot market averaged 3.4 million trades a
day or an average of 170 trades per second. While this is a hectic pace of
market activity, the mean trade size was small—Rs.23,655 or $577. BSE was
at 1.5 million trades a day, with a similar trade size. The picture, then, is one
of a very high trading intensity for small trade sizes. The small trade size in
India is accentuated owing to the fact that the minimum market lot in which
transactions can be conducted is one. In other words, it is possible to place an
order for one share on the trading system.

There has been dramatic growth in trading intensity. Both exchanges were
at 0.1 million trades a day in 1996–1997. In a decade, the BSE has grown by 15
times and the NSE by 31 times.

Almost all listed firms are listed on BSE. NSE listing requirements are stiff, and
most firms do not qualify for these. Some BSE-listed firms are also listed on NSE.
A small set of firms are only NSE-listed. By and large, the exchanges compete
for *order flow* for cross-listed stocks. Competition for listings is not an important
feature of the competition between the NSE and BSE, since the regulatory and
legal environment supports multiple listings and listing fees are low.

When a firm is traded on both the NSE and BSE, both prices are directly
comparable since they both pertain to T+2 settlement. The two prices are
tightly bound by arbitrage. The official NSE closing price is the value weighted
average (VWA) of the last 30 minutes of trading. Since the NSE has more trading
of most stocks, the NSE closing price is the preferred measure of price on the
Indian equity market. Neither exchange offers sophisticated order placement

and order matching mechanisms such as a market-on-close order, or a call auction.[4]

NSE members have roughly 50,000 trading screens across the country and BSE members have roughly 25,000 trading screens. Put together, there are roughly 75,000 screens, each of which is associated with a human dealer who is often a conduit for an order flow coming in over the telephone. Both exchanges are demutualized, and there is an infinite supply of memberships that can be accessed any time. For all practical purposes, any important member firm has memberships on both exchanges. The important firms have offices all over the country for the purpose of interacting with geographically dispersed order flow.

While Bombay is the financial capital of the country, and almost all institutional turnover (including that of foreign investors) originates in Bombay, a considerable amount of trading originates from cities outside Bombay. Table 4.3 shows the important cities in the sum of NSE and BSE turnover, as seen in January 2007. In this month, NSE and BSE turnover summed to Rs.2.6 trillion or $59.4 billion.

Bombay is, obviously, very important, with $38 billion of turnover in a month, accounting for a shade under two-thirds of the turnover. This turnover reflects a combination of institutional turnover (since almost all institutional investors are in Bombay) and the noninstitutional business originating from Bombay. There were seven other cities that have at least $0.5 billion of turnover.

TABLE 4.3   Geographical Breakdown of Equity Spot Market Turnover (January 2007)

City	Turnover		
	Billion INR	Billion USD	Share (%)
Bombay	1,691	38.3	64.4
Delhi	263	6.0	10.0
Kolkata	190	4.3	7.3
Ahmedabad	79	1.8	3.0
Chennai	39	0.9	1.5
Bangalore	27	0.6	1.0
Hyderabad	23	0.5	0.9
Jaipur	21	0.5	0.9
Others	293	6.6	11.2
Total	2,627	59.4	100.0

---

[4]There is no official way for an investor to achieve a transaction at the official NSE closing price. One possibility consists of placing 30 orders, one per minute, in the last 30 minutes.

What is somewhat remarkable is that *after* these major centers are counted, a considerable amount of activity is left out: the Others in the table account for $6.6 billion of turnover a month or 11.2% of the total.

4.1.2   MARKET INDEXES

There are three important groups of market indexes in India: The BSE Sensex, Nifty & Nifty Junior, and the CMIE Cospi. The oldest and most prominent index in India is the BSE Sensitive Index, known as the BSE Sensex. The BSE Sensex was created in 1986. The set of companies that formed the index was chosen by a committee. It was a market-capitalization weighted index of 30 listed firms. Daily data is available from April 1979 onward, where the returns prior to 1986 were back calculated keeping the set of companies fixed for the seven year period from 1979 to 1986. The committee was likely to have chosen firms which did well in the 1979–1986 period. This is likely to have generated an upward bias in the apparent returns on the BSE Sensex.

The index set that was selected in 1986 was held fixed till 1996. This is likely to have generated a downward bias in index returns during the 1986–1996 period. In a substantial reshuffle of the index components in 1996, as many as 13 of the 30 stocks were changed on one day. After 1996, the index set has been monitored and maintained on a regular basis. In 2002, the BSE Sensex shifted from market capitalization weights to "floating stock weights." Here, the weightage of a company in the index is proportional to the shares held by investors who might possibly sell the shares.[5]

The events of 1986, 1996 and 2002 imply that while the BSE Sensex has a long time-series going back to April 1979, it suffers from inconsistencies in methodology. An additional difficulty when using the Sensex is that a total returns index, which incorporates capital gains and dividends, is not available.

The most important alternative to the BSE Sensex is an index published by the National Stock Exchange (NSE). Since 1995, the NSE has been India's biggest stock market. In 1996, a new index named the NSE-50 or Nifty was released. This was calculated as a market capitalization weighted portfolio containing 50 stocks. The full name of the index is now "S&P CNX Nifty," reflecting an involvement of Standard & Poors from 1999 onward. While the BSE Sensex is calculated using prices from the BSE, the NSE-50 is calculated using prices from the NSE.

---

[5] The measurement of floating stock in India presents several difficulties. Hence, "float weights" should be treated as only broadly indicative of the ownership structure.

The 50 firms that go into the NSE-50 index are chosen using a methodology that focuses on liquidity. The stocks are required to deliver low transactions costs while doing portfolio (or basket) trades to buy or sell the index portfolio. Basket trades of Rs.5 million at a time are simulated for these computations. Basket trades are simulated using four snapshots of the limit order book every day on NSE, so as to achieve measurement of the impact cost suffered when doing basket trades. Firms with a higher market capitalization naturally have bigger transaction sizes in these simulated baskets. The simulations use exact data from NSE, and thus accurately measure the transactions costs associated with doing basket trades. This mechanism ensures that the index series is not contaminated by illiquid stocks, and that index returns are genuinely attainable to an investor who would have to implement such basket trades on the market. The time-series for the NSE-50 from March 1996 onward consistently uses these rules and is hence an internally consistent time-series. The time-series was pushed back to July 1990, where high trading frequency was used as a proxy for low transactions costs. Through this imputation strategy, a time-series of the NSE-50 index is available from July 1990 onward.

Another useful index which uses the same methodology is Nifty Junior. This contains the set of 50 stocks which satisfy the liquidity criteria, but are not big enough to qualify for inclusion into the NSE-50 index. The sets of stocks in Nifty and Nifty Junior are guaranteed to always be disjoint sets. It is hence easy to compute a composite index of the 100 most liquid firms of India, as a weighted average of the two returns, with weights proportional to the market capitalization. This merged index has been given the confusing name CNX-100. The most interesting feature of Nifty Junior has been the remarkable returns over the 10.57 years of its history, with data that starts from November 4, 1996. While Nifty returned 4.82 times (16.04% per year) over this period, Nifty Junior returned 8.1 times (21.89% per year) over the identical period (both figures exclude dividends). The outperformance of many active fund managers, when compared with Nifty, was about their having an exposure to Nifty Junior.

The two major financial sector applications of market indexes are in index funds and index derivatives. Derivatives based on the NSE-50 trade at the NSE in India, and at the SGX in Singapore. In India, over 99% of the index derivatives trading volume is based on the NSE-50 index. The NSE-50 is the largest single underlying on exchange-traded derivatives in India. The BSE Sensex had 7% market share in July 2005 in the index fund market. ETFs are available on Nifty, the BSE Sensex and Nifty Junior.

A comprehensive set of stock market indexes, spanning different sectors as well as the entire economy, comes from the Centre for Monitoring Indian Economy (CMIE). The CMIE indexes are calculated using a consistent methodology from 1990 onward. The largest of the index portfolios calculated at CMIE (called Cospi) recomputes a set of eligible stocks every day, containing all firms with a historical trading frequency above 66%. In June 2007, Cospi consisted of 2,663 stocks, which had a market capitalization of Rs.41.78 trillion which constitutes the universe of actively traded equity in India. For all practical purposes, there is no meaningful equity market beyond these 2,663 firms.

The remaining listed companies, which are not in the Cospi set, are highly illiquid and contain a small amount of market value. For all practical purposes, they are not in the public equity investment universe. However, they are interesting targets for PIPE (private investment in public equity) investment, particularly because the rich data availability that is induced by listing requirements makes it easy for a private equity investor to thoroughly study them at low cost. Some of these firms are ordinary illiquid firms, but there is a possibility of outlandish stock prices, weak accounting data, outlandish valuations and weak corporate governance. These firms are the wild frontier of listed space, and for the bulk of this chapter, we pay no attention to this group. Most of this chapter focuses on the active Indian equity which we define as the CMIE Cospi firms.

CMIE releases the Cospi and a detailed breakdown of 254 industry indexes organized in a tree structure. Table 4.4 shows one example of the tree structure of indexes that is available. Level II below the overall Cospi is the Metals & metal products, where there are 191 firms in all with a market value of Rs.2.85 trillion. The overall Metals & metal products index is broken down into two Level III indexes for Ferrous metals and Non-ferrous metals. One of the sub-indexes available under the Ferrous metals index is for Steel (a Level IV index). And finally, one of the sub-indexes available below this, at Level V, is for companies making stainless steel. This rich tree-structured collection of market indexes permits an accurate understanding of industry-level stock market fluctuations.

CMIE also releases the daily time-series of the number of stocks in the overall Cospi, its market capitalization and the P/E. The strengths of Cospi are that a single consistent methodology is in place from 1990 onward, a large universe of stocks is captured, and a detailed range of industry indexes are available. The weakness of the Cospi family is that these index sets are relatively illiquid, which introduces noise in the index time-series and impedes the direct utilization of the indexes in financial products such as index funds and index derivatives.

4.1.3 CHARACTERISTICS OF THE INDEXES

Figure 4.1 shows the long time-series of the level of Cospi (in log scale), and of the P/E ratio of Cospi. Cospi started at 100 in mid-1990 and has risen twenty-fold in the following years. When India opened up in the early 1990s, at first

TABLE 4.4   Tree-Structured Industry Indexes from CMIE: An Example

| | 25 May 2007 | |
Industry	Number of firms	Market capn. (Rs. billion)
Metals & metal products	191	2,850
Ferrous metals	160	1,832
Pig & sponge iron	14	24
Pig iron	6	16
Sponge iron	8	8
Steel	68	1,353
Finished steel	55	1,341
Stainless steel	5	2
Ferro alloys	8	9
Castings & forgings	15	48
Metal products	63	407
Steel tubes & pipes	26	148
Structurals	6	76
Metal tanks & fabrications	9	22
Steel wires	3	4
Fasteners	3	2
Other metal products	16	155
Non-ferrous metals	31	1,018
Aluminum & aluminum products	16	360
Aluminum	4	347
Aluminum products	12	13
Other non-ferrous metals	8	286
Copper & copper products	7	371

the index rose sharply, with a P/E ratio which touched 50. However, the fierce competitive pressures which came about upon opening up generated considerable difficulties for a large number of firms and many years were spent in a process of firm failure, restructuring of firms, and rearrangement of control of assets through mergers and acquisitions. The index P/E ratio dropped all the way to 10.

In the late 1990s, the global IT boom—based on the Y2K problem and on the rise of the Internet—had a profound effect on Indian software stocks, with the P/E rising to 35. This was followed by another difficult period for the market. From 2002 onward, Cospi fared extremely well, reflecting strong earnings growth and the global recovery after the brief recession of 2001. In this period, the remarkable returns of the index were based on stable P/E ratios and meteoric growth in earnings. The lowest P/E ratio in this period was 9.74 and the highest was 50.33. The median P/E ratio was 16.57. The 25th and 75th percentile—the

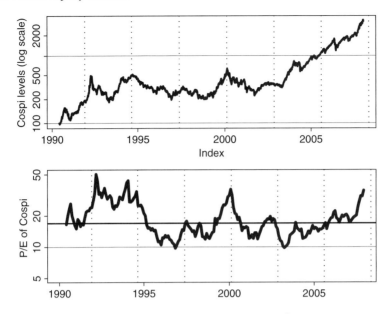

FIGURE 4.1   Time-Series Characteristics of Cospi

TABLE 4.5   Valuation of Market Indexes
(March 30, 2007)

Index	P/E	P/B	D/P
Nifty	18.40	4.87	1.25
Nifty Junior	18.48	3.49	1.13
CNX-100	18.41	4.61	1.23

interval between which the index P/E lay with a 50% probability—work out to 13.9 and 22.29.

Valuation characteristics of various indexes, at the end of March 2007, are presented in Table 4.5. Very large values of the P/B ratio are found in India, reflecting the low accounting value of equipment purchased in the past owing to a high inflation environment. The P/E ratio and the dividend yield involve all values at current prices, and are thus immune to this problem. The P/E of both Nifty and Nifty Junior were near 18.41, which is the overall P/E ratio of the CNX-100 index which represents the merger of Nifty and Nifty Junior. Dividend yields in India are relatively low, with a yield of 1.23% for the CNX-100 index.

4.2   LIQUIDITY

4.2.1   Impact Cost of Nifty and Nifty Junior

Impact cost is a good measure of liquidity in that it accurately measures the transactions costs faced when placing market orders on the electronic market. As an example, for Nifty, NSE calculates the basket of stocks which have to be purchased, with market capitalization weights, in order to buy and sell Rs.5 million ($125,000) of Nifty. Using three to four snapshots of the limit order book every day, NSE reports the average impact cost for doing program trades.

For Nifty Junior, NSE reports impact cost for doing a transaction of Rs.2.5 million ($62,000). This is a disproportionately large transaction, because the market capitalization of Nifty Junior is only 15% of that of Nifty. In both cases, these are plausible transaction sizes for index funds and generous sized transactions for arbitrageurs who are able to do smaller baskets.[6]

As Table 4.6 shows, in the case of Nifty, the impact cost at a Rs.5 million transaction, which used to be roughly 0.25% in 1996, had dropped to 0.2% in 2001 and dropped sharply to 0.08% by 2007. The impact cost for the Rs.2.5 million basket of Nifty Junior dropped from 0.24% in 2003 to 0.14% in 2007. The liquidity of Nifty Junior is thus roughly where Nifty was in 2001–2002. In CNX-100, 87% of the weightage belongs to Nifty stocks. Hence the impact cost of CNX-100 transactions is slightly worse than that of Nifty. A program trade for the 100-stock CNX-100 basket gets executed in under a second on NSE. Hence, there are no practical impediments for doing direct spot-futures arbitrage for any of the three indexes.

TABLE 4.6   Impact Cost (%)

Period	Nifty	Nifty Junior
2001	0.20	
2002	0.12	
2003	0.10	0.24
2004	0.09	0.24
2005	0.08	0.16
2006	0.08	0.16
Jan–Apr 2007	0.08	0.14

[6]The round market lot, which is the minimum quantity of shares that can be purchased, is one in India. Hence, little imprecision is introduced by rounding to the nearest market lot when computing the basket of shares that is traded when doing a program trade for the index. The smallest feasible index basket transaction sizes are roughly Rs.1 million ($25,000).

4.2.2 RESILIENCE OF LIQUIDITY

The first aspect of liquidity is a static concept: When an order is placed, by how much does the actual execution price degrade, when compared with a benchmark price? This is accurately measured using impact cost, as described above.

The second aspect of liquidity is resilience. A resilient financial market is one which is able to absorb large shocks and rapidly revert to efficient pricing and high levels of liquidity. The issue of resilience is relevant regardless of the direction of the shock: a large upward or downward movement is equally challenging for market efficiency. When a large order is placed in a market that lacks resilience, it takes a long time for liquidity and price to restore to normal levels. When a market lacks resilience, negative price shocks can adversely affect liquidity. The most extreme version of a lack of resilience is a case where market institutions collapse when there is a large price shock, and trading stops completely.

Resilience is important from two points of view. At an analytical level, resilience is a necessary condition for market efficiency. In an efficient market, prices rapidly revert to fundamentals, regardless of whether the shocks are from the order flow or from news. At a more practical level, poor resilience directly translates to liquidity risk. At future dates, economic agents face the risk that they might not be able to execute transactions as required, or the cost of transacting might be prohibitive.

In order to obtain some insight into the resilience of the Indian equity market, we closely examine the experience of two large price shocks on the equity market—the 36% drop in the price of Infosys over two days starting 10 April 2003 and the 12% drop in the market index on May 17, 2004.[7]

Example: Nifty on May 17, 2004. General elections took place in 2004 with an unexpected outcome. In response to negative news, the Nifty dropped by an unprecedented 21% in the first two hours of trading on May 17, 2004. At the end of the trading day, the market closed with a largest-ever one-day drop of 12%. The CMIE Cospi index, which is a more comprehensive index covering all significant Indian equities, also dropped by 12%. Despite such a large drop, the equity market institutions did not collapse. Instead, markets stayed open for business.

What is more, the liquidity in the market remained sound. Table 4.7 presents the evidence of the number of trades that were executed on the National Stock Exchange and the Bombay Stock Exchange during the period. We also look at

---

[7] This comparision is based on Thomas (2006b), which goes on to compare the impact of price shocks on liquidity of the equity and debt markets. The main finding there is that while the equity market appears to have considerable resilience, this is not the case with the debt market.

the number of shares that were traded at the time. Both the number of trades
and the number of shares traded show no drop in value around May 17, when
the index drops significantly.

Price discovery at this time was concentrated on the index derivatives market
(with the largest activity being focused on Nifty futures trading). Here too the
liquidity remained strong, as can be seen in the data on number of contracts
traded in the last column in Table 4.7. This experience compares well with,
say, the October 1987 crash on the New York Stock Exchange, when liquidity
vanished in response to a 21% drop in the index.

Example: Infosys on April 10, 2003. On April 10, 2003, Infosys Technologies, one of the biggest firms in the country, announced a gloomy earnings
outlook. Infosys signaled that it was unlikely to be able to maintain the high

TABLE 4.7   Liquidity in the Indian Equity Markets around May 17, 2004

Date	CMIE Cospi index	NSE + BSE turnover (No. of trades)	(No. of shares)	Index futures (No. of contracts)
Pre-event				
May 3	741.97	1,649,915	245,354,000	333,921
May 4	755.92	1,531,144	235,415,000	275,337
May 5	762.92	1,515,675	241,438,000	231,047
May 6	774.88	1,563,617	273,661,000	238,171
May 7	764.70	1,612,551	284,350,000	253,403
May 10	750.96	1,465,055	242,245,000	278,484
May 11	717.84	1,381,364	227,157,000	274,407
May 12	723.11	1,662,059	247,569,000	292,879
May 13	722.57	2,231,378	363,509,000	484,365
May 14	660.18	2,307,533	389,614,000	497,610
Event				
May 17	582.27			
Post-event				
May 18	627.36	1,889,804	294,170,000	272,737
May 19	658.61	2,065,262	307,024,000	306,470
May 20	653.67	1,840,805	273,963,000	272,847
May 21	656.47	1,605,056	215,305,000	336,866
May 24	674.29	1,631,292	220,922,000	309,148
May 25	673.13	1,741,467	229,012,000	365,793
May 26	673.68	1,658,692	224,941,000	333,396
May 27	667.18	1,523,038	204,337,000	353,083
May 28	635.19	1,835,976	259,607,000	294,658
May 31	619.22	1,816,211	237,583,000	284,215

earnings growth associated with the software industry. The valuation of the market dropped sharply and dramatically. Over a two-day period, the price fell by 36%, one of the largest-ever price changes over two days for a large stock in India. However, as Table 4.8 shows, the supply of liquidity on the market remained steady. The number of shares transacted per day, summing across NSE and BSE, rose sharply on the date of the announcement (10 April) but then fell back to pre-event levels.

Table 4.8 shows details of the liquidity as the news broke on 10 April 2003. The average level of turnover, prior to the event, was 1,025,670 shares per day. The event was associated with a massive *increase* in trading, as myriad speculators participated in price discovery. From April 10 to April 17, turnover *increased* to the range of 2 to 6.5 million shares a day. The highly negative news event did not generate a negative impact upon liquidity. After this news was absorbed into the price, the liquidity of the market returned to normal conditions. The mean turnover in the 30 trading days from April 23 onward was 1,169,973 shares per day, which was insignificantly different from the mean turnover of the 30 days prior to April 10.

TABLE 4.8   Price and Turnover of Infosys in April 2003

Date	Adj. closing price (Rupees)	NSE + BSE turnover (Number of shares)
Pre-event		
Apr 4	1,073.80	1,119,145
Apr 7	1,095.72	963,174
Apr 8	1,058.13	954,262
Apr 9	1,037.99	979,878
Event		
Apr 10	762.44	4,822,068
Apr 11	663.34	6,524,268
Apr 15	714.92	3,412,717
Apr 16	756.13	2,586,204
Apr 17	740.85	2,122,830
Apr 21	733.15	1,261,185
Apr 22	729.92	1,322,230
Post-event		
Apr 23	720.75	1,056,386
Apr 24	724.46	1,610,804
Apr 25	727.48	749,380
Apr 28	723.21	810,668

4.3   DERIVATIVES

There is equity derivatives trading on stock market indexes and 186 individual stocks. In both cases, futures and options are traded, with maturities from one to three months. Almost all derivatives trading takes place at the NSE. The trading system is identical to the spot market: it is an electronic limit order book market, there are no market makers and trading runs from 9:55 A.M. to 3:30 P.M. exactly as is the case with the equity spot market.

The National Securities Clearing Corporation (NSCC) is the central counterpart for net settlement obligations of all clearing members for equity spot and derivatives trades on the NSE. NSCC runs a realtime SPAN-style risk management system. Despite the extremely high transaction intensity at NSE, the instant a trade takes place, the position of the purchaser and the seller are updated at the *client* level, and a fresh SPAN margin calculation is done.[8] It has been in business since 1996 and has weathered substantial market events such as the crash of May 17, 2004, when large spot and derivatives positions were present. This has helped induce confidence in the risk management system. At the same time, the general sense in the market is that the capital requirements, and position limits, on NSE are exceedingly conservative and are impeding the ability of equity derivatives to fully perform their functions of enabling speculation and hedging.

Table 4.9 shows the structure of equity derivatives turnover at the NSE in the month of April 2007. Over the entire month, notional turnover amounted to $151.1 billion. There were 20 trading days in the month, so this works out to an average of $7.56 billion per day. The end-of-day open interest has typically been slightly below twice the one-day turnover. Contract sizes in India are small, so turnover when measured by number of contracts is very high.

TABLE 4.9   Structure of NSE Equity Derivatives Notional Turnover in April 2007

	Turnover		
Component	Rs. billion	Billion USD	Share in total (%)
Individual stock futures	2,966	72.7	48.1
Individual stock options	171	4.2	2.8
Index futures	2,055	50.4	33.3
Index options	972	23.8	15.8
Total	6,164	151.1	100.0

[8]These calculations are done using a system called *Parallel Risk Management* (PRISM).

When measurement is done by the number of contracts, NSE is the second largest exchange in the world in stock futures and the third largest exchange in the world in index futures. The Nifty futures is one of the top 20 contracts of the world by this measure.

It is difficult to express negative views on the Indian equity *spot* market. This is a critical role that is played by the index and stock derivatives markets: the Nifty futures and the stock futures feature a free play between positive and negative views. Hence, in practice, the lack of a short selling and stock borrowing mechanism in India only impedes reverse cash and carry arbitrage; it does not interfere with price discovery.

Turnover in stock futures and stock options is dispersed over a large number of underlyings. In contrast almost all the index derivatives turnover is concentrated in one index, the Nifty. As a consequence, a full 51% of the notional turnover pertains to one underlying—Nifty. The near month Nifty futures is India's most liquid financial market.

Figure 4.2 shows the depth of the limit order book for the near month Nifty futures. This liquidity supply schedule shows the impact cost obtained for all transaction sizes. As an example, a purchase of Rs.1 billion—i.e., a single market order of value Rs.1 billion—gets executed at a one-way impact cost of 20 basis points. A sell order for Rs.1 billion of the Nifty futures (shown in the graph as a transaction with a negative size) gets a somewhat inferior execution, with a bigger impact cost.

In the real world, a customer might seldom place a single market order of a billion rupees or roughly $25.5 million. A customer faced with such a requirement might place a limit order at the touch (i.e., halfway between bid and offer) and wait for the market to chip away at this order. Or, a customer faced with such a requirement might dribble out five market orders of $5 million each. In this sense, the information shown in the graph measures the transactions

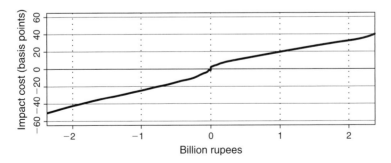

FIGURE 4.2   Impact Cost on Near Month Nifty Futures (mid-2007)

costs suffered under stringent conditions: a requirement to implement the entire transaction in a single market order.

4.3.1 MARKET EFFICIENCY AND ARBITRAGE

While banks are a natural class of financial firms with an interest in low-risk short-dated investments, the present regulations prohibit the participation of banks on the equity derivatives market. Insurance companies and pension funds are also absent in equity derivatives arbitrage. There are three kinds of players who are engaged in equity derivatives arbitrage:

Foreign institutional investors: FIIs have the skills and the permissions required to do equity derivatives arbitrage. However, the rules which block algorithmic trading have impeded the establishment of the IT systems which dominate arbitrage globally. FIIs are believed to do a few large sized arbitrage transactions when acute mispricings surface, but are not engaged in millisecond-to-millisecond trading.

Mutual funds: The existing regulations make it possible for mutual funds to launch dedicated products where assets under management will be deployed into arbitrage strategies which require cash. As an example, such mutual funds can do cash and carry arbitrage since they have cash, but not reverse cash and carry arbitrage since they do not have shares. In May 2007, Rs.25 billion of assets under management were held with 9 mutual fund products which were specialized in arbitrage.

Small securities firms: Perhaps the most important players in arbitrage are small securities firms. Given the ban on algorithmic trading, the way in which arbitrage is being done is through pairs of human traders facing computer screens. As an example, one person may watch the NSE Infosys order book while the other watches the BSE Infosys order book. Alternatively, one trader might watch the Infosys spot on NSE and another the Infosys futures on NSE. Each pair of traders places arbitrage transactions all through the day, and obtains a profit by removing mispricings.

There are perhaps thousands of such screens in the country. These firms dominate the millisecond-to-millisecond arbitrage order flow. However, they tend to be undercapitalized and are unable to solve many important mispricings. As an example, there have been many days when the spot-futures basis is negative. Given the absence of stock lending,[9] what this calls for is large institutional long-only investors who are able to sell shares on the

---

[9]For recent efforts on short selling backed by borrowed securities, see http://ajayshahblog.blogspot. com/2007/12/sebis-move-on-short-selling.html.

spot market and buy the cheap futures. This arbitrage is not feasible for the small securities firms.

4.3.2 DERIVATIVES TRADING ON NIFTY JUNIOR AND CNX-100

Index futures and options trading is available for Nifty Junior and CNX-100, in addition to Nifty. As described above, Nifty Junior is the second tier of stocks which do not make it into Nifty. Apart from this, it uses the identical methodology as that used in Nifty. The mechanism of index construction ensures that Nifty and Nifty Junior have no common members. CNX-100 is the merged index of the members of Nifty and Nifty Junior—it is the index of the top 100 liquid stocks of India.

Nifty Junior is more volatile than Nifty. In the recent period, from January 1, 2003 onward, Nifty had a daily volatility of 1.47% while Junior had 1.66%. All three indexes have high correlations. The correlation between Nifty and Junior is 0.85 while that between Nifty and CNX-100 is 0.995. The correlation between Junior and CNX-100 is 0.893. Derivatives trading on Nifty Junior, and on CNX-100, opens up many interesting possibilities:

- Index fund investors can go beyond the front-line bluechip stocks of Nifty, and buy Nifty Junior index funds, so as to delve into less liquid and smaller stocks.
- CNX-100 is a more-diversified broad Indian index than Nifty. CNX-100 index funds would be better than Nifty index funds at reflecting the broad Indian market movements. It would make a better proxy for broad market movements, and is likely to correlate better for well-diversified portfolios.
- The second tier stocks (Nifty Junior) have differing fluctuations when compared with the biggest stocks. A position which is long Nifty Junior and short Nifty would be focused on the difference between the movements of Nifty and the movements of this second tier of stocks.
- Many stock speculators buy a stock and short the index in order to hedge against broad market movements. For many stocks, superior hedging is obtained by using both Nifty and Nifty Junior in this hedging.[10]
- 37 of the 50 stocks in Nifty Junior, which make up 87.3% of the market capitalization, have stock futures trading. Hence, it is possible to do

---

[10] The calculation of hedge ratios in this case involves the estimation of a market model where stock returns are explained with two regressors: Nifty returns and Nifty Junior returns. As an example, consider Reliance Petroleum. Using Nifty alone, the beta is 0.58 and the market model R^2 is 0.39. Using both indexes yields a beta of 0.04 on Nifty and a beta of 0.49 on Nifty Junior, and an improved market model R^2 of 0.48.

futures-futures arbitrage between Nifty Junior futures and stock futures, for the bulk of Nifty Junior. For the remaining 13%, it would be necessary to use the spot market.

- It is, of course, easy to construct arbitrage positions between Nifty, Nifty Junior and CNX-100 because the latter is just a weighted average of the other two.
- Index funds on both Nifty and Nifty Junior are available.[11] They can be used for writing covered calls on both indexes. Once again, it is possible to put together a portfolio of the two, with a 13% weight on Nifty Junior, and achieve a long position on the CNX-100.

4.4   RISK AND RETURN

4.4.1   THE EQUITY PREMIUM

How big is the equity premium, i.e., the excess returns obtained (on average) by holding the equity index when compared with the short-dated government bond? Estimation of the equity premium requires knowledge of the long-run expected returns on the equity index. In India, as in most emerging markets, this simple question is difficult to answer because of constraints on data. The data infrastructure required is a *long* time-series of the interest rate on short-dated government bonds, and a corresponding time-series of a well-maintained and correctly computed stock market index. In emerging markets, these elements of the statistical system are weak, so arriving at an estimate of the equity premium requires engaging in guesswork based on imperfect statistical estimates.

All equity indexes are fairly volatile—with a daily standard deviation of 1% to 2.5%. This implies that we have poor statistical efficiency when trying to discern the average returns on equity. Very long time-series of data are required to obtain sharp estimates. Further, only the span of this data helps in attaining statistical efficiency—delving into high-frequency data does not help. Conversely, evidence about the returns on equity over short periods (such as 2000–2007) is of highly limited value in judging the average returns to the equity index, given wide confidence intervals.

As shown in Section 4.1.2, there are many difficulties with the three alternatives for stock market indexes in India. The BSE Sensex has a long time-series but there are many flaws in the methodology. The Nifty has a sound methodology, but the price index is only observed from July 1990 onward, and a total returns index is not observed. The Cospi has a sound methodology, is reported

---

[11] Index funds on Nifty are mainstream. JUNIORBEES, from Benchmark, is an ETF on Nifty Junior.

TABLE 4.10 Compounded Nominal Returns on Stock Market Indexes

Index	4/1979–12/1990	1/1991–3/2007	Full period
BSE Sensex (price index)	19.93	16.97	17.98
Nifty (price index)		16.43	
CMIE Cospi (total returns index)		18.05	
INR/USD	7.05	5.50	6.14

inclusive of dividends, but data is only available from July 1990 onward, and index funds or index derivatives on Cospi are not available (see Table 4.10).

For the full time period of nearly 28 years, from April 1979 to March 2007, the compounded average return on the BSE Sensex was 17.98%. Focusing on a shorter time period from January 1991 till March 2007, we are able to compare this against Nifty and Cospi. The Nifty return is essentially the same. The Cospi return is 100 to 150 bps higher, which is consistent with a dividend yield of 1% to 1.5%. These comparisons of average returns across different indexes for a 16-year period are reassuring in the sense that the three different indexes, covering very different groups of stocks, have similar returns. These estimates should, of course, be interpreted with caution owing to the imprecision associated with short time series. As an example, the full period for the BSE Sensex has data for 28 years only, and assuming a daily index standard deviation of 1.5%, the 95% confidence interval around the mean works out to have a width of ±8.8%.

If a dividend stream of 150 bps, which seems to characterize the present, is added into the full period returns on the BSE Sensex, this gives us an estimated 28-year nominal total return of 19.5% per year. Over this same period, the INR/USD exchange rate depreciated by 6.14% per year. The nominal INR return of 19.5% per year then translates to returns of 12.5% expressed in USD.

The equity premium is the gap between investments in short-dated government bonds and investment in the stock market index. A market for government bonds did not exist over these 28 years, so it is not possible to estimate the equity premium. It is, however, possible to estimate inflation over this period—which works out to 8% per year. Hence, we may say that the real rate of return on an Indian stock market index works out to 10.6% per year. To summarize, the historical evidence suggests that over the last 28 years, returns on the Indian stock market index were:

- 19.5% per year in nominal INR
- 10.6% per year in real INR
- 12.5% per year in nominal USD

While pinning down the historical experience is important and useful, macro-economic conditions in the next 25 years are likely to be very different when compared with the last 28 years. Looking forward, what might we expect in the next 25 years? It appears reasonable to project inflation of 4%, a short interest rate r_f of 5%, and an equity premium of 8 percentage points. This implies nominal equity index returns of 13% in INR (inclusive of dividends).

If the P/E is stable, an ex-ante estimate of future index returns of 13% can be rationalized as 2% dividends and 11% nominal earnings growth. This is consistent with 4% inflation and 7% GDP growth. An equity premium of eight percentage points into the future appears audacious, at a time when equity premium estimates in industrial countries are much lower. However, three elements of qualitative rationale can be offered in favor of a substantially bigger equity premium than is found in industrial countries.

Equity ownership has percolated to only perhaps 1% of the households in the country, so far. There will be large one-time returns over the next 25 years when this number goes to 50%. Pension funds—so far—have 0% equity investment. There will be large one-time returns over the next 25 years when the pension funds buy $500 billion of equity assets. Finally, India has a low correlation with global indexes. But global asset managers have thus far only got $100 billion or so invested in India. This is a miniscule number when compared with the global investable pool. When Indian asset prices shift to something related to India's β against a world equity index in an ICAPM, there will be a one-time rise in prices. This phenomenon will also be seen in the next 25 years.

4.4.2   SHARPE'S RATIO OF INDIAN EQUITY

The Sharpe's ratio (SR)—averaged annual return divided by annualized volatility—expresses the reward-to-risk ratio. Table 4.11 shows the SR for some indexes for some time intervals. Data for Nifty and the CMIE Cospi are available from mid-1990 onward. Nifty is a price index of 50 stocks while Cospi is a total return index with a very large number of stocks (going to 2,500 stocks by mid-2007). Cospi hence has better diversification and superior returns. The

TABLE 4.11   Reward-to-Risk Ratio of Some Market Indexes

Index	Sharpe's ratio	95% Conf. interval
Jun-1990 to Jun-2007		
Nifty (price index)	0.57	0.079–1.044
Cospi (total returns index)	0.65	0.145–1.118
S&P 500 (price index)	0.57	0.061–1.057
Jan-1969 to Jun-2007		
S&P 500 (price index)	0.44	0.128–0.778

Sharpe's ratio of Nifty works out to 0.57 while Cospi stands at 0.65. Over the identical time period, the SR of the S&P 500 (price index) works out to 0.57, which is coincidentally the same value as that of Nifty. In other words, the superior returns of Nifty, when compared with the S&P 500, are in the same proportion as the higher volatility of Nifty.

While such point estimates are commonly reported, they have poor statistical precision. Table 4.11 also shows a 95% confidence interval for these estimates.[12] Very wide confidence intervals are seen: the SR for Cospi ranges from 0.145 to 1.118. When the SR for the S&P 500 is calculated over a longer period, this gives improved statistical precision. Using data from 1969 to 2007, the SR of 0.44 has a confidence interval from 0.128 to 0.778. When compared with these values, the Indian indexes appear to have a slightly superior reward-to-risk ratio. Given the lack of statistical precision, we should not make too much of the differences in SR seen in Table 4.11. US and Indian equities have similar Sharpe's ratios. The higher volatility of Indian equity is broadly "paid for" with proportionately higher returns.

4.4.3   CHARACTERISTICS OF INDIVIDUAL STOCKS

In describing the characteristics of the individual stocks, we focus on the 2,661 firms in the Cospi index. We explore four features of these stocks:

1. Size—measured by market capitalization, measured in million USD.
2. Total risk—measured by annualized volatility. Bigger numbers convey bigger total risk.
3. Beta—the percentage change in stock price which takes place, on average, for a 1% change in the Cospi index. Bigger numbers convey a greater sensitivity to fluctuations of the overall market.
4. R^2—the proportion of total risk that is associated with fluctuations of the market index. Lower numbers convey a greater extent of stock-specific fluctuations (see Table 4.12).

TABLE 4.12   Summary Statistics about 2,661 Cospi Firms

Feature	Minimum	Q1	Median	Mean	Q3	Maximum
Market capitalization (Mln. USD)	0.05	2.13	9.09	311.25	58.76	43,038.81
Total risk (annualized vol)	14.37	54.73	72.40	81.86	101.61	414.96
Beta	−3.23	0.77	1.05	1.02	1.32	6.52
Market model R^2	0	0.04	0.12	0.14	0.22	0.60

[12]The 95% confidence interval for the SR is calculated using bootstrap inference.

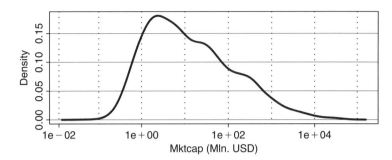

FIGURE 4.3   Distribution of Market Capitalization of 2,661 Cospi firms, February 2007

The market capitalization of the firms ranges from $0.05 million to $43 billion. Figure 4.3 shows the distribution of this market capitalization. Half the firms lie between the 1st quartile of $2.13 million and the 3rd quartile of $58.76 million. There is a a long tail going all the way up to $43 billion. This pulls up the average firm size to $311.25 million.

The total risk attains very high values, ranging from a minimum of 14.37% annualized to a maximum of 414.96% annualized. The mean and median of the total risk amounts to roughly 80% annualized, which is roughly a daily standard deviation of 5%. Cospi stocks are extremely volatile. The most tame quartile has values of total risk ranging from 14.37% annualized (roughly 0.9% per day) to 54.73% annualized (roughly 3.5% per day), which are comparable to the typical stock volatility that is found in industrial countries. Half the betas lie between the 1st quartile of 0.77 and the 3rd quartile of 1.32. The extreme values that lie at the left edge and the right edge of the distribution partly reflect extreme outliers where market model estimation has not worked well. As expected, the mean and median beta is near one.

In many developing countries, price discovery for stocks is dominated by index fluctuations. In these countries, there is really only one risk factor: country risk. This problem is exacerbated by poor disclosure, so that stock speculators have relatively little good information about firms to go by, using which firms can have idiosyncratic fluctuations of their own, which reflect firm-specific information production by speculators, and not just the fluctuations of the politics and macroeconomics of the country. Under such circumstances, diversified portfolios of equity yield little gains from diversification.

Indian stocks do not exhibit this malady. Half the values of the market model R^2 lie between 0.04 and 0.22. The highest value for the market model R^2 stands at 0.60. This suggests a substantial extent of stock-specific fluctuations, and opportunities for substantial gains from diversification. In most emerging

TABLE 4.13   Market Capitalization in the Size Deciles

Decile	Minimum	Maximum	Sum	Percent to total
	(Million USD)			
Small	0	1	156	0.02
2	1	2	332	0.04
3	2	3	575	0.07
4	3	5	993	0.12
5	5	9	1,787	0.22
6	9	19	3,511	0.42
7	19	39	7,393	0.89
8	39	102	16,970	2.05
9	103	353	55,462	6.70
Big	358	43,039	7,41,048	89.47

markets, fund managers are used to thinking that a 10-stock or 20-stock portfolio exhausts opportunities for diversification. In the Indian case, there are substantial gains to diversification even in going from 50 stocks (Nifty) to 100 stocks (CNX-100), as shown earlier.

In order to obtain further insights into the Cospi firms, Table 4.13 breaks up the universe of 2,661 firms into deciles by size. Each size decile contains roughly 266 firms. The characteristics of these deciles are shown in Table 4.13. As an example, decile 6 contains 266 firms with a market capitalization ranging from $9 million to $19 million. These firms add up to a market capitalization of $3.511 billion, which constitutes 0.42% of the overall market capitalization of the Cospi set. The main feature of this table is the domination of the biggest decile (decile 10). A full 89.47% of the overall Cospi market capitalization is accounted for by the 266 firms in the top decile, which have a market capitalization ranging from $358 million to $43 billion. This group of firms has a market value of $741 billion. This table is particularly useful when an investor has a clear sense of the range of firm sizes that make up the investment universe of interest. As an example, a fund manager who likes to invest in firms with a size range from $5 million to $100 million is able to see that these are found in deciles 5, 6, 7 and 8. Each decile contains 266 firms, so four deciles contain an investment universe of 1,064 firms. Adding up from the table, these firms have a total market capitalization of $29.661 billion or 3.58% of the overall market capitalization of Cospi. In summary, an investor who treats firms with a market capitalization from $5 million to $100 million as his investment universe faces 1,064 firms in India which have a market value of $29.661 billion, which make up 3.58% of the overall Indian market capitalization.

TABLE 4.14   Risk Characteristics of Size Deciles
(medians within each decile)

	Total risk	Beta	Market model R^2
Small	122.349	0.823	0.023
2	99.954	0.919	0.040
3	92.754	0.997	0.055
4	80.748	1.071	0.091
5	77.838	1.117	0.109
6	72.483	1.165	0.138
7	62.110	1.162	0.180
8	60.567	1.148	0.200
9	50.269	1.061	0.230
Big	42.047	1.005	0.273

Table 4.14 goes on to show the risk characteristics of these size deciles. Within each decile, the median value of the 266 firms is reported. This table has many fascinating features. The remarkably large values for total risk, seen in Table 4.12, prove to be strongly related to *size*. The bottom decile has a median total risk of 122.349%. This drops *monotonically* to 42.047% for the top decile. The largest two deciles (decile 9 and 10) have values of 50% annualized or below, which are like the values seen in industrial countries. Median betas have an interesting pattern, with low betas in the bottom 2 deciles, high betas in deciles 5 to 8 and then betas of 1 at the top 2 deciles. Deciles 5 through 8 appear to be carrying higher systematic risk; conversely, important free lunches of diversifications appear to be available by going to decile 4 and below.

Small and medium sized stocks in India have enjoyed spectacular returns. Table 4.14 suggests that to some extent, this is simply systematic risk. In the case of Nifty—the biggest 50 companies of India—a market model regression using Cospi as the index reveals a beta of 0.9977. The Nifty Junior, which is the second rung of liquid stocks, has obtained much better returns than Nifty. However, it has a beta of 1.1549. The superior returns to Nifty Junior appear to be largely a return to beta. The market model R^2 also rises *monotonically* with the size deciles: from a very low value of 0.023 at decile 1 to a modest value of 0.273 at the top decile. Once again, this emphasizes the prospective gains from diversification which are available using the stocks in deciles 1 through 4.

Turning to the characteristics of random portfolios formed using these stocks, Figure 4.4 shows the average portfolio volatility (on an annualized basis) that is obtained by forming random portfolios of various sizes. For each portfolio size shown, thousands of equally weighted portfolios are formed, at random, from

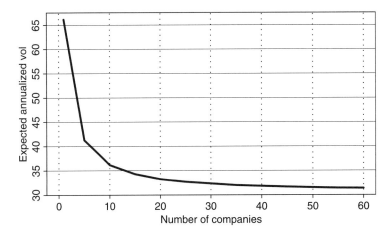

FIGURE 4.4   Volatility of Random Equally Weighted Portfolios

the universe of the CMIE Cospi stocks. The average volatility of these randomly chosen portfolios is reported.

The results show that on average, the individual stock has an annualized volatility of 65%. Volatility drops dramatically by going to portfolios with 10–20 stocks. The bulk of the gains are obtained by going to 50 stocks and beyond. These results are not directly comparable with the volatility of Nifty or Cospi or the other indexes in the country, because (a) these indexes do not use equal weights, and (b) they harness larger stocks, which have lower volatility to start with. The results in Figure 4.4 involve higher volatility because the universe from which stocks are drawn is the full membership of the CMIE Cospi, but the weights used are equal.

4.5   ROLE OF INDIAN EQUITY IN GLOBAL PORTFOLIOS

Indian equities are interesting in global portfolios owing to high expected returns and low correlations with global risk factors. In order to empirically understand the relationships, we analyze a database consisting of four indexes: the US S&P 500, the UK FTSE-100, the Japanese Nikkei 225 and the Indian Cospi (the broad market index). In all four cases, weekly returns are considered from July 1990 to May 2007, and all four indexes are re-expressed in US dollars.

Table 4.15 shows the summary statistics of these four indexes. While the Indian Cospi index had the highest returns (12% in USD), it also had the highest volatility (28.3% per year). The correlations of the Cospi against the other three countries had low values of 0.155, 0.12 and 0.119. This suggests substantial gains from diversification by placing Indian equities into global portfolios.

TABLE 4.15   Properties of Four Indexes (expressed in USD)

July 1990–May 2007	Cospi	FTSE-100	Nikkei 225	S&P 500
Mean annualized returns	12.0	6.7	−2.3	8.5
Annualized returns volatility	28.3	15.7	24.4	14.9
Correlations:				
Cospi	1.000	0.155	0.120	0.119
FTSE-100		1.000	0.340	0.571
Nikkei 225			1.000	0.265

TABLE 4.16   Changing Correlations

Period	FTSE-100	Nikkei 225	S&P 500
July 1990–Sep 1994	0.005	−0.032	−0.049
Sep 1994–Dec 1998	0.079	−0.047	0.110
Dec 1998–Feb 2003	0.203	0.266	0.154
Feb 2003–May 2007	0.443	0.389	0.364
Overall	0.155	0.120	0.119

For an illustrative calculation, a portfolio optimization was applied to this data, seeking to replicate the average returns of holding the US S&P 500 index fund, while obtaining the lowest possible portfolio volatility. The weights in this optimized portfolio worked out to 17.1% in India, 29.4% in the UK, 0.76% in Japan and 52.7% in the United States. The key difficulty with such reasoning lies in changing correlations over time. As India has globalized, correlations with world portfolios have gone up. Hence, the importance of Indian equities in world portfolios is exaggerated when such past performance is utilized in computations.

In Table 4.16 the overall dataset is broken into four sub-periods, each of which is 4.2 years long. This shows a vivid increase in correlations over time, reflecting India's rapid globalization. As an example, while the correlation with the S&P 500 was 0.119 for the full period, it was 0.364 in the last period which runs from February 2003 to May 2007. At the same time, even in the fourth period, correlations with India remained low. In the fourth period, correlations with the S&P 500 were 0.715 for the UK and 0.463 for Japan. The correlation between Japan and the UK was 0.453. The lowest values in the correlation matrix for the fourth period are those between India and the other countries. This suggests that the benefits of improved diversification continue to apply when Indian equities are brought into global portfolios.

Architects of India's Financial Markets

Montek Singh Ahluwalia was one of the pioneers in pushing for the establishment of India's first serious financial regulator, the Securities and Exchange Board of India (SEBI), in the late 1980s. He was Finance Secretary at the Ministry of Finance in the critical years of the early 1980s when major events and reforms took place on the equity market.

Jaimini Bhagwati was the Joint Secretary heading the Capital Markets Division at the Department of Economic Affairs, Ministry of Finance, when Yashwant Sinha was finance minister, at the time when the critical decisions of 2001—the end of weekly settlement and *badla* trading on the stock market, the shift to rolling settlement and the substantial enlargement of derivatives trading—were taken.

Architects of India's Financial Markets

C. B. Bhave was Executive
Director at SEBI in charge of the
secondary market in the early
1990s. Working closely with
P. J. Nayak, who was then the
Joint Secretary in charge of
Capital Markets at the Ministry
of Finance, he helped emphasize
that the agenda for reforms on
the equity market should be
about shifting the spot market
to rolling settlement, shifting to
electronic trading, and doing
netting by novation at a clearing
corporation. He went on to head
the dominant depository in
1995 and then to become
Chairman of SEBI in 2008.

As Joint Secretary
in the Ministry of
Social Justice and
Empowerment,
Anand Bordia
understood that
emphasizing the
State as the source
of pension
payments was not
scalable and
sustainable. He set
up Project OASIS,
headed by Surendra
A. Dave and
administered by
Gautam Bhardwaj,
which designed the
New Pension
System.

Surendra A. Dave, an economist who had a lifetime of experience in running public sector financial firms, was tapped to be the first chairman of SEBI in 1988. He went on to head 'Project OASIS,' setup by the Ministry of Social Justice and Empowerment, which designed the New Pension System.

L. C. Gupta was member of SEBI in the early 1990s, and one of the pioneers in thinking about the equity market in new ways. He headed an expert committee in 1997 which set the stage for the establishment of the equity derivatives market.

Nimesh Kampani first worked with Morgan Stanley in establishing J M Morgan Stanley, an Indian subsidiary of Morgan Stanley and then struck out on his own in 2007 with J M Financial, though he is still Chairman of J M Morgan Stanley India Company Pvt Ltd.

Architects of India's Financial Markets

Uday Kotak, had securities broking and investment banking partnerships with Goldman Sachs but bought Goldman out in 2006. He cofounded Kotak Mahindra Bank in 1985 as a finance company with Anand Mahindra, and then converted it into a bank in 2003. In addition to running the Bank, he is Chairman of Kotak Securities.

Hemendra Kothari led a fine private investment bank and securities house named DSP Financial Consultants Ltd, and entered into a joint venture with Merrill Lynch to create DSP Merrill Lynch, which has become one of the leading debt and equity underwriters in India and has won the Euromoney award for the overall best private banking services for four consecutive years as of 2008.

Percy Mistry was a member of L. C. Gupta's committee on derivatives, and chairman of the 'Mumbai as an International Financial Centre' committee of 2006, which set out a roadmap for thinking about the integration of Indian finance into the world of global finance.

Ravi Narain was part of two very important teams in the history of Indian financial markets. First, he was a member of Surendra Dave's small team that was seconded from the Industrial Development Bank of India (IDBI) to create SEBI. He then became part of the core founding team, again from IDBI and led by R. H. Patil, to create the National Stock Exchange. He went on to become the second head of NSE after Dr. Patil.

S. Narayan was Finance Secretary at the Ministry of Finance and was the most important person in translating the New Pension System from ideas to action.

Architects of India's Financial Markets

P. J. Nayak was the Joint Secretary running the Capital Markets division at the Department of Economic Affairs, Ministry of Finance, in the early 1990s at the time of the early reforms of the equity market. Among other things, he played a major role in the drafting of the depositories legislation. He went on to head Axis Bank and turned it into one of India's best run banks.

R. H. Patil was the first leader at the National Stock Exchange of India. Nobody thought NSE would succeed, but it turned into India's biggest financial exchange. Dr. Patil went on to found the Clearing Corporation of India (CCIL) which created a major transformation in the way the debt market operated.

Raghuram Rajan, a chaired Professor at the University of Chicago, winner of the Fischer Black Prize awarded by the American Finance Association for outstanding original research in finance and the former (and youngest ever) Economic Counselor and Director of Research at the IMF, headed the influential High Level Committee on Financial Sector Reforms in 2008.

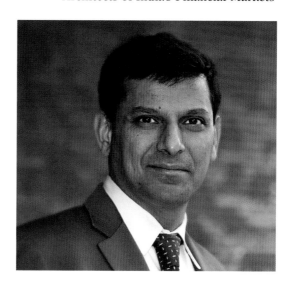

C. Rangarajan was RBI Governor in the critical period of the early 1990s, where a currency market was set up, capital controls were eased, and the automatic monetization of government debt was ended. He went on to become the governor of a state, head the Twelfth Finance Commission, and head the Economic Advisory Council to the Prime Minister for Manmohan Singh.

Architects of India's Financial Markets

U. K. Sinha was Joint Secretary of the Capital Markets Division at the Department of Economic Affairs, and played a critical role in the establishment of the New Pension System. He went on to head the United Trust of India UTI.

Jayanth Varma, Professor at the Indian Institute of Management, Ahmedabad, has been actively involved in all aspects of the equity market from the early 1990s onwards. He briefly served as a member of SEBI, and was chairman of a committee that defined SEBI's regulatory stance for the equity derivatives market in the early years.

CHAPTER 5

Government Bonds

Government debt is the second largest securities market in India by value. Large fiscal deficits have implied a considerable scale of government bond issuance. As a consequence, the Indian government bond market capitalization grew sharply from Rs.1.2 trillion in 1996 to Rs.11 trillion in 2006.

However, the market has not developed as rapidly as the size of the outstanding debt has increased. Liquidity is poor, localized to a few securities, and unreliable. In times when interest rates are low, the liquidity has been high, and when interest rates rise, the liquidity tends to drop sharply. Despite the high volatility of interest rates, interest rate derivatives are highly inadequate.

The largest issuer of government debt is the central government (referred to in this chapter as GOI for "Government of India"), although there have increasingly been debt issues by state governments as well. As with other countries, GOI bonds define the riskless yield curve, and have a considerable significance.

In this chapter, we describe the products that make up the government bond market and derivative products based on government debt, the market mechanisms under which these products trade, and the regulatory framework.

5.1   PRODUCTS IN THE GOVERNMENT DEBT MARKET

As in most other debt markets in the world, the Indian market is divided into short-term debt products—which tend to be indicative of monetary policy in that country—and long-term debt.

5.1.1   SHORT-TERM PRODUCTS

Short-term products are *money market products*, and have short maturities, typically within a year. And like money market products worldwide, they are issued and traded at a discount to face value. There are three key elements of this market:

1. Borrowing and lending is done by the central bank, Reserve Bank of India (RBI), as part of the conduct of monetary policy. In many countries, the policy rate of the central bank is unambiguously defined. In India, there are two distinct rates at which the central bank borrows and lends, the repo rate and the reverse repo rate. These rates are generally quite far apart; there is a substantial bid-offer spread. Hence, the short rate is not unambiguously pinned down by monetary policy in India, as it is in many countries.

    In September 2007, the reverse repo rate was 6% and the repo rate was 7.75%. There was a bid-offer spread of 175 basis points. The short rate can fluctuate between these two values based on market forces. On a typical day, transactions only take place at one of the two rates.
2. The call money market is a non-collateralized interbank dealer market for overnight funds. This market involves credit risk, for there is no collateral. However, the government has not allowed any important bank in India to fail. Hence, the credit risk is negligible.
3. A collateralized borrowing and lending obligations (CBLO) market is an exchange-traded repo, where there is no credit risk owing to the presence of collateral. Participation in the CBLO market is not limited to banks.

Treasury Bills (T-bills—issued by the GOI) are short-term products and are standardized securities, unlike the previously discussed bilateral contracts. T-bills in India have maturities of 3 months, 6 months and 12 months, and are issued and traded like their long-dated counterpart, the Treasury Bonds (T-bonds), also issued by the GOI.

5.1.2 LONG-DATED GOVERNMENT DEBT

Longer maturity government debt products are the Government of India Treasury Bonds (ranging from greater than a year up to 30 years). Treasury bonds issued by the GOI have the following characteristics:

*   The face value of all treasury products, both bonds and bills, is Rs.100.
*   The maturity of bonds issued goes from over a year, all the way out to 30 years.
*   All GOI bonds are *coupon bearing bonds*, with coupons being paid semi-annually. The maturity and the coupon of each bond is defined at the date

of issue. In September 2007, there were 174 bonds outstanding. There are no zero coupon bonds traded, for all practical purposes. There is also no effort to create a "strips" market as in the United States where investment banks strip T-bonds to sell zero coupon instruments.

An example of the standard nomenclature of a GOI bond is "7.99% CG2017," where "CG" stands for "Central Government," "2017" denotes that it matures in 2017, that the bond pays an annual cash flow of Rs."7.99" which is split in two payments of Rs.3.995 every six months from the date of issue of the bond and the final redemption on the bond is Rs."103.995" (the face value of the bond plus the final coupon payment).

Table 5.1 shows the outstanding debt as of 2007, with maturities and the size of the stock of bonds at each maturity. From this table, we can see that even though the span goes out to 30 years, the majority of outstanding bonds have maturities between 5 and 15 years.

Most developing countries find it difficult to achieve a long-dated government bond market. Markets are averse to holding long-dated government bonds when there is inflation risk. India has apparently achieved considerable success with a local-currency thirty-year bond market. This is puzzling, given the lack of a well-specified monetary policy framework, and given the considerable inflation risk that is present (Figure 5.1).

This achievement is less impressive than it appears when government bond issuance is placed in the larger context of financial repression. Government forces banks, insurance companies and pension funds to hold a considerable amount of government bonds. Government is able to issue long maturity bonds,

TABLE 5.1   Year of Maturity of Outstanding Central GOI Debt, as of September 2007

Year of maturity	Stock (Rs. billion)	Year of maturity	Stock (Rs. billion)	Year of maturity	Stock (Rs. billion)
2007–2008	181	2016–2017	1,141	2026–2027	194
2008–2009	440	2017–2018	1,008	2027–2028	164
2009–2010	956	2018–2019	425	2028–2029	110
2010–2011	856	2019–2020	280	2031–2032	27
2011–2012	736	2020–2021	110	2032–2033	304
2012–2013	741	2021–2022	459	2034–2035	294
2013–2014	760	2022–2023	470	2035–2036	710
2014–2015	690	2023–2024	210		
2015–2016	762	2025–2026	167		
Total stock					
(Maturity < 2017)	6,122	(Maturity < 2027)	10,392	(Maturity < 2037)	12,195

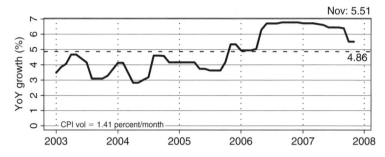

FIGURE 5.1   High Volatility of CPI

knowing that there are captive buyers. Hence, the Indian success in stretching the yield curve is based only partly on the growing mass of sophisticated institutional investors—such as insurance companies—who have a natural need for long-dated bonds. It is largely based on old-fashioned financial repression, and not on a sense, in the mind of the market, that inflation deep in the future is highly predictable.

Changing Patterns in Maturity of GOI Bond Products

The pattern of issue maturity for Treasury bonds has been shifting over the last decade. If we look at the maturities of bonds that were issued a decade ago compared to those today, we see that the term structure of issued bonds has been growing longer over this period. Table 5.2 shows the issued bond maturities: the longest maturity bond issued in 1997–1998 was at 13 years, in 2001–2002 it was at 20 years, and in the most recent period of 2006–2007, the longest dated bond was issued at 30 years.

This evolution of maturity also needs to be seen in the context of fiscal difficulties and financial repression. In this decade, India had acute difficulties with massive fiscal deficits. The elongation of maturity was partly about making deficit financing more convenient for the government. With long-dated bonds, the problem of repayment was postponed deep into the future, and short-term rollover risk was avoided.

Banks, the natural buyers of government bonds, were ill-equipped for holding long-dated bonds. Ordinarily, banking regulation and supervision is expected to ensure that large maturity mismatches do not develop on the books of banks. However, in India, large mismatches did come about, as documented in Patnaik and Shah (2004).

TABLE 5.2 Maturity of GOI Debt Issued
at Different Points in the Last Decade

Maturity (Years)	Size of issue in: (Issue size in Rs. billion)		
	1997–1998	2001–2002	2006–2007
2			60
3		25	
4	30	40	
5	50	60	60
6		30	60
7	80	40	50
8	30	60	60
9	60	30	170
10	30	165	
12	30	110	280
13	20	95	50
15		150	
16		15	90
17		15	90
18		15	
19		15	
20–30		70	130
> 30			270
Total	330	935	1,280

Changing Patterns in Turnover of GOI Bond Products

Along with changes in the issue maturity of Treasury bonds, the patterns of traded volumes across maturities have also been changing. If we examine where along the term structure the market traded a decade ago compared to those today, we see that the market has shifted to trading longer maturity bonds on average. Table 5.3 shows the top most-traded securities in March of 1998, 2002 and 2007.

Some interesting observations about Table 5.3 are

- The identities of the most-traded securities change from year to year, reflecting the changes in the securities that are issued every year.
- The most active market trades tend to be in maturities of 4–13 years.
- While the mean maturity traded more than doubled between 1998 and 2002, it dropped again between 2002 and 2007. So there has not been a consistent trend toward trading longer maturities.

TABLE 5.3   Most-Traded Securities in a Given
Month

Name of bond	Monthly traded volumes (Rs. billion)	Maturity (Years)
March 1998		
11% CG2002	9.2	4
13.05% CG2007	7.5	9
TB 364D	7.4	<1
TB 364D	6.9	<1
12.69% CG2002	4.3	4
March 2002		
11.50% CG2011A	171.3	9
9.85% CG2015	63.0	13
11.03% CG2012	55.0	10
9.81% CG2013	48.0	11
11.40% CG2008	33.3	6
March 2007		
7.37% CG2014	15.9	7
8.07% CG2017	15.2	10
6.65% CG2009	14.7	2
11.90% CG2007	7.6	<1
9.39% CG2011	7.6	4

- Traded volumes jumped in 2002 compared to 1998. This dropped off again to low levels in 2007, even though the volumes were better in 2007 compared to 1998.

The last observation of Table 5.3 merits a closer look at the liquidity of the GOI bond market. The interest rates in the Indian economy had undergone a steep drop in levels starting from 2001, lasting all the way to 2004. During this period, the liquidity of GOI bonds went up sharply. However, this liquidity was not resilient: when interest rates started going up, the liquidity dropped in relation.

The picture in Figure 5.2 depicts this inverse relationship between liquidity and market levels. We measure the liquidity of the GOI bond market using the market *turnover ratio* (TR).[1] We compare the behavior of the market turnover

---

[1] Turnover Ratio is measured as Traded Volumes in a given period for all the GOI bonds divided by the Market Capitalization of the bonds, expressed as a percentage.

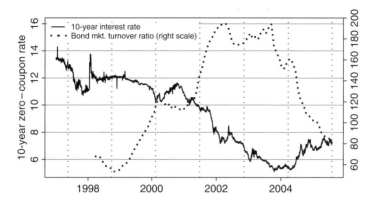

FIGURE 5.2   Bond Market Liquidity vs. Interest Rate Levels

with the 10-year interest rate, and observe that the liquidity in this market does have an inverse relationship with levels.

5.1.3   ISSUANCE OF GOI DEBT

The RBI is the investment banker for the central government, and runs auctions to issue GOI bonds and T-bills. In the 1980s, government deficits were funded by a mix of (a) forcing banks to buy bonds at below-market rates and (b) money creation. In the early 1990s, as part of market-oriented reforms, there was a conscious effort to move away from these distortionary practices. While substantial force-feeding of bonds continues, the prices of bonds are at least overtly determined in an auction. In addition, a ways and means agreement was signed between the RBI and the Ministry of Finance, prohibiting deficit financing through money creation.

Treasury bills are issued to the market on a regular calendar by the RBI. The calendar is fixed and released to participants at the beginning of the financial year by the RBI. Auctions are "sealed bid," price–based auctions. They are announced around four to five days before the date of the auction. The bids have to be submitted to the Head Office of the RBI which is located at the south end of Bombay. The RBI announces the maturity and the coupon as well as the the quantity of the issue. Internally, the RBI also sets the reservation price for the bonds, and reserves the right to not issue the bonds if the prices offered are below the reservation price. The winning bids are awarded their bid quantities at their respective prices. If the bond is oversubscribed, the winners receive proportional allotments of the issue. Earlier auctions saw a number of failed auctions with the bonds devolving on the RBI. However since 2004, very few of the bonds issued have devolved back on the RBI.

5.1.4   BUYERS OF GOI DEBT

There is a large captive demand for GOI debt in India today in the form of banks, insurance companies and pension funds which are forced to buy government bonds. A particularly important category among these are public sector financial firms. The government owns over 51% of these. The government promises that the risk of failure is zero; it will support these firms to an unlimited extent. These firms, thus, serve as an effective collection mechanism for the government, sourcing household savings from all over the country, and using this to fund the fiscal deficit.

In the Indian financial sector, state ownership is pervasive:

- Around 72% of the commercial banking sector is the public sector: this covers about 28 public sector banks among a total of 81 commercial banks.[2]
- The Life Insurance Corporation (LIC), which has a market share of approximately 85% of the life insurance market, is a public sector firm.
- The largest provident fund, the Employees Provident Fund Organization (EPFO), is the equivalent of a mandatory pension fund for government employees as well as employees of large firms. The EPFO is also a public sector financial firm.

Other firms who form the demand-side of GOI debt are

- Primary Dealers (PDs), who act as market makers for the placement of GOI debt. They are obliged to place bids in the auction for the issuance of government bonds, as well as provide liquidity in the secondary market for these bonds. There are 17 PDs in the Indian GOI bond market.
- Mutual funds. Other than the state-promoted Unit Trust of India (UTI), mutual funds and asset management companies are relatively new entrants into the Indian financial sector. Therefore, these firms are much smaller in size compared with the financial firms listed above. However, they are less constrained by restrictions on investments and are an active participant in the GOI debt market (see Tables 5.4 and 5.5). In the last ten years, there has been a rapid growth in the number and size of debt fund schemes,

---

[2]Of these, 25 are private commercial banks and 28 are foreign banks.

TABLE 5.4   Patterns of GOI Debt Ownership

Financial firm	1997	2001	2005
	(Rs. billion)		
Commercial banks	1,302	2,767	4,949
Public Sector banks	1,085	2,268	3,911
LIC	383	843	1,885
UTI	24	45	19
EPFO	19	87	221
PDs	0	77	22
Others	353	876	2,656
Total	1,929	4,537	9,296

TABLE 5.5   Share in Settlement Volume

Financial entity	2002	2005
	(in %)	
Primary dealers	27.82	31.13
Development financial institutions	2.36	1.84
Mutual funds	8.10	6.31
Public Sector banks	28.37	23.35
Private Sector banks	16.53	15.48
Co-operative banks	3.77	4.46
Foreign banks	12.80	17.18
Others	0.25	0.27

which took place with the shift to a market-based regime for interest rates.

- The remainder—such as charitable institutions, trusts and societies, nonfinancial firms and individuals—often somewhat confusingly termed retail investors. Of these, firms and individuals do not have regulatory constraints on their investment in government debt. But trusts and charities are forced to invest largely in government bonds. In addition, these investments are held to maturity. This makes for a captive audience for government bonds that do not contribute to the liquidity of these instruments.
- Foreign financial institutions. Foreign investors can buy GOI bonds domestically. However, the limit of total foreign institutional investor investment in GOI bonds is $2.6 billion. Unless there is a more serious policy effort to

raise this limit, foreign FIs are unlikely to be a large participant in the GOI bond market.

Since most of these are public sector firms, they become captive demand for the GOI bonds. Put together, these public sector financial firms control assets in the order of Rs.24 trillion.

Within this set of buyers, only banks and PDs are permitted to actively bid in the bond issue auction of the RBI. Insurance companies and provident funds, as well as individuals, may also bid in the auction but only with noncompetitive bids. These bids carry a quote for a quantity that can be purchased at the market. Thus, only banks and PDs contribute to discovering the price of a GOI bond in the primary market.

Table 5.4 shows the ownership structure of government bonds. Of the Rs.9,296 billion of government bonds present in 2005, Rs.4,949 billion were with the banks, of which Rs.3,911 billion were with the public sector banks. This table also shows that the Life Insurance Corporation (LIC) and Employee's Provident Fund Organization (EPFO) are fast-growing buyers of government bonds, as are others constituting the new financial firms such as private mutual funds, private insurance companies and foreign institutional investors.

Table 5.5 shows a very different picture when it comes to *transactions*. Public sector banks accounted for only 23.35% of settlement volume in 2005. LIC and EPFO accounted for almost no transactions.

5.2 MARKETS

In the early 1990s, a major scandal erupted connected with falsification of records in the government bond settlement system. This led to sharp changes in the settlement system. Apart from this, the debt market has been an area of halting and incremental change, particularly when contrasted with the revolutionary progress achieved by the equity market.

5.2.1 SETTLEMENT

Debt market reform started with the injection of computer technology into the bond depository—the Securities General Ledger (SGL). SGL membership is a closed club controlled by RBI, comprising primarily banks and primary dealers. All other economic agents hold government bonds thorough constituent SGL accounts held with SGL members. It has also become possible for investors to hold balances of government bonds at the National Securities Depository

(NSDL). Today, all GOI bond settlement takes place either through the SGL or NSDL. Physical certificates have been eliminated.

5.2.2 Reporting Platforms

In June 1994, NSE set up a trade reporting system called the Wholesale Debt Market (WDM). The broad framework was that of continuing with the pre-existing OTC market, based on telephone calls between players, and requesting participants to report trades on the WDM.

In fact, few trades were reported intra-day. WDM became a useful source of data at the end-of-day, but did not make a significant difference to the debt market.

5.2.3 Clearing Systems

Policymakers then decided that risk management at the clearing corporation was a place to make progress on the bond market, even if the trading system remained a non-transparent OTC market. This led to the creation of the Clearing Corporation of India Limited (CCIL), which is owned by a consortium of large financial firms. CCIL started operations in February 2002 as the clearing corporation for spot market transactions for all RBI-registered entities. These latter entities were distinguished as those market entities who had a direct SGL account with the RBI. CCIL stood to guarantee both the buyer and the seller a spot in GOI bond trade by using the same set of margining principles that improved the liquidity on the equity market. This was convenient for market participants for two reasons: (a) transactions no longer suffered from counterparty default risk and (b) CCIL helped bring about many efficiency improvements in transaction processing.

CCIL was so successful in launching a new clearing service for bond trades that by the end of 2002, CCIL had also expanded operations to include clearing foreign exchange transactions. Once again, these services were restricted to members of the SGL club.

The essence of a clearing corporation is to eliminate credit risk between two counterparties who do not know each other. Clearing corporations improve the liquidity of financial markets by bringing in new players who are not incumbent club members. With the establishment of CCIL, it should have been possible to eliminate entry barriers into the bond market, i.e., to eliminate restrictions on becoming part of the SGL club. However, this was not done. For this reason, a substantial part of the potential benefit from the creation of CCIL has not been harnessed.

5.2.4 TRADING VENUES

Largely speaking, the government bond market is an OTC market. RBI has set up a Negotiated Dealing System (NDS) in an attempt to bring new trading technology into the market. In a remarkable decision by world standards, the central bank is the owner and operator of NDS.

NDS set out to learn the business practices of the OTC market and encode them in software. This made little difference to the market. In recent years, there has been an effort to set up a new system, named NDS-OM, which offers computerized order matching for government bonds. Hence, there are now four important elements for trading interest rate products in the Indian market:

1. An OTC bond market, where conversations take place by telephone;
2. NDS-OM, where order matching takes place;
3. The OTC call money market; and
4. The electronic CBLO market.

In the government bond market, there are two trading venues: the OTC market and order matching at NDS-OM. Regardless of which venue is used, almost all transactions go to CCIL for risk management and SGL for settlement. Access to the bond market is limited to the SGL club.

At the short end, there is the call money market—an uncollateralized market which is limited to banks—and the CBLO market—an exchange-traded repo without entry barriers. CBLO turnover has grown very well. CBLO is a pioneer in two key innovations: the use of order matching, and breaking with the SGL club. While all other aspects of the bond market are limited to the SGL club, access to the CBLO market is genuinely open.

5.2.5 DERIVATIVE PRODUCTS ON GOVERNMENT DEBT

Figure 5.3 shows the time-series of the short rate and the long rate. Both these interest rates have been quite volatile. This naturally throws up a need of risk management. In particular, with a system of financial repression, where key institutional investors are forced to buy government bonds and often hold excessive interest rate risk, a natural response could have been to lay off risk using interest rate derivatives.

Despite these features, interest rate derivatives have been slow to emerge in India. An OTC market has sprung up, primarily involving Forward Rate Agreements (FRA) and Interest Rate Swaps (IRS) involving large financial firms.

All FRAs are executed as OTC deals between two counterparties that are comfortable trading with each other. They can also be intermediated by a broker.

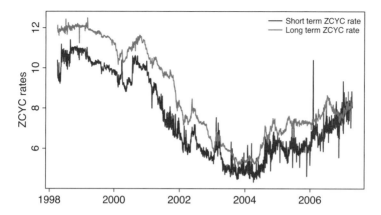

FIGURE 5.3   Indian Zero Coupon Yield Curve (ZCYC) Rates at 3 Months and 10 Years from April 1998 Onward

In either case, each counterparty takes on the credit risk of the other, typically for durations of two weeks to six months. The reference rate that is typically used to settle these products are short-term rates that are polled from the market using a methodology similar to that of LIBOR. Of these, the NSE Mumbai InterBank Offer Rate is polled by the NSE and is a well-known benchmark. Other reference rates popularly used are those polled by Bloomberg and Reuters.

The RBI has viewed interest rate derivatives with considerable suspicion, and worked to prevent market development. As an example, when interest rate futures trading began on exchanges, RBI came out with a rule requiring banks to only hold short positions. By forcing banks—the largest participants in the bond market—to not participate on both sides of the interest rate futures market, the interest rate futures market was hobbled from the start.

Similarly, the growth of the OTC market has been hobbled by a rule created at RBI which forces nonbank firms to not transact with each other. Every OTC derivative must have one counterparty that is a bank. This gives RBI a mechanism to control the growth of the OTC market through the powers that flow from banking regulation.

5.3   REGULATION AND MARKET ACCESS

The divergent trajectories of the equity market and the debt market are striking. The equity market has achieved genuine liquidity, genuine speculative price discovery, and has become India's most important financial market. The debt market has languished. Many computer systems have been built; many IOSCO

TABLE 5.6   The Moribund Government Bond Market

Feature	2003–2004	2004–2005	2005–2006	2006–2007	2007–2008
Number of bonds traded over 4 times/week	27	14	9	6	
Number of gilts that sum to 90% of turnover	26	33	15	11	11
Share in turnover of the top traded bond	11	23	18	33	36
Bond market turnover (billion USD)	365	216	164	221	

recommendations are met. However, the soul of a market—speculative price discovery—has been rigorously excluded.

A key feature of the bond market is the role of the Reserve Bank of India. The RBI has severe conflicts of interest: through functions in monetary policy, public debt management, banking regulation, deposit insurance, ownership of the depository and exchange, etc. In addition, the RBI carries the baggage of decades of a philosophy of control. A liquid financial market is, too often, viewed as a threat to control.

In 2006–2007, one element of the conflicts of interest of the RBI began to be shifted out of the RBI. This is the task of public debt management, now in the process of moving to a Debt Management Office (DMO) which serves the Ministry of Finance directly. However, there are many miles to go before the remaining hurdles are solved, and a liquid bond market is achieved. In the meantime, a plausible scenario is that of the blossoming of a rupee-denominated interest rate derivatives market outside the country, which will dominate price discovery.

5.4   ELUSIVE LIQUIDITY

The broad strategy of public policy on the Indian market has failed to deliver a liquid and efficient bond market. This is visible in the statistics shown in Table 5.6.[3] The number of bonds that have at least one trade over four days a week has dropped to single digits. The top 11 bonds account for over 90% of turnover. The biggest single bond (by turnover) accounts for one-third of overall turnover. And, in a fast-growing economy with a massive fiscal deficit, it is surprising to see that the turnover of the bond market has declined over the years.

---

[3] This is drawn from *How to brighten dark side of negotiated dealing system* by Manish Sabharwal and Digant Bhansali, in *The Economic Times*, 23 October 2007.

CHAPTER 6

Corporate Bonds

The corporate bond market involves all bonds that have credit risk, i.e., bonds issued by all entities other than the Central Government. This includes not just the bonds issued by private Indian firms but, more significantly, bonds issued by sub-national agencies such as state governments (SG) and municipalities, as well as the Public Sector Units or Entities (PSU/PSE) which are firms where the majority shareholder is the central or state government.[1]

In India, the corporate and sub-national bonds that are raised in the market are largely privately placed, have very low trading, and suffer from severe lack of transparency in pricing and liquidity. It is much smaller in size than the GOI bond market as seen in Table 6.1. Unlike some areas of Indian finance where progress has been taking place, the share of corporate debt in the overall bond market has actually been dropping.

In this chapter, we look at products, participants, market mechanisms, and some policy issues.

6.1 THE PRODUCTS

By definition, corporate bonds are bonds issued by firms and sub-national bonds are issued by any other state-level entity than the Central Government of India. Both financial firms (e.g., banks) and nonfinancial firms issue bonds. A distinction that is important among firms is that of government ownership. The corporate bond market generally assumes that public sector firms cannot fail, because they are backed by a guarantee from the State.

---

[1] A deeper examination of the bonds issued by state governments inevitably becomes an examination of the fiscal soundness of sub-national governments. On this subject, see Kishore and Prasad (2007).

TABLE 6.1   Resources Raised from the Debt Markets

	2000–2001		2004–2005	
	Rs. billion	% of total	Rs. billion	% of total
Total debt raised	1,850.56		2,050.81	
Of which				
Corporate	565.73	31	594.79	29
Government	1,284.83	69	1,456.00	71

6.1.1   STATE GOVERNMENT BONDS

Compared to the stock of central government bonds, issues of bonds by the state government are significantly smaller. In 2005–2006, issues from the SG were just under Rs.0.2 trillion, whereas the Central Government issued Rs.1.3 trillion in the same period. This difference in size also shows up in the stock of bonds: outstanding stock of State Government bonds were around 500 billion compared to the Central Government at around 10 trillion in 2005–2006.

Until 2005, when important reforms took place through the 12th Finance Commission,[2] bond issuance for state governments was done by the central bank, RBI. RBI used to auction bundles of bonds for a group of states; bidders had to take a group of states and could not choose one. This auction mechanism has been discontinued, and state government bond issues have been unbundled.

Maturities of SG bonds typically run between 5 and 15 years. SG bonds share the same characteristics as the GOI bonds:

- The face value of both bonds and bills is Rs.100.
- All GOI bonds are coupon bearing bonds, with coupons being paid semi-annually.
- An example of the standard nomenclature of an SG bond would be "7.91% Maharashtra SDL 2016," where "2016" denotes the maturity date, that the bond pays an annual cashflow of Rs.7.91 and that it is issued by the State of Maharashtra.
- There are no zero coupon bonds issued by state governments, for all practical purposes.

The issues done by the SGs in the last two years are listed in Table 6.2. All the bonds issued in these two years have a maturity of 10 years.

[2]A finance commission is appointed in India every five years to preside over the sharing of tax revenues between the centre and the states.

TABLE 6.2   Issues by State Governments,
2005–2007

Issuer	2005–2006	2006–2007
	Rs. billion	
Andhra Pradesh	19.56	27.26
Arunachal Pradesh	0.47	1.08
Assam	8.80	8.57
Bihar	7.28	0.00
Goa	0.83	1.00
Gujarat	6.02	0.00
Haryana	5.21	0.00
Himachal	4.69	5.11
Jammu&Kashmir	2.98	6.91
Jharkhand	3.64	4.01
Karnataka	4.15	0.00
Kerala	18.08	21.68
Madhya Pradesh	12.61	14.20
Maharashtra	15.80	17.38
Manipur	2.05	0.99
Meghalaya	1.58	1.92
Mizoram	1.15	1.25
Nagaland	2.54	2.93
Orissa	5.06	0.00
Punjab	11.99	9.81
Rajasthan	10.41	14.98
Sikkim	1.04	1.15
Tamil Nadu	16.19	18.14
Tripura	1.37	0.35
Uttaranchal	5.68	3.69
Uttar Pradesh	30.03	32.48
West Bengal	17.14	13.36

6.1.2   PSU BONDS

A public sector enterprise (PSU) is a firm owned by an arm of government—the central government, a state government, or a municipality. They can be straight bonds or structured obligations, which are specific to a particular project. The maturity of these bonds issued by SOEs are typically between 5 and 15 years, whereas the typical term of a municipal bond can typically go up to seven years out. Bonds issued by PSU financial firms, particularly banks, are the biggest single element of this market.

Given the majority ownership by the Central Government, the perception is that these bonds are of a very high credit quality, regardless of the fragility of the issuing firm. In addition, some of these bonds also have a tax-exempt status.

6.1.3 BONDS ISSUED BY PRIVATE FIRMS

Corporate debt issued by firms is either in the form of short-term instruments called commercial paper (CP) or corporate debentures/bonds (CB). CPs are borrowings done with maturities between two weeks and a year, while corporate bonds have longer maturities. Typical corporate bond maturities are between three to seven years in India today.

CBs can have significantly different structures compared to those issued by the government or by PSUs. CBs do not necessarily have semi-annual coupons, nor are these cash flows always a fixed value. The most signficant difference between CBs and the rest of the corporate bond instruments is that several CBs have embedded options in them: either these contain *call* options, which give the company the right to pre-pay and close the obligations in the bonds before maturity, or they contain *put* options, which give the bond holder the right to convert the bonds into equity shareholding at a predetermined price. These latter are also referred to as warrants in India.

In the 1990s, Indian company law imposed a ceiling on the coupon rate that a corporate bond could offer. Many firms felt that their bonds would not be attractive at this ceiling. They set about bundling warrants with corporate bonds in order to get past this problem. Table 6.3 shows the structure of borrowing of the nonfinancial firms observed in the CMIE database for 2006–2007. Of the

TABLE 6.3 Structure of Borrowing from the Nonfinancial Firms in the CMIE Database (2006–2007)

Component	Value (Rs. trillion)
Total borrowing	8.10
Of which:	
Bank borrowing	3.81
Short term	1.77
Long term	2.03
Foreign borrowing	1.55
Bonds	0.60
Borrowing for corporations	0.52

total borrowing of Rs.8.1 trillion of all these firms put together, the biggest component was bank borrowing (Rs.3.81 trillion) followed by foreign borrowing (Rs.1.55 trillion). The bond market accounted for only Rs.0.6 trillion. A comparison against the past is bleak. In 2001–2002, total borrowing was lower at Rs.5.7 trillion. However, at that time, bonds were *more* important at Rs.0.77 trillion.

6.1.4 STRUCTURED DEBT PRODUCTS

Securitization of loans made by banks—either to individuals or to firms—has started taking place in India. Loans to individuals are either mortgage loans for housing (where the structured products are called mortgage-backed securities, or MBS) or loans to purchase assets (called asset-backed securities, or ABS) which have primarily been personal loans to purchase automobiles, commercial vehicles, construction equipment and two-wheelers. There are also structured products on loans to firms such as Corporate Debt Obligations (CDOs), Loan Sell Offs (LSOs) and Partial Guarantee Structures (PGs).

Of these, ABS is the largest and is growing the most rapidly (Table 6.4). The MBS market has not grown as much, despite the growth in the housing finance market. MBS products, unlike those of ABS, have a relatively long maturity. This makes it more vulnerable to interest rate risk, which might be a factor going against this product having good liquidity. As can be seen in the table, structured products on loans to firms form a much smaller fraction of this market.

Securitization products are created under Trusts or Special Purpose Vehicles (SPVs) that hold the legal ownership of the assets underlying the structure. The ownership of the assets under SPV is distinct from the balance sheet of the trustees/creators of the SPV. Every product that is issued is a Pass Through Certificate (PTC) and is rated individually. The rating for a PTC is typically differentiated from the rating on a debt product by the letters "(SO)" in the

TABLE 6.4   Trend in Volumes of Structured Products (Rs. billion)

Component	2001–2002	2002–2003	2003–2004	2004–2005
ABS	12.90	36.40	80.90	222.90
MBS	0.80	14.80	29.60	33.40
CDO/LSO	19.10	24.30	28.30	25.80
PG	4.00	1.90	0.00	16.00
Others	0.00	0.40	0.50	10.00
Total	36.80	77.70	139.20	308.20

rating. Therefore, a rating of "AAA(SO)" stands for a AAA-rated Structured Obligation. Investors in the PTCs only buy the rights to the cash flows from the assets, not the assets themselves.

6.1.5 BUYERS OF CORPORATE DEBT

The buyers of corporate bonds are almost the same as the buyers of GOI bonds:

1. Banks, insurance companies, mutual funds, the central provident fund and companies are large buyers in the market for SG bonds and PSU bonds.
2. Along with these, other companies and individuals are also buyers of CPs and CBs.
3. Trusts, Associations and Funds as well as Non-Resident Indians (NRIs) also form a bulk of the demand-side for CDs, Bank and Municipal bonds.
4. There are very few retail investors that directly invest in corporate bonds.
5. Foreign institutional investors (FII) can buy corporate bonds, but only to the limit of USD 1.5 billion. This is an even smaller limit compared to FII limits on the ownership of GOI bonds of $2.6 billion. Given these limits, FIIs cannot be expected to be a serious participant in pricing and trading corporate bonds in India.

While the above are active participants in the bond market, they all face both regulatory and economic restrictions on their roles. The economic restrictions come in the form of the tax benefits faced by different buyers: some corporate bond holders are exempt from taxes, while others are not. Firms pay a tax at source on dividends and bond cash flow redemptions (called Tax Deducted at Source, or TDS). When these bonds are held in pension funds, insurance companies or at mutual funds, they are exempt from the tax. However, companies, individuals and banks are not exempt from paying the tax. This causes a disparity in the prices at which a trade can take place between counterparties who are tax-exempt compared with those who are not. This has an adverse impact on the liquidity of the corporate bond market.

The regulatory restrictions are two-fold:

- The buyers face restrictions on what they can or cannot buy in the corporate bond market.
- Bond holders face restrictions on when they can sell the bonds they hold.

For example, pension fund managers are regulated to invest under 10% of the funds collected in corporate bonds that are investment grade. In addition, these funds are permitted only to buy and hold the bonds, and cannot be traded. There are similar restrictions on fund managers of trusts and related associations. Regulations limit the amount of investments and the type of bonds that insurance companies can make in corporate bonds, although they have fewer restrictions on holding the bonds once they are purchased. Mutual funds are smaller, but they have the least restrictions on the manner of their participation in the corporate bond market, and have been the source of activity in the corporate bond market since 2000.

6.1.6 INFORMATION ABOUT CREDIT RISK IN INDIA

The lack of information enabling the assessment of credit risk across different bonds in the country is one significant bottleneck in trading corporate bonds. Over and above a knowledge of the interest rates and the term structure of interest rates in the economy, there are two key elements that are crucial to understanding and managing credit risk in a bond portfolio.

The first is what is the probability of default associated with a particular bond. There are several well-established models that can be used to identify key ratios that indicate whether a firm is close to default or not by looking at the balance sheet data of the firm. Once the time of the default has been identified, there is a well-known approach to calculate the probability of default likely for the firm. However, while there are good sources of clean and consistent data for the balance sheet of an Indian firm, it is very difficult to identify the point at which the default has actually taken place. Typically, information about the time of default is available at banks; however, this is not publicly available. Unlike in the United States where the declaration of Chapter 11 is a clear instance of a firm's bankruptcy in India, information about firm default would become public only when the company was reported to the Bureau of Industrial and Financial Reconstruction (BIFR), which was the agency in charge of recovering assets from the nonperforming assets (NPA) of a bank. However, the time taken to report a firm to BIFR was five to seven years after the actual date of default. This delay compounded the uncertainty about the point of default, and was a bottleneck to estimating the default probability for Indian firms. In the period between 2000–2005, information about company defaults was available on the website of the Reserve Bank of India (RBI). Banks in India were required to report to the RBI a record of all the loans having default on a payment, which the RBI then posted on its website. The records contained the name of the bank, the branch at which the default took place and the name of the defaulting entity, as well as the size of the loan. The date of the loan repayment was not available in this data. However, it was easy to identify the year of default by a firm using this data, not available previously.

Today, all data about defaulting firms are reported by banks to a credit information bureau called the Credit Information Bureau of India, Ltd. (CIBIL). This is an information network where only banks are permitted membership. The membership enables the banks access to the information about defaulting firms (as well as individuals) and their loan characteristics. In India, the RBI has made it mandatory for public sector banks to become members of CIBIL. This data is not available to nonbanks. Hence, the availability of information about defaults has actually worsened in recent years. The Centre for Monitoring Indian Economy (CMIE) has a database of defaults constructed from reports of defaults, as well as from newspaper reports of firms defaulting on obligations for a period of time between 1990–2000. An analysis of this shows that there were approximately 633 defaults in 33,874 firm-years. This set the average probability of default of an Indian firm to be 1.8% between 1996–2000.

Another critical element needed to assess the credit risk of a loan is the loss given default. This is the amount of the loan that cannot be recovered once default takes place. One recent report shows that the loss given default faced by banks on commercial loans greater than Rs.5 million was a bit over 73% (as seen in Table 6.5), while those on retail loans was a little better at 65%. This would imply that default would be expected to have a significantly negative impact on a bank's portfolio because of an increase in credit risk.

6.1.7   CREDIT RATINGS IN INDIA

The last source of information about default rates for Indian firms come from the *credit rating agencies*, or the CRAs.[3]

TABLE 6.5   Loss Given Default at Various Banks for Commercial Loans Greater Than Rs.5 million, 1998–2007

	Loss given default (%)
Bank 1 (Mid-sized)	62.6
Bank 2 (Small)	81.0
Bank 3 (Mid-sized)	84.9
Bank 4 (Small)	73.8
Bank 5 (Large)	64.7
Bank 6 (Large)	80.6
Bank 7 (Mid-sized)	66.5
Average	73.4

Source: Arindam Bandopadhyay, NIBM, 2007.

[3]For an early critique of the credit rating industry, see Raghunathan and Varma (1992).

In India, any corporate bond has to be rated before it can come to market, independent of whether the bond is publicly issued or privately placed. Furthermore, every bond has to be re-rated by the CRA once a year. This policy framework forces issuers to incur the costs of rating. These ratings can be obtained by paying one of three CRAs in India: the Credit Rating and Information Services of India Ltd. (CRISIL), Credit Analysis and REsearch Ltd. (CARE), and the Investment Information and Credit Rating Agency of India, Ltd. (ICRA).

Ratings nomenclature in India follows the nomenclature for credit ratings worldwide. The first level of differentiation is between long-term debt and short-term debt. Long-term debt ratings are alphabetical with the best credit quality being typically denoted as "AAA" down to "C" denoting substantial risk and "D" denoting a defaulted security. Short-term debt ratings have a different rating nomenclature with "PR+/PR1+/F1+" standing for low-default risk, and "PR3/P3/F3" standing for high-default risk.

These ratings are crucial to the pricing of bonds, particularly since several potential buyers of corporate bonds in India face regulatory restrictions on

1. The credit rating that defines an "investment grade" bond, and whether it is an "investment grade" for the buyer.
2. Whether the bonds held in the portfolio can be traded. For example, pension funds regulation, until recently, constrained the fund to hold assets until maturity.

The first credit ratings are available for bonds of Indian firms from 1991 onward. While the earlier data is thin, there was a significant number of bonds rated from 1995 onward. Thus, there is a reasonably good history of credit ratings available for firms in India. The longest credit ratings available are the CRISIL ratings database, a source of several aspects of default characteristics. For example, in the period between 1996 and 2002, there were about 2,400 rating events involving 640 firms. Of these rating events, there were 100 upgrades, 620 downgrades and 1,635 re-affirmations. The database can be used to calculate default rates in India across different credit ratings. CRISIL reports default rates across credit ratings for India in the period from 1992–2006 as shown in Table 6.6.

We see from Table 6.6 how default rates have shifted in the last six years. The data is for the credit ratings published by CRISIL, and shows that the default rate has dropped for most of the credit classes. For example, the default rate for the investment grade bonds in India has dropped from 0.87% to 0.48%. Another aspect of default rates that can be assessed with the credit rating history is the transition probability from one credit rating to another. This is the probability that a "AAA" bond drops to a "AA" credit rating over a year. The transition probability matrix for CRISIL credit ratings can be seen in Table 6.7. For example,

TABLE 6.6   CRISIL Average One-Year Default
Rates in 1992–2006 and in 2000–2006

| Rating | Default rates (%) | |
	1992–2006	2000–2006
AAA	0.00	0.00
AA	0.00	0.00
A	0.98	0.63
BBB	3.36	4.00
Investment	0.87	0.48
Speculative	18.72	11.73

TABLE 6.7   CRISIL Average One-Year Transition Probabilities
in 1992–2006

| | Transition probabilities (%) | | | | | |
	AAA	AA	A	BBB	C	D
AAA	97.58	2.42	0.00	0.00	0.00	0.00
AA	2.39	89.88	6.65	0.58	0.00	0.00
A	0.00	3.73	82.64	7.31	0.70	0.98
BBB	0.00	0.32	5.60	73.60	1.92	3.36
C	0.00	0.00	0.00	5.88	8.83	29.41
D	0.00	0.00	0.00	1.23	70.37	28.40

there is a 2.42% probability that a AAA-rated bond will change to a AA rating
over the next year.

6.1.8   The LINK WITH CREDIT RATING AND PRICING OF CORPORATE BONDS

In order to understand the pricing of corporate bonds, we first look to the
demand for the bonds in the market. Long-term savings in the Indian economy
target investments in pension funds and insurance companies. Fixed deposits
at banks have typical maturities of between three to five years. These form the
bulk of the demand for corporate bonds and ought to logically be the drivers
of the liquidity for corporate bonds in the market, and in turn, will drive the
prices and the spreads in corporate bonds over the default rate.

Financial institutions with the longer-term investment horizon ought to have substantial weight in the liquidity and pricing of these bonds. For instance, the Provident Fund for the central and state government employees, EPFO, has assets under management (AUM) of Rs.1.75 trillion and a focus on investing over the long investment horizon. However, the EPF has regulatory restrictions on what credit exposure they can take in their portfolio. This automatically means that the funds that could improve the pricing and liquidity of the corporate bond market do not participate in these markets as much as their counterparts in other countries.

Even with restrictions on their investment choices, given that the size of the economy stands at $1 trillion, a savings rate in the economy that stands at 35% implies that the demand for investment grade corporate bonds far outstrips the supply of such bonds. This means that the liquidity in the market for corporate bonds is skewed toward higher volumes in "investment grade" bonds and practically no volumes in lower credit grades. This can be seen in Table 6.8 which is a snapshot of traded volumes reported in the corporate debt market in August 2005.

For bonds with better liquidity in the secondary market, the credit spreads can be calculated using the bond prices. The higher the credit rating, the smaller the spreads, as can be seen in Table 6.9 (Bose and Coondoo, 2003). Since the trading in the secondary market is confined to investment grade bonds, it is difficult to estimate a credit spread to use to calculate the price for the other corporate bonds in the market. This is despite the fact that all corporate bonds have to be rated before they can be issued in the market. This becomes a problem for any issuer trying to raise debt in the market with an issue that has a rating of noninvestment grade. This lack of liquidity in the corporate bond market in India becomes a bottleneck, particularly for issuers like the State Governments that attempt to use the corporate bond market to manage their fiscal deficits and are not able to get an investment grade rating on their bonds.

TABLE 6.8 Trading Volumes across Credit Ratings (Aug. 2005)

Rating category	Traded value (Rs. million)	Market share (%)
AAA	1,810	84.0
AA+	220	10.0
AA	25	1.2
AAA(So)	9	0.4
P1+	4	0.2
PR1+	3	0.1
UR	3	0.1

TABLE 6.9   Average Spreads in Rating Category Estimated
Using Bond Prices of Nonconvertible, Nonfinance Company
Debentures, 1997–2001

Rating category	Average spread (%)
AAA	2.49
AA	3.04
A	3.38
BBB	3.71
D	11.62

6.2   MARKETS

The corporate bond market in India, as elsewhere in the world, is an Over-the-
Counter (OTC) telephone market. Counterparties strike deals either directly
on the phone or through a bond market broker, who acts as an intermediary to
the deal. While there have been several institutional improvements of the GOI
bond, only a few of these appear in the corporate bond market in India. And
the consensus is that these reforms have not sufficiently helped improve the
liquidity of the corporate bond market in India; rather, liquidity has worsened
in the market since the time that reforms processes started.

6.2.1   SETTLEMENT

All corporate bonds today are settled in dematerialized form at the equity market
depositories, regardless of how they are issued, or how many counterparties
were involved in the issue. Each corporate bond is issued a unique International
Securities Identification Number (ISIN) and held in electronic credit for any
investor. For example, the National Securities Depository Ltd. (NSDL) has
issued a total of 37,465 ISINs for debt instruments of which 9,562 are active.
The value of the demat bonds held at NSDL is shown in Table 6.10. Coupon
payments and redemptions are credited to the clients' accounts, in a similar
fashion as dividends credited on behalf of equity shareholding.

One of the barriers holding back higher levels of trading in the corporate
bond market is the different application of taxes across the end buyer of the
bond. Insurance companies and mutual funds are exempt from taxes because
of being pass-through financial firms. However, banks are not. This means that
the price of corporate bonds would differ depending upon the buyer of the bond
in a particular transaction. This is another cause of friction in easy trading of
corporate bonds.

TABLE 6.10   Corporate Debt, Dematerialized at NSDL

| | Rs. billion | | |
Issuer	Nov. 2007	Nov. 2006	Change in %
Corporate Debt	4,369	3,674	19
Commercial Paper	462	233	98
Securitized Paper	812	605	34
Certificates of Deposit	1,398	730	92
Government Debt	70	59	19

6.2.2   Primary Market

Corporate debt instruments are issued today in India through either the *auction* route, similar to the one used to issue GOI debt, or through *private placements*. Some of the SG bonds are issued using an auction mechanism. The auction for an SG bond with a fixed coupon and a fixed maturity is announced 4 to 5 days before the auction. The auction is a multiple-price auction, where the winning bids are awarded the quantities bid. However, for most of the corporate bond market today, the issue mechanism of choice is private placement. This is irrespective of whether these are bonds of private firms or PSUs. The process of a public issue is considered too onerous, time consuming and expensive compared to the privately placed route.

Table 6.11 lists the size of the bonds privately placed in India in 1996, 2000, 2004, as well as who the issuers of the bonds were each year. The issue of corporate bonds (as defined by the set of issuers in the table) was the largest in the period 1999–2001. After this, the volumes issued in the market dropped and have only slowly been building up to those seen more recently.

In the case of a private placement, a bank/investment bank acts as an intermediary, prices the bond and offers it to a network of clients. Such a placement can be done in a very short period of time. Typically, the biggest buyers are pension funds and mutual funds. Pension funds have restrictions on buying corporate bonds which have credit ratings that are worse than AA, while mutual funds can invest in a bond with any credit rating. Pension funds have restrictions on selling the bonds once they have been purchased, while mutual funds can trade the bonds to suit the risk profile of their investments. However, pension funds have assets under management that are orders of magnitude larger than that under management at mutual funds. These observations have a significant impact on the ratings of bonds that are issued in the corporate bond market as can be seen in Table 6.12.

TABLE 6.11   Corporate Debt and Their Issuers, 1995–2005

	Rs. billion		
Issuer	1996–1997	2000–2001	2004–2005
Public Sector Companies	165.8	432.9	451.9
State Level Undertakings	27.3	113.1	35.2
Municipalities	0	1.2	1.3
Private Firms (All)	18.1	91.7	101.9
Private Firms (Nonfinancial)	11.3	67.4	53.5
Public issues of bonds	70.2	41.4	41.0

TABLE 6.12   Size of Outstanding Corporate Bonds, Corporate Structured
Obligations and Their Related Credit Rating, Aug. 2005

	Corporate bonds		Structured obligations	
Rating class Bond / SO	No. of issues	Issue size (Rs. billion)	No. of issues	Issue size (Rs. billion)
AAA[4]/MAAA[5]	955	926.09	19	31.16
AA+/LAA+/MAA+	320	196.05	6	1.75
AA/LAA/MAA	175	132.48	5	2.63
AA-/LA-	31	12.72	15	17.00
A+/LA+	16	15.45	24	30.42
A/LA/MA	16	15.12	136	123.28
A-	12	10.63	10	19.00
BBB+	11	8.33	3	2.00
BBB/LBBB	8	7.22	2	8.40
B	6	2.57	1	7.18
No Ratings	82	99.06		

6.3   SECONDARY MARKET TRADING

Corporate bonds can be listed and traded on the exchanges that trade equity in
India. For example, corporate bonds can be traded on the electronic limit order
book of the equity segment of the National Stock Exchange (NSE) and BSE-F

[4]"AAA" is the rating for the bond.

[5]"MAAA" is the rating for the SO.

TABLE 6.13 Estimates of Traded Volumes and Fraction of Turnover in
Secondary Market Trading on the NSE/WDM

	Turnover (Rs. billion)		% of Turnover	
Securities	2004–2005	2005–2006	2004–2005	2005–2006
Government Securities (Central and State)	7,248,097	3,455,832	81.69	72.67
T-Bills	1,248,069	1,052,184	14.07	22.13
PSU Bonds	109,061	68,572	1.23	1.44
Institutional Bonds	69,043	53,119	0.78	1.12
Bank Bonds CDs	26,917	20,084	0.30	0.42
Corporate Bonds CPs	168,100	104,184	1.89	2.19
Others	3,650	1,260	0.04	0.03
Total	8,872,937	4,755,235	100.00	100.00

segment at the Bombay Stock Exchange (BSE). The NSE also has a segment
called the Wholesale Debt Market (WDM) which is an electronic platform to
trade bonds. However, the real secondary market for corporate bonds is an
OTC market. Very low volumes are traded on the equity platforms of NSE
or BSE, if at all. The traded volumes reported on the WDM segment of the
NSE are trades reported to the exchange rather than actually traded on the
exchange.

Table 6.13 shows the changes in traded volumes of corporate bonds, broken
up further across different kinds of corporate bonds. Again, the pattern of
liquidity is the same: there is a secular decrease in the turnover reported of all
the corporate bonds.

6.4   REGULATION AND NEXT STEPS FORWARD

Traditionally, the Indian corporate bond market has been a relatively unregulated one. As with the GOI bond market, the regulatory and supervisory focus
was on the participants in the market, rather than on the instruments themselves. However, the decreasing activity in the corporate bond market raised
alarm bells in the policy circles about the urgent need for reforms in the
corporate bond market. A high level Expert Committee on Corporate Bonds
and Securitization was announced in the Finance Minister's budget speech of
2005–2006. The report of the Expert Committee was submitted in December
2005. Several of the recommendations regarding what is required for progress in

the corporate bond market involve an improvement in the market microstructure of the corporate bond markets. These included:

- Enabling electronic systems of trading, clearing, and a more efficient
  settlement of bond trades.
- Improving institutions for transparency of price information and access
  to trade.
- Removing differences in the tax treatment for investing in bonds among
  different kinds of participants in the market.
- Removing differences across different kinds of products due to the Stamp
  Duty charged by State Governments on bond issuers.

The report focused on improvements in the market microstructure of the
corporate bond market, as well as improving the coherence of the tax system
in dealing with corporate bonds as an asset class. One outcome of enabling an
electronic exchange for corporate bond trading would bring the regulation of
corporate bonds under SEBI.

6.4.1 STRENGTHENING CREDITOR'S RIGHTS

Even with an improvement in the market microstructure targeted at improving
the tradeability of corporate bonds, the real issue remains that Indian Financial
Institutions have very weak rights as a creditor when a default takes place. The
operational processes to recover value for the creditor on a defaulted loan is
lengthy and costly. This is the main deterrant to any financial entity actively
participating in the corporate bond market.

Traditionally, when a firm defaulted on payments to a bank, the bank would
go through an ever-greening of loan for a certain length of time. This would
imply that it would be a while before the bank foreclosed the loan and applied to
the BIFR, which took charge of the recovery of assets from the defaulting firm.
This process could take from five to seven years. In this period, the assets of
the firm would suffer erosion in value, and the recovery would be much lower
than if there was a more prompt recovery process.

The most recent attempt at better defining creditors' rights under the situation of bankruptcy is the Securitization and Reconstruction of Financial
Assets and Enforcement of Security Interest (SARFAESI) Act of 2002. The Act
explicitly vests the lender with secured credit with powers to take possession
of, and sell, the assets of the debtor to recover their dues. The intent of the Act
was to shorten the time to recovery of the due once the debtor had defaulted
on its payments. While SARFAESI is a step forward, it only improves creditors'
rights for secured credit.

In the same year that the SARFAESI Act was passed, the Ministry of Finance also called for the creation of an asset reconstruction company to take charge of the recovery of nonperforming assets (NPAs) to replace the BIFR. The first one that was set up was the Asset Reconstruction Company of India, Ltd. (ARCIL). The total NPA accumulated at the ARCIL until the end of 2007 was Rs.224 billion out of a total of 622 cases of default. The amount recovered until that point was Rs.12 billion out of a resolution of 204 cases.

Despite the empowerment of the creditor promised by the SARFAESI, the implementation of the Act to strengthen creditors' rights has not been an entire success. The first case of a bank using SARFAESI to recover their dues was in early 2004 when ICICI Bank claimed Rs.14 billion from Mardia Chemicals, one of the NPLs in the ICICI Bank portfolio. Mardia Chemicals got a stay order from a court, and the court ruled in favor of Mardia Chemicals which was given 60 days within which to attempt a repayment to ICICI Bank.

The lack of a bankruptcy code, and improved values for the loss given default—particularly for unsecured credit—continues to be a critical constraint holding back the possibility of having a meaningful corporate bond market.

CHAPTER 7

Commodity Futures Markets

The Indian commodity futures markets are both very old and very new.[1] They began in 1875 with a cotton exchange, barely a decade after the Chicago Board of Trade opened its doors for futures trading. But they went through a transformation between 2000 and 2003 with significant regulatory liberalization and the creation of three new national, electronic exchanges, each listing scores of products. Today, there are 23 exchanges in India listing futures on physical commodities, including the three national exchanges. For historical reasons, commodity exchanges have been governed by a different law—the Forwards Contract Regulation Act (FC(R)A)—and overseen by a different regulator—the Forward Markets Commission (FMC)—than have financial derivative exchanges. So in India, we find that commodity derivatives are traded on exchanges that are separate and distinct from the exchanges on which financial derivatives are traded. This makes India more like Japan, which has separate laws, regulators and exchanges for physical commodities and financial derivatives and less like the United States and Europe, where physical and financial derivatives trade side by side on exchanges like the Chicago Mercantile Exchange and Euronext.Liffe.

7.1 A LITTLE HISTORY

Cotton was the first product to be traded on an organized exchange in India in 1875. This was followed by a group of oilseeds, then jute, then wheat and then many other commodities. These contracts traded on local exchanges

---

[1] For further reading in this field, see Thomas, 2003 and 2005.

throughout the country, with markets and prices fragmented due to the high cost of moving both goods and information around.

After independence from the UK in 1947, however, commodity futures trading came under increasing pressure as the country moved down a socialist path. Prime Minister Nehru had watched from prison as the capitalist countries got mired in the Great Depression of the 1930s, while the Soviet Union seemed to be making significant progress. So when Nehru came into power, planning was in and markets were out. Thus the government in 1952 banned cash settlement and options trading under the Forwards Contract Regulation Act.

The ban was subsequently extended to all forward trading after several years of drought at the end of the 1960s caused supply shortages and soaring prices. A large number of farmers whose crops had failed defaulted on their forward contracts, many of them actually committing suicide. The government shifted policy again in the 1970s and permitted trading of forwards on a small set of nonessential commodities, but the volumes never reached their pre-ban levels. Trading had moved underground to OTC contracts, which had the additional advantage of avoiding taxes. To this day, the underground OTC market dwarfs the liquidity of the visible exchanges. Commodity futures then tended to be traded on a large number of small regional exchanges, which typically had active trading in only one or two products.

As part of the overall liberalization of India's markets, between 2000 and 2002 the law was changed, regulations were rewritten, many restrictions on commodity futures trading were lifted, and the framework was put in place to allow the creation of a new type of pan-Indian commodity exchange, which traded on screens and listed a multitude of products. This helped the new exchanges gain economies of scale when compared with the pre-existing regional exchanges.

The first of these new national, electronic exchanges out of the box was the National Multi-Commodity Exchange of Ahmadabad (NMCE), which started November 2002. A year later two more exchanges opened their doors in Mumbai—the Multi-Commodity Exchange (MCX) and the National Commodity Derivatives Exchange (NCDEX), which is partially owned by the NSE. A fourth exchange, the National Board of Trade in Indore, has been on the list to achieve national status, but has not yet converted from floor to screen and actively trades only one product.

In what follows, we describe the products, i.e., the commodities and the design of the futures contracts. Next, we focus on the market for these commodity derivatives with brief descriptions of the trading, clearing and settlement systems, with special attention to the new national exchange infrastructure that has been put in place since 2002. This includes some innovations and differences between markets in India and outside, such as the process that is in place today to obtain reference prices for the underlying commodities. We examine the behavior of trading volumes and the behavior of the futures price vis-à-vis the spot price. Last, we look at the current regulations that form the underlying legal infrastructure for commodity derivatives trading in India.

7.2   PRODUCTS IN THE COMMODITY DERIVATIVES MARKETS

The Forward Markets Commission notes 153 different products as being listed and available for trading on India's 23 commodity exchanges, although less than half of these products actually see significant trading. Most of these commodities are shown in Table 7.1.

While there are several agricultural products listed in Table 7.1, most of the trading is in the nonagricultural products. Table 7.2 shows the value of daily turnover for all exchange traded financial products in India. We can see that about a quarter of the volumes in the commodity derivatives markets tends to be agricultural. The remaining volume comes from nonagricultural products, mainly gold, silver and energy. Much of the trading in energy and metals tends to be during the Indian evening when the energy and metals markets in New York and London are open. To a substantial extent, customers of local exchanges are held in place by capital controls, and prices in India merely reflect the fluctuations in New York and London through active arbitrageurs.

TABLE 7.1   Commodities with Listed Products on Indian Exchanges

Nonagricultural	Agricultural
Energy (crude oil, brent crude oil, furnace oil, natural gas)	**Pulses** (chana, masoor, moong, tur, urad, yellow peas)
Precious Metals (gold, silver)	**Grain** (barley, parboiled rice and basmati rice, wheat)
Base Metals (aluminium, copper, lead, nickel, tin, zinc)	**Oils and oilseeds** (castor oil, coconut cake and oil, cotton seed and oil, groundnut seed and oil, mentha oil, mustard seed and oil, palmolein, soya bean and soya oil, sesame seeds)
Ferrous Metals (steel, sponge iron)	**Spices** (cardamom, chili, cumin/jeera seeds, jaggery/gur, pepper, sugar, turmeric)
Polymers (polyethylene, polypropelene, polyvinyl chloride)	**Nonedible Agriculture** (cotton and cottonseed oilcake, guar seed and guar gum, mulberry coocoons and silk, raw jute and jute bags, rubber)
	Others (cashew, coffee, potato)

TABLE 7.2   Average Daily Volumes on
Indian Financial Markets, March 2007

Market	Average daily volumes (million USD)	
Commodity derivatives of which	3,400	
Agriculture		890 (27%)
Nonagriculture		2,510 (73%)
Equity derivatives	7,925	
Equity spot	2,040	
Government bonds spot	1,020	

Note also the comparison in volume between the equity derivatives markets and commodity derivatives. Equity derivatives have been trading on national electronic exchanges since 2000, while commodity derivatives trading on a similar platform began at the end of 2003. In a relatively short span of just over three years, commodity derivatives markets have reached more than 40 percent of the size of equity derivatives.

7.2.1   MOST ACTIVE CONTRACTS

In order to get a sense of which contracts have been most important, we list the 15 commodity contracts that were the most active as of the middle of 2007, in Table 7.3.[2]

Out of the national electronic exchanges, MCX and NCDEX account for 14 of the 15 most active contracts. NMCE has no contract among the top 15. The other exchange—the National Board of Trade of Indore (NBOT)—has a soy oil contract that trades roughly the same volume as NCDEX. This is NBOT's only active contract and NBOT is not a national electronic exchange.[3]

MCX dominates in metals and energy and these contracts are the most active commodities contracts in India. MCX's gold, copper, silver, zinc, nickel and crude oil contracts accounted for 71% of all commodity futures trading in mid-2007. The contracts that are most uniquely Indian are the agricultural

[2]These numbers are as reported by the Forward Markets Commission (FMC), which is the commodities derivatives regulator. We have converted the value of trading in crore rupees for a two-week period—that is reported by FMC—into the average daily value of trading in million USD, using a Rs.40 per USD exchange rate and 12 trading days, since the commodity exchanges are open 6 days a week.

[3]NBOT has the licenses to start national trading but has not yet operationalized this.

TABLE 7.3   Top 15 Futures on Physical Commodities: Average Daily Value of Trading for June 1–15, 2007

	Commodity	Exchange	Trading volume (Crore rupees/14 days)	Trading volume (Million USD/day)	Share of total (%)
1	Gold	MCX	26,795.88	558	18
2	Copper	MCX	26,409.80	550	18
3	Silver	MCX	20,405.04	425	14
4	Crude oil	MCX	13,702.11	285	9
5	Zinc	MCX	12,821.65	267	9
6	Jeera	NCDEX	7,035.88	147	5
7	Nickel	MCX	6,212.78	129	4
8	Guar seed	NCDEX	4,508.68	94	3
9	Pepper	NCDEX	4,165.32	87	3
10	Soy oil	NCDEX	4,044.52	84	3
11	Soy oil	NBOT	3,857.83	80	3
12	Gold	NCDEX	3,209.65	67	2
13	Chana	NCDEX	2,685.29	56	2
14	Soy oil	MCX	2,586.21	54	2
15	R/M seed	NCDEX	2,132.78	44	1
Top 15			140,573.44	2,929	93
All contracts			150,796.26	3,142	100

Source: Forward Markets Commission, Fortnightly Dissemination of Data, June 22, 2007.

contracts, and here, NCDEX dominates. The agricultural contracts in the top 15 accounted for 29% of total volume.

The only contracts in the top 15 that actively trade simultaneously on multiple exchanges are the soy oil contracts on three exchanges, and the two gold contracts on MCX (89% share) and NCDEX (11% share), which reinforces the general rule that in the long run liquidity in any specific contract tends to gravitate to a single exchange.

A bit of explanation is appropriate for the contracts that are uniquely Indian and sound strange to Western ears.

Jeera is the ancient spice known in the West as cumin, and best known for its use in Indian and Mexican cooking. It is also used as an ingredient in Indian Ayurvedic medicines. India is the number one consumer of cumin. It is also the number one producer, with most of the spice being produced in the states of Rajasthan and Gujarat. Acreage planted, and production, can be quite volatile. Cumin is planted in October/November and harvested four months later. This is a relatively dry season in India and unexpected rains during the February–March harvest can have a very negative effect on both the size and quality of the crop.

Guar is a plant with beans in pods, like pea pods. When the beans are young they can be eaten as a fresh vegetable. But when allowed to mature, the beans, called guar seeds, are ground into flour known as guar gum. Because the endosperm of the guar seed forms a gel when mixed with water, guar gum is used as a thickener, stiffener and stabilizer in foods such as softserve ice cream, cheeses, instant puddings and cold meats. It also has industrial uses in the production of paper and textiles and in drilling for petroleum. Around 80% of the world's guar comes from India, out of which about 70% comes from the state of Rajasthan, with Jodhpur in western Rajasthan as the major delivery center for futures trading. It is a monsoon-fed crop and price volatility is driven chiefly by variations in monsoon rainfall. Both guar seed and guar gum are traded on Indian exchanges, although most trading is in the seeds. Guar is also produced in Pakistan and in the high plains of Texas where it's known as cluster beans.

Chana, called chick peas or garbanzos in the West, is a pulse (the dried seed of a leguminous peapod-like plant) that is split, boiled, pureed and mixed with spices to make one of the many types of dal, a staple of many Indian meals. Chana is an important source of protein in a largely vegetarian culture. About a third of all pulse production in India is chana. India accounts for about 65% of world production, but only imports a small amount. Price volatility is driven by the rains.

Rapeseed-Mustard Seed (or R/M for short) represents a combination of the two seeds which are bought, sold and marketed together because the two plants are from the same species and the oils exhibit the same properties. It is the second most important oilseed in India, after ground nuts (peanuts to Americans). The seeds are crushed to create oil and oil cake (similar to crushing soybeans to obtain soybean oil and soybean meal). The oil is used for cooking and in a number of both food and industrial applications, including the manufacture of biodiesel. It is the third most important vegetable oil in the world after soybean and palm oil. The oil cake is mainly used for animal feed. Rapeseed and mustard seed are planted in September and October and harvested in February and March.

Gold ETFs

In addition to the gold spot and the futures market, one more market in India trades gold on a nationwide platform—the Exchange Traded Fund (ETF) on gold trading on the equity market, NSE. This is also a national trading platform with access to the same retail order flow as the national commodity derivatives exchanges. These funds are offered by mutual fund companies. The first two companies with gold ETFs were the Benchmark Asset Management Company (GoldBeES, March 2007) and the Unit Trust of India (GoldShare, April 2007).

The ETFs target the retail order flow with a minimum unit size of 10 grams of gold and a market lot size of one contract. The units are dematerialized like all equity shares in India. These ETFs were launched on the NSE first in March 2007. By July 2007, ETFs on gold had roughly Rs.5 billion of assets under management, and an average daily traded volume of Rs.10 million a day.

7.2.2 CONTRACT SPECIFICATION

Contract specifications vary with the underlying commodity. However, there are some common features:

1. Exchanges trade only commodity *futures*—there are no commodity options traded in India.
2. The shortest maturity contracts are one-month contracts. The longest possible contracts listed are twelve-month contracts.
3. Expiration dates vary, but NCDEX has almost all its expiration dates on the 20th of the month and MCX on the 5th, the 15th or the 20th on a contract by contract basis.
4. Indian exchanges have experimented with partial cash settlement procedures, such as giving the seller the option to deliver the product or settle in cash. These experiments have not worked well and virtually all commodity contracts today have mandatory delivery for parties who hold their positions beyond expiration.

For each commodity, other important aspects of contract design are the size of the contract and the grade of commodity that is delivered at settlement. In general, the size of the contract tends to be small in order to be accessible to a target audience that includes farmers, merchants and individuals. In some cases, such as bullion, there are two contracts: one at a size tailored for a retail audience, and another larger sized, more commercial contract. For example, two gold futures trade simultaneously, one at a contract size of 1 kg and another at a contract size of 100 grams. Generally, commodity contracts in India are about a fifth the size of commodity contracts traded in the United States.

The grade of the underlying good for contract settlement is largely determined by the quality of the commodity that is widely available in the local markets. This is typically the case in agricultural commodities, where the local product is available from different locations all over the country, and there is no unique standardized quality of the underlying. Sometimes, this means that the grade used for price settlement differs from season to season, or month to month, an uncertainty that makes it inevitable that the liquidity of long-dated futures contracts suffers.

This problem does not arise with bullion and energy commodities. Here, the grades are largely set by the standards on international commodity futures contracts. Taking gold as an example once again, MCX does the daily settlement of Indian gold futures loss/profits on the London Bullion Market Association price of 995 purity gold.

7.3 MARKETS

Spot as well as derivative markets for commodities have existed in India for centuries. However, the traditional markets were local markets built for local access, spread all across the length and breadth of the country. In the traditional Indian commodity derivatives markets, instead of one exchange trading multiple commodities, each *commodity* would have *multiple* exchanges. Each exchange would be set up in, or close to, the region where the commodity was produced. As elsewhere in the world, all the exchanges were associations of brokers. Today, these markets are very different due to some liberalization in the underlying product markets and the reforms in the financial sector. The regulatory framework for commodities means that spot markets are still localized, with multiple markets all over the country.[4] The government still has power to control the supply and the pricing of several commodities in the country. However, with dropping trade barriers, prices of most commodities are determined by import parity pricing, rather than solely by local conditions.

In the case of commodity derivatives markets, reforms have seen a more significant development of institutions that enable a manifold increase in the size and accessibility of commodity derivatives in India. These developments started at the end of 2003, and the commodities markets are still in the process of transition toward an equilibrium between the spot and the futures markets.

7.3.1 TRADING

The traditional commodity derivatives exchanges were organized as local open-outcry marketplaces with broker-owners that co-ordinated the order flow between buyers and sellers. Often, the futures markets traded a single commodity, such as cotton, chana or chile peppers. These have traditionally served as localized pools of liquidity and price discovery. Such fragmentation meant that there was little progress toward standardization of grades of commodities or toward the development of a benchmark price for any single commodity.

[4]This is discussed more in Section 7.5 on the regulatory and legal framework for commodity spot and derivatives markets.

The structure of the market today has changed. There are now 24 commodity derivatives exchanges in India. In addition to the older local, open-outcry exchanges, generally focusing on a single commodity, there are three electronic exchanges today which offer a single trading and clearing platform across the nation.

1. National Multi-Commodities Exchange (NMCE) in Ahmedabad, Gujarat
2. Multi-Commodities eXchange (MCX) in Bombay
3. National Commodities Derivatives EXchange (NCDEX) in Bombay

These exchanges are unlike the traditional exchange in almost every aspect: they are owned by financial entities rather than by brokers. Regulations mandate that a single entity can own more than 10% equity in an exchange. This makes for a dispersed shareholding that includes foreign ownership as well. For example, Fidelity International is a shareholder in MCX and the Goldman Sachs Group has invested in NCDEX. The new exchanges all trade multiple commodities. For the commodities they trade, the new exchanges have become the best source of liquidity. When a commodity trades on one of the new national exchanges, traded volumes tend to move away from the traditional local exchange that used to be the center of liquidity for that commodity onto the new national exchange.

The exchanges run trading sessions during the same trading hours between 10 A.M. and 3:30 P.M. In addition, the new electronic exchanges also run trading sessions for a limited set of commodities in the evening hours between 6 P.M. and 8 P.M. (All of India is on the same time zone, which is GMT + 5.5 hours.)

On the new electronic exchanges, the order flow comes from all across the nation onto a single electronic order book, where the orders are matched into trades by a computer on the principle of price–time priority. The electronic order book has anonymous orders to buy and sell. This set of orders is visible to all market participants. Thus, for the first time in the country, both the orders as well as the traded prices for commodity derivatives are visible in real-time. The accessibility of the electronic order book on a common national platform has led to an unprecedented level of transparency of commodity trading in India. Superior levels of price transparency have become available not just for the futures contracts but also for the underlying spot market prices (as described in Section 7.3.2). The transparency and the accessibility of the prices has led to the futures markets prices gradually becoming the benchmark that traders use to price their trades on the spot market.

This makes for a fiercely competitive environment among the exchanges. The exchanges can compete in terms of what products they can trade futures on. Further, when the same underlying is traded on multiple exchanges, the specifics of the contracts that each trade are often slightly different in an attempt

TABLE 7.4   Gold Futures Contracts on MCX and
NCDEX

	MCX	NCDEX
Size	1 kg	1 kg
Quality	995 purity	995 purity
Delivery	Ahmedabad	Mumbai
Additional	Mumbai	Ahmedabad
Daily price limit	3%	4%
Expiry	5th day	20th day
Position limit	2 metric tons	2 metric tons

to cater to user requirements. For example, the contract specifications for gold
on NCDEX and MCX are seen in Table 7.4.

7.3.2   POLLING PRICES OFF SPOT MARKETS

Commodity futures exchanges require accurate measurement of the spot price.
In addition to being used for measurement of spot prices to assist traders on
the futures market, it is also a crucial input for the surveillance and the risk
management functions at the exchange. Since all trades are cleared through
a clearing house at the end of each day, all member positions have to be marked-
to-market daily. There is typically low liquidity on newly launched contracts,
and thus, the exchange traded futures price may not be the best indicator of the
value of the positions. In addition, the volatility calculated using the exchange
traded futures price is almost certainly not the best measure for volatility of the
underlying commodity. Lastly, for all contracts, there is a need to continually
monitor the underlying commodity price to ensure that the futures and the spot
markets are constantly aligned and converge properly at expiration, and that
there is no rampant malpractice affecting the futures market prices.

In India, in the absence of the availability of reliable spot price data, commodity futures exchanges had an incentive to develop high quality systems
to obtain these prices directly. The incentives are larger for agricultural commodities, since grades are numerous and standardization is difficult. Prices are
difficult to gather and disseminate, with consistency in quality and in real-time,
from spot markets that are fragmented across regions and grades, especially
with trading that is floor-based and open-outcry. However, the efficient and fair
functioning of a futures market is dependent on observing a fair market price
of the underlying commodity.

Therefore, one innovation that emerged along with the new national electronic exchanges is a process to collect and disseminate price information, in

real-time, on the underlying commodities for which the exchange trades futures. At NCDEX, there are processes to gather spot market prices in a timely manner and at frequent intervals within the day. This spot price information is then disseminated through the exchange trading terminals all over the country. The process involves:

1. Identifying key regional markets for the specific grade of the underlying commodity,
2. Identifying key market dealers for the commodity,
3. Polling bid and ask prices prevailing in the market at time, at regular intervals,
4. Collating polled prices from different locations to a central data warehouse,
5. Statistically testing the veracity of all the polled bid and ask prices for any indication of price manipulation by any single dealer or a coalition of dealers,
6. Calculating the trimmed mean bid and ask prices,
7. Transmitting this trimmed mean to the exchange terminals, and from there, to the rest of the market as the real-time benchmark price for the commodity.

The price polling mechanism is not a new one—price polling is used to calculate the London Inter-Bank Offer Rate (LIBOR). However, there are several distinct differences that the commodities exchanges have to deal with that are not issues of the LIBOR.

Unlike the LIBOR which is polled by the British Banker's Association—an association of 199 banks operating in the UK—the spot price polling process in India is outsourced to third-party information vendors. The entire process of polling dealers, collating information, testing information, and calculating the summary statistic is in the hands of the information vendors. In India, these vendors are CMIE (Centre for Monitoring Indian Economy), CRISIL (Credit Rating Information System of India Ltd.), and NCMSL (National Collateral Management System, Ltd.). Of these, CMIE and CRISIL are independent firms while NCMSL is a wholly owned subsidiary of NCDEX.

The exchanges play an important role in determining the key regional markets as well as the market dealers who are polled. Since the dealers are present at the local markets spread all across the country with no single national registry of dealers, identifying these dealers can be quite a problem. Secondly, which market and which set of dealers to poll is influenced by the grade of the commodity specified in the contract design. A change in the grade could mean a change in the dealers to be polled. Thus, unlike the LIBOR, where a stable set of banks can be readily accessed, the identification of the correct dealers in the Indian commodity markets is a difficult and moving target.

Once the markets and the dealers are identified, the information vendors put the machinery of price polling, collection and verification into play. Spot commodity prices are typically disseminated from the exchanges three times a day. For instance, NCDEX receives prices at the start of the day (10:45 A.M.), past noon (1 P.M.), and at the end of the trading day (4 P.M.). This requires a network to span the geographical spread of India, and to have a capacity for numerical analysis and reliable data transmission—quite a challenge in a developing market like India.

To illustrate the magnitude of the effort, in 2005 CMIE polled prices for 34 commodities over 52 markets. This meant polling data from 90 locations spread over an area of 3.3 million square km. This amounted to approximately a million phone calls in the year. In order to keep the data timely, there cannot be a wide interval between receipt of the individual prices by the price polling vendor and receipt of the tabulated information by the exchange. Receiving the data at the CMIE head office in Bombay to transferring the final price takes between 15 and 20 minutes.

The gap between the polling and collation of prices and dissemination is further complicated by the critical step of testing the veracity and the consistency of the dealer quotes. Since the quality of the dealer network cannot match the credibility of the top banking and financial institutions in an international financial center like London, the simple process of trimming the data and calculating a mean used to calculate LIBOR cannot be used for Indian commodity prices. There, the quotes are collected from eight dealers, out of which the highest two and the lowest two quotes are discarded, and a mean calculated from the remaining quotes.

For Indian commodities, there are often situations where there are only a handful of dealers that are willing to, or available to, quote market reference rates. In such situations, the price becomes extremely vulnerable to manipulation by a dominant dealer or a dominant cartel of dealers. At CMIE, the process of calculating a mean does not, therefore, involve trimming the data (removing the extremes of the data) in the fixed manner as for the LIBOR. The data for a given commodity is first tested for signs of manipulation. This process depends upon the extent of variation in the data. If there is manipulation, it is likely that different subsets of the data can yield significantly different reference prices. The statistical process employed to test for manipulation is call the adaptive trimmed mean, where the amount of trimming depends upon the extent to which different subsets yield different prices. When using this process, it is possible that the mean reference price is calculated with a large amount of data trimming, and sometimes with no trimming at all.

This entire process of spot price collection has become part of the new information network put into place to support commodity derivatives trading. This new level of price transparency both for futures as well as spot prices has very positive implications for any endeavor with an exposure to commodities prices, starting from the farmers with their cropping decisions, to financial institutions and their funding decisions, to wholesale dealers in these commodities.

7.3.3 MARKET PARTICIPANTS

Currently, customers do not have direct market access to commodity derivatives markets. Access is available only through exchange members. There are three types of members on the exchange: Professional or Institutional Clearing Members (PCM), Trading and Clearing Members (TCM) and Trading Members (TM). PCMs offer pure clearing services, and do not have any proprietary trading positions. TCMs have their own proprietary positions, which they clear through their own clearing accounts. TMs take positions on behalf of their clients, which they clear through either TCMs or PCMs.

Each exchange permits membership using the eligibility criteria of the firm's net worth. In addition, different exchanges charge different fees for membership to the exchange. The range of the Net Worth Criteria (NC) as well as the Fees and Deposits (F&D) for membership on NMCE, MCX and NCDEX are as seen in Table 7.5. For a comparison, we use similar numbers for a membership on the National Stock Exchange's equity derivatives markets. Market participants on the commodities exchanges do not include any of the traditional financial institutions. Currently banks are not permitted to take commodities exposure in their portfolios. Regulation also does not permit foreign brokerage firms or foreign institutional investors membership on the exchange. Thus, the profile of market participants are retail: this category includes Indian brokerage firms, private firms and individuals.

TABLE 7.5 Range of Membership Fees and Net Worth Criteria on the National Exchanges

| | (Figures in thousand USD) | | | |
| | Commodities | | Equity | |
Member type	F&D	NC	F&D	NC
Professional Clearing Members	40–320	125–15,000	883	750
Trading and Clearing Members	40–200	125–185	883	245
Trading Members	40	125	700	245

The range of values stand for the differences between costs and criteria at MCX, NMCE and NCDEX.

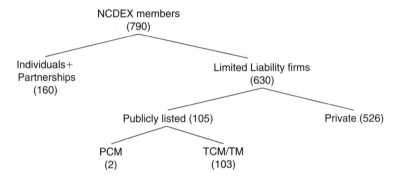

FIGURE 7.1   Structure of NCDEX Membership

Figure 7.1 shows the structure of membership of NCDEX. Of the 790 members, 160 are individuals or partnerships and the remainder are limited liability firms. Of the 630 limited liability firms, 105 are listed. Of these, two are clearing members.

A number of the brokerage firms are commodity derivatives affiliates of the same brokerage firms that have memberships on the equity derivatives markets. Since the regulatory framework does not permit the same firm to have joint membership of equity as well as commodity derivatives firms, almost all the large equity derivatives brokerage firms have set up separate brokerage firms with membership on the commodity derivatives exchanges as well. On the streets of India, it is typical to see signs put up by securities firms offering both equity and commodity futures trading. Technically, this requires distinct firms, but for all practical purposes the firms are unified.

7.3.4   CLEARING AND SETTLEMENT

As with futures exchanges elsewhere in the world, the clearing process involves netting by novation where the clearinghouse becomes the counterparty to the net settlement obligation of all clearing members. Initial margin and marked-to-market margin are used in the risk management of the clearinghouse.

Initial margin is calculated using a variant of the CME SPAN. At NCDEX, there is real-time calculation of initial margin requirements during trading time at the client level. In other words, when a trade takes place, the position of the buyer and the seller is updated and a fresh initial margin calculation is done. This is compared against the capital placed with the clearinghouse ahead of time.

As is typical with futures exchanges elsewhere in the world, a very small part of the open interest results in delivery at the expiration of the futures contract. At NCDEX, a trade that ends with physical settlement involves delivery based on warehouse receipts. The buyers taking physical delivery must have depository accounts at both the depositories, NSDL and CDSL. Traders who aim to make physical delivery, deposit their goods before settlement at an NCDEX-accredited warehouse, with the quality of the commodity certified by an approved exchange assayer. After the quality has been certified and the goods have been deposited, the warehouse issues a receipt to the seller in the form of an electronic credit statement into the seller's depository account.

7.4   MARKET OUTCOMES

An issue with starting any new market is that liquidity is an elusive feature. In India itself, the equity derivatives that today are well traded with deep trading volumes and tight pricing between futures and the underlying, were trading at low volumes for two years after their start in 2000. Commodity derivatives markets trading has always been well entrenched in India and these markets have transited remarkably well to the new infrastructure of a small number of multiple-commodity, single national electronic marketplaces.

Table 7.6 shows total trading volumes in the top commodity exchanges, as well as the top traded products on the exchange. The table shows that liquidity for a specific commodity tends to accrue to one specific exchange. For example, bullion and metals contracts are the top trades at MCX, Bombay, while NCDEX, Bombay is the agricultural futures exchange.

Trading volume falls off sharply beyond the two top national, multi-commodity exchanges. MCX is the top exchange with volumes of around USD 60 billion in March 2007, with NCDEX clearly below with about a third of the volumes at around USD 20 billion. A feature that is not captured in Table 7.6 is the volatility of these rankings. While the top two exchanges have held their positions for several years now, five of the next six had changed their ranking only three months after this table was compiled.

At any given time there are a number of contract months available for trading in each commodity. For example, as this chapter is written, it is July 12th. NCDEX has active trading in Chana (chick pea) contracts for July, August, September, October, November and December. This allows hedgers or speculators to take positions a month out, two months out, even a year out in many cases. It is an almost universal phenomenon that the front month always has more trading activity than any of the more distant months, at least until contract expiration draws near and people who want positions but not delivery will roll into the next month out. Traders want to position themselves where the

TABLE 7.6   Monthly Volumes on the Top Commodity Exchanges, March 2007

Market	Popular contracts	Volumes (million USD)
MCX, Bombay	Copper, gold, silver, crude oil, zinc	56,626
NCDEX, Bombay	Jeera, pepper, guar seed, channa, soy oil	19,482
NMCE, Ahmedabad	Pepper, rubber, gold, zinc, aluminium	1,220
NBOT (National Board of Trade), Indore	Soy oil	1,490
Chamber of Commerce, Hapur	Mustard seed	510
Ahmedabad Commodity Exchange Ltd, Ahmedabad	Castor seed	705
The Surendranagar Cotton & Oilseeds Association Ltd, Surendranagar	Kapas (cotton)	136
Rajkot Seed oil, Bullion Merchants Association Ltd, Rajkot	Castor seed	135

The popular contracts are listed in the order of decreasing volumes traded in the month.

most liquidity is, where it is easiest and cheapest to enter and exit the market. The only time serious liquidity starts to build in the deferred months is when participants with clear commercial needs for specific deferred months begin to place orders in those more distant months.

So if we look at volume and open interest in the front month as a percent of volume and open interest in all months combined, this gives us some feeling for how speculative the market is. The more that activity is concentrated in the near month (i.e., as the ratio approaches 100%), the more likely the contract is being used for mainly speculative purposes. When the share of trading in the front month is small (as it moves away from 100%), it suggests substantial commercial participation.

Table 7.7 shows these ratios for the five most important nonagricultural commodities as well as the five biggest agricultural commodities. Foreign exchange and equity futures worldwide tend to have most of their trading and open interest concentrated in the front or nearby month. There is a clear difference between the two groups. The agricultural commodities have substantially lower concentrations of trading activity in the front month suggesting that there is more commercial activity in these contracts compared to the nonagricultural contracts.

The concentration of volume and open interest in metals and energy is quite high, typically above 70%. Crude oil, for example, has 79% of the open interest in the front month. While this is substantially higher than the agricultural

TABLE 7.7   Patterns in Near Month Contract Open
Interest (OI) and Traded Volumes (TV) as a Fraction of
the Open Interest and Traded Volumes Summing across
Contracts of all Maturities, March 2007

Commodity	Near month/All months (Figures in %)	
	Open interest	Traded volume
Gold	74.80	69.92
Silver	84.29	88.86
Copper	82.63	89.27
Crude oil	79.18	75.12
Zinc	68.27	57.05
Guar seed	12.38	5.76
Channa	27.46	5.45
Soy oil	26.21	22.73
Pepper	19.07	18.72
Jeera	46.96	24.09

commodities (six times the front month concentration of guar seeds), it is
also six times the level shown in the equivalent crude contract at NYMEX. On
July 11, 2000, for example, NYMEX crude oil listed 71 different contract months
and had only 11.6% of the total open interest concentrated in the front month
contract.

7.5   REGULATION AND LEGAL FRAMEWORK

The two important pieces driving the legal and regulatory framework in the
commodities markets are the Essential Commodities Act, 1955 (ECA), and the
Forwards Contract Regulation Act, 1952 (FCRA).

7.5.1   SPOT MARKET REGULATION

The markets trading the underlying commodities are licensed, regulated and
monitored by the state governments where they are set up. The regulatory
powers are based on the Essential Commodities Act of 1955, which is an "act to
provide for the control of the production, supply and distribution of, and trade
and commerce in certain, commodities." This act defines a set of commodities
as "essential commodities." In addition, the ECA gives the central government

the right to categorize any commodity trading in the country as an essential commodity. The original set of essential commodities includes sugar, cotton, jute and automobile components. Interestingly, other than a broad category of foodstuff, the Act does not specifically mention wheat or rice. For these commodities, the ECA empowers the central and state governments to control the supply of the commodity available. This includes the right to

- Control the production of the commodity.
- Set the price at which the commodity can be bought or sold, and
- Regulate the storage of the commodity, to the point of taking action against those with inventory of the commodity.

This means that the same commodity can have different controls on supply and pricing across different states. This has significant implications for the arbitrage linking futures and spot prices in the country. Futures contracts trade on a national platform with a uniform price, but with deliveries at different points across the country. Arbitrage linking the futures with the spot could vary depending upon where the arbitrageur is receiving or making delivery. What is more difficult to predict and factor into the arbitrage is that these arbitrage linkages get broken when the state government changes policy affecting the supply of the commodity in the state. For example, a change in the import subsidies on gold meant that states with well-developed ports, like Kerala and Gujarat, would become more important supply centers for gold. This could shift the patterns of optimal delivery from the arbitrage point of view.

7.5.2 DERIVATIVES MARKETS REGULATION

Regulation of derivatives trading on physical commodities is a work in progress. The legal framework for commodity derivatives in India has its basis in the Forwards Contract (Regulation) Act (FC(R)A) of 1952, though there have been amendments over time. By this law, the only commodity derivatives permitted in India are forward or futures contracts on physical underlyings. In addition, contracts that reach the day of maturity have to settle with physical delivery. The law does not permit trading on any underlying that is not physically deliverable. Therefore, the legal framework has to be amended to trade derivatives based on an index like a commodities index futures contract, or futures on the monsoon where the level of rainfall during the monsoons would become the underlying. Options contracts are forbidden by the FC(R)A of 1952.

The overseer of all commodity futures markets, including the new big national exchanges, is the Forward Markets Commission (FMC). The FMC is a department of the Ministry of Consumer Affairs, Food and Public

Distribution, much like the predecessor agency to the US Commodity Futures Trading Commission was a unit within the US Department of Agriculture. The Commission is based in Mumbai and must have between two and four members. As of now, the FMC does not have the full power to take punitive action against criminals in the commodity derivatives markets. An amendment of the FC(R)A of 1952, which includes permitting options trading on commodities as well as further empowering the regulator, has been pending since 2006.

For historical reasons, commodity futures trading is placed with the Department of Consumer Affairs, rather than the Ministry of Finance. And to complicate matters, the jurisdiction of the spot markets for commodities lies with the state governments, rather than the central government. All of this has several implications for a very different path of development of commodity derivatives in India compared to these markets in the United States and Europe:

- There are and must be separate exchanges for physical commodity derivatives and financial derivatives. This has resulted in certain inefficiencies because the large electronic commodity exchanges have adopted the same market microstructure as the two equity derivatives exchanges, and it would make economic sense to tap economies of scale to use the existing infrastructure of these equity derivatives exchanges. But as is often the case worldwide, politics trumps economics and this is not currently possible.
- There are separate regulators for commodity trading and for securities trading. While the Forward Markets Commission (FMC) regulates commodities markets, the Securites and Exchange Board of India (SEBI) regulates the securities markets. And while SEBI is a relatively strong regulator, the FMC is a much weaker stepsister buried within the Department of Consumer Affairs.
- For commodities, the policies of market development have been dominated by issues of India's agriculture policy and food security policy rather than issues toward improved market efficiency, price transparency, and risk management as with other financial markets. This has caused instances of market disruptions with extreme price increases or drops in essential commodities. Essential commodities are those agricultural commodities in the Government of India's food security program, including wheat and gram. During 2006 and 2007, the government banned futures trading in tur, urad, wheat and rice. This was due to the belief that futures markets had contributed to commodity price inflation, even though commodity price inflation was a worldwide phenomenon. Such banning of products has injected uncertainty in the minds of traders who ask what will be banned next.

CHAPTER 8

Real Estate

India is huge. With 1.2 billion people, even India's modest 1.46% population growth rate (there are 89 countries with faster growing populations) still creates 48,000 new souls each day that have to be fed, clothed and sheltered. While many of these people are in relatively dire poverty, and therefore are not in the market to purchase or rent real estate, the rapidly growing middle class is in increasing need of places to live, offices in which to work and malls in which to shop. And with the economy growing at 8–9% per year, it is clear that industrial and commercial capacity is also being added at a pretty fast rate. It is these two factors, population growth and economic growth, which are the main drivers in the real estate market. As in any country, there will be periods of under-expansion and over-expansion on the supply side of this market, with prices and lease rates reacting accordingly, but the press of population and economic growth will require a long-term expansion in residential, commercial and industrial real estate development.

8.1 PRICE TRENDS IN REAL ESTATE

Real estate markets in most countries experience cycles. The supply and demand for real estate are rarely in balance for long. As this is written in early 2008, it appears as though prices have turned soft in many urban areas. Too quick a run up in prices combined with rising mortgage rates has made residential property much less affordable and has begun choking off demand. Prices in Mumbai, Delhi and Bangalore had at least doubled in four years and mortgage rates have risen about 300 basis points since 2005 and there were signs that prices had begun to fall in some of the hotter markets. However, no one was forecasting anything like the huge drop in property prices that occurred earlier from 1995 to 2002 in India.[1] The reason for this was that India seemed poised to continue its very rapid economic growth rate, which would continue to drive rising salaries, especially in the IT sector. This would continue to swell the numbers of the Indian middle class, giving them the ability to fulfill their dreams of housing ownership.

These fundamental economic forces should continue to cause a long-term rise in property values along with the prices of the stocks of companies involved in property development. But the fact that the market will often under- and overvalue properties and stocks at any given time means that the investor must carefully choose entry and exit points. Real estate investors will watch occupancy rates as well as the market prices and rental rates to determine whether they should expand or contract their activities. While local investors can often gain this information anecdotally, it is useful to have more objective measures of these prices.

The problem in India is that most price information is still anecdotal. Journalists will quote how the price of a flat in a particular building or township has risen 40% over the past year. This information is easier to process for local analysts who know all these properties than it is for the more distant observer. Some information is a bit more organized. For example, an international property consultant, Cushman and Wakefield, publishes the average price of properties in nine areas in and around Delhi in the Saturday edition of the *Times of India*. The data are expressed as the price per square yard and shows the change from six months prior and one year prior. These average prices are calculated by having student interns call property dealers in each of the areas covered.

India is working on developing aggregate indicators of the health of the real estate market. One of the key indicators of housing health used in the United States is Housing Starts, published monthly by the Census Bureau in the Department of Commerce. A housing start involves beginning land excavation to put in the foundation for a new residence. In India, the RBI has created a Technical Advisory Group to develop a Housing Startup Index, and as of November 30, 2007, the Group had met twice.

Singer-songwriter Bob Dylan once said that you don't need a weatherman to know which way the wind blows. Likewise, you don't need a national real estate index to know that property prices have been advancing quite sharply over the past half decade in cities in many parts of India. Currently, India is estimated to have over 60 cities with populations exceeding one million (the United States has nine) and a very large number of technology parks, industrial parks and integrated townships are being built in Mumbai, Delhi, Bangalore,

---

[1]For example in the report *India Property Sector* released on September 27, 2007, Credit Suisse First Boston saw a 10–15% correction in prices within the coming year, but nothing like the 60% drop in prices from 1995 through 2002.

Hyderabad, Pune, and scores of other locations. Indian newspapers and magazines have been filled with stories of spectacular price increases in many of these cities.

8.2   ACCURACY OF PRICES

Prices of land and real property reported to the government are often significantly understated because both buyers and sellers have an incentive to report a price lower than the one actually paid and received for the property. Let's take a typical transaction. Buyer and seller agree to transfer a flat at Rs.40 lakh (about $100,000).[2] Furthermore, they agree to do 10 lakh by check (called white money) and 30 lakh in cash (called black money, because its tough to trace and tax). It appears to the government that the property sold for 10 lakh (the visible white money) which becomes the relevant number for both the stamp tax paid by the buyer and capital gains taxes paid by the seller.

Stamp taxes, which are essentially title transfer taxes, are set at the state level, or by the central government for Union Territories[3] such as Delhi, India's capital. The stamp tax in Delhi, for example, is 8% for men and 6% for women (a little piece of social engineering intended to get property into women's names to empower and protect them). Right next door to the Union Territory of Delhi is Uttar Pradesh (Pradesh is Hindi for State). And while Delhi has one of the lowest stamp taxes, UP has one of the highest at 10%. Capital gains taxes are assessed at the federal level and range from 10 to 30%, depending upon income. So reporting a lower-than-actual sales price benefits both parties. The thing that prevents the reported price from getting too ridiculously low, aside from pure credibility, is that banks finance a percentage of the reported price. So, in the above example where the actual sales price is Rs.40 lakh, but the reported price is Rs.10 lakh, a bank willing to loan 75% of the reported purchase price would be lending only 18.75% of the actual purchase price. Those who need bank financing would be likely to report something closer to the real price. While there are no official statistics on this, it is felt that on average transaction prices are reported at 40% of their true levels, meaning that 40% of the purchase price is given by check and 60% is given in cash.[4] There

---

[2]Remember that one lakh is 100,000 and one crore is 100 lakh or 10,000,000, and throughout this chapter we will use the exchange rate of 40 rupees per US dollar. See Appendix C.

[3]India is composed of 28 states and seven Union Territories, even though these numbers change from time to time and Delhi is on its way to shifting from being a National Capital Territory to a State. Union Territories are administered by the central government.

[4]*Income Tax Department Mulls Capital Tax on Property Deals* by Prashant K. Sabu and Siddharth Zarabi, November 28, 2007, Delhiscoop.com.

has been a recent shift here in that a number of Non Resident Indians (NRIs) have been purchasing investment properties in Tier 1 and Tier 2 cities and paying fully with white money. In addition, senior executives from banking, financial markets, information technology, and other such emerging businesses have been purchasing high-end properties as their primary residence, using bonuses as their down payments and financing the rest with mortgages from various housing finance companies. They too have been paying with white money.

The government also began calculating circle rates in 2007, which are more realistic rates by area and set by property experts. The prices reported for transactions for stamp tax and capital gains tax purposes can be no less than these circle rates. Delhi, for example, has been divided into eight circles (A through H), with a minimum rate for each circle varying from $150 per square foot for the cheapest circle to $1,077 for the most expensive circle, as of November 2007. In Maharashtra, so-called Ready Reckoner rates play a similar role. These are rates set by the State and stamp taxes are based on either the reported transaction price or the Ready Reckoner price, whichever is higher. At the beginning of 2008, these rates were raised 35 to 50% on average throughout the state, but even more in Mumbai neighborhoods—121% in Goregoan (home to film city, Bollywood), 127% in Malabar Hill (home of the famous Malabar Hanging Gardens), and 140% in Worli.

8.3   PROPERTY DEVELOPMENT

There are four basic phases in property development: land acquisition, gathering permits, construction planning, and actual construction. Each of these phases takes time, although construction planning can overlap the two earlier phases to some extent.

Land acquisition can be easy if the desired plot is owned by a single entity, but this is rarely the case for large developments. One developer with whom we spoke described a project which involved the acquisition of land parcels from 70 different farmers. And although they try to keep the acquisitions quiet, this rarely happens and later purchases typically take place at higher prices. In this case, all 70 acquisitions were made within 12 months.

Next comes the gathering of permits. Even though the permit process has been simplified, the time and cost (particularly the nonofficial cost, which is paid in order to reduce the time to market) involved is not trivial.[5] The permit process varies from state to state, but there are a number of permits

---

[5]See Section 8.7 on the sensitive subject of corruption.

that must be obtained to develop a property. Some of the major ones are as follows:

1. Intimation of Disapproval (IOD) is, despite the name, a letter of approval issued by the local or state authorities. This permit enables the builder to apply for building permits and submit their plans for approval.
2. Commencement Certificate Issued by the Building Planning Authority enables the builder to start construction.
3. The Change of Land Use (CLU) is granted by the Chief Minister of the relevant state. The Chief Minister is equivalent to a state governor in the United States. Often the acquired land is zoned for uses other than those the developer has in mind, and the project can move forward only after the Chief Minister has approved a change in land use.
4. An Environmental Clearance must be granted by the central government's Ministry of the Environment for all projects. The process has been simplified in that today only the Ministry of the Environment has to sign off on projects. Developers used to have to go to both the state government and central government ministries of the environment.
5. The Municipal Corporation must affirm that the planned project meets all of its bylaws and rules. The project architect must show all the blue prints so that the Municipal Corporation ensures that setbacks, sewer connections, electrical connections, access for emergency vehicles and other aspects of the plan are appropriate and in compliance.
6. Finally, the Fire DCP must ensure that fire codes and traffic entry and exit plans are met. This unit will often receive a referral from the Municipal Corporation. This process is the easiest because many of these issues will have already been covered under the Municipal Corporation's permit, and the Municipal Corporation will often inform the Fire DCP that these standards have been met.

Construction cannot begin until the first five permits have been obtained. The whole permit process takes a minimum of two years for smaller development companies and one year for large, experienced companies.

The construction process is the nuts and bolts of the whole project. The construction unit could be a part of the development company or the developer could outsource to a construction firm. Construction is the most time consuming act of the whole process. A commercial project may take four years; a large residential project could take four to seven years; while a large township could take much longer. The time, of course, depends also on the size of the development. For example, the DLF Group announced in 2007 that it would create two integrated townships in West Bengal. The smaller one, a 95-acre township at Durgapur about 160 km northwest of Kolkata, was expected to take four years to complete. The massively larger 4,840 acre township at Dankuni, only 25 km northwest of Kolkata, was expected to take 10–12 years. The Dankuni project was expected to employ 40,000 people and require an investment of $8.25 billion. It would include an industrial park, a stadium, hospitals, multiplexes and housing for all income classes. It will utilize land from 20 different villages (mouzas) and those losing land will be compensated by either receiving a free flat in the new township or receiving a two-cottah plot (60 cottahs equal one acre) on which they can build their own house. In addition, each family would receive $50 for moving.[6]

8.4   SEGMENTS OF THE OVERALL REAL ESTATE MARKET

In India, as elsewhere, the major real estate sectors are residential, commercial and industrial. But there are some twists. Within the commercial sector, there are many IT parks being developed; within the industrial sector, there are many Special Economic Zones (SEZ); and within the residential sector, there is a specific, high-profile category called slum redevelopment.

8.4.1   RESIDENTIAL

Residential property values in many parts of India have risen substantially. Mumbai is the most expensive and a new record was set in November 2007 with a flat in a prized building at the end of Nariman Point going for $8.5 million. It was a nice 3,475 sq ft seventh-floor apartment and was sold by Citibank to a UK-based NRI for $2,446 per sq ft.[7] Delhi is the second most expensive city in India. For example, Assotech is developing the tallest building in the National Capital Region at 121.6 meters with apartments in the building selling for over $1 million each.[8]

---

[6]*DLF Group to Set Up 4,840-Acre Township*, Business Line, February 20, 2007, and *DLF's Durgapur Township Project*, Business Line, August 23, 2007.

[7]Citibank auctioned off the flat by first calling for sealed bids, then bringing the five highest bidders into its offices in the Bandra Kurla Complex and allowing them to bid against one another to determine a final winner. The UK-based NRI had to raise its original bid by 21% to win the property. *Mumbai Flat Sells for a Record Rs.34 Crore*, in *The Times of India*, November 22, 2007.

[8]*Assotech in Talks with Canadian Firm for Raising $40 m*, in Business Line, December 15, 2007.

8.4.2 SEZs

The Special Economic Zone (or SEZ) is a geographic area within a country that for some period of time is completely or largely exempt from taxes. Governments allow the creation of these tax-free areas in order to stimulate economic activity and employment growth. Indian SEZs are modeled on the Chinese SEZs created in 1978 by Deng Zhao Ping. The Special Economic Zone Policy was announced in April 2000 and some 19 SEZs were approved over the next six years. SEZs were designed to be engines of economic growth and were made attractive to operate by minimizing regulation and taxes.

The Government further showed its commitment to the SEZ concept with a major piece of legislation called the Special Economic Zone Act of 2005, which was passed by Parliament in May of that year and signed by the President on June 23, 2005. The Department of Commerce then had to create the rules to implement the Act and received about 800 suggestions in reaction to its draft rules which it then tried to incorporate into its final rules. This is India as a democracy. Of course, developers must submit 25 copies of their application to become an SEZ. This is India as a bureaucracy. The final rules, all 94 pages of them, took effect February 10, 2006 and new SEZ notifications began arriving three months later on May 16, 2006. The first was a pharmaceutical SEZ created by Divi's Laboratories Ltd. on 105 hectares (a hectare is 2.471 acres) in the state of Andhra Pradesh.[9]

The 94 pages of SEZ rules require minimum sizes (10, 100 or 1,000 hectares, depending on the type of SEZ), two-meter-high barbed wire fences around free-trade and warehousing zones, contiguous land parcels with no public thoroughfares, proof the developer either owns the land or has leasehold rights for at least 20 years and many other things.[10] There are, of course, exceptions to much of this under specified circumstances. For example, the minimum sizes are reduced for certain activities, such as services and biotech, and for certain states.

The Act indicates that the objectives of SEZs are higher economic growth, greater employment, increased investment in infrastructure, and more international trade. The SEZ Act did stimulate the creation of new SEZs. In the six years before the Act, 19 SEZs were established. In the two and a half years after the Act (as of August 2007) another 366 were

[9]Ministry of Commerce and Industry, *Background Note to Special Economic Zones in India*, at http://sezindia.nic.in/HTMLS/about.htm.

[10]Ministry of Commerce and Industry, Special Economic Zone Rules 2006, February 10, 2006, http://sezindia.nic.in/HTMLS/sez-rules2006.pdf.

approved.[11] Most SEZs appear to be IT related, although others have focused on textiles, footwear, jewelry, pharmaceuticals, paper, semiconductors, biotechnology, electronics, power, automobiles, high tech engineering products and services, port services, animation and gaming, food processing, aluminum, and nonconventional energy.

The land in the SEZs varies widely. The smallest approved was 5.17 hectares for WIPRO Ltd. in Bangalore in July 2006. The largest was 2,648 hectares for Mundra Port and Special Economic Zone Ltd., the largest private port in India, for multi-product purposes in Mundra, Gujarat.

The specific benefits of choosing the SEZ structure include duty-free import and export, 100% income tax exemption for the first five years, 50% for the next five years, and 50% on reinvested profits for the third five years. There are other State and Central Government tax breaks and benefits as well.

There are two stages to creating an SEZ. First, the developer sends a proposal directly to the Central Government's Board of Approval, or to the State Government, which forwards it to the Board of Approval. Either way, there are things that the State must do and approve before the Board of Approval will act. This is the approval stage. As stated above, there have been 366 SEZ approvals since the passage of the SEZ Act. The second stage is that once the developer demonstrates he has taken all final steps, including financing, the Board of Approval will then notify the SEZ and it can begin operations. At this writing 142 of the 366 approved SEZs (39%) have been notified. The Board of Approval is chaired by the Secretary of the Ministry of Commerce and has 18 other members, generally senior level officers from other relevant ministries. Note that there can be foreign direct investment in SEZs and foreign companies can set up branch manufacturing operations within SEZs.

8.4.3   THE REAL ESTATE NEEDS OF THE FINANCIAL SECTOR

When one thinks of financial markets in India, one thinks of a single city—Mumbai. Even when there were still 23 stock exchanges spread around India in the mid-1990s, Mumbai (called Bombay until 1995) accounted for the bulk of stock trading and was the country's undisputed center of finance. But Mumbai is an old city with more than 13 million people crowded onto seven small islands connected by landfill. It has a highly stressed infrastructure and little room to grow. Much of the city's financial activity was located in South Mumbai and as a rapidly growing financial sector drove rents in the area to unaffordable

---

[11]Ministry of Commerce, Fact Sheet on Special Economic Zones (on August 29, 2007), http://sezindia.nic.in/HTMLS/Factsheet-on-SEZs.pdf.

levels, it became clear that some serious real estate development was needed to relieve the increasing pressure on South Mumbai. As of September 30, 2007, a CB Richard Ellis Survey found that Mumbai (at $190 per sq ft per year) had the second most expensive office space in the world after London's West End (at $329).[12] Delhi was the eighth most expensive city while as a comparison, Midtown Manhattan came in at number 12 (with $101). One of the first of these attempts at real estate development targeting the financial markets was the International Finance and Business Centre (IFBC) set up in the north of the city.

The planning began back in 1971 by the Mumbai Metropolitan Region Development Authority. The resulting development is known as the Bandra Kurla Complex. A number of major financial institutions have relocated to this North Mumbai enclave. These include the National Stock Exchange, the ICICI Bank, the Unit Trust of India, the State Bank of India, Citibank, and the Securities and Exchange Board of India (SEBI), the government entity that regulates them all. There is also a large diamond market called the Bharat Diamond Bourse[13] expected to open its doors by the end of 2007. With eight towers spread over 20 acres in the Bandra Kurla Complex, the market expects to house about 2,500 small and large diamond traders.[14] The National Commodity and Derivatives Exchange (NCDEX)—one of the two major commodity exchanges—chose Bandra Kurla as its first home when it launched in 2003.

Despite this attempt to relieve the pressure, it is not enough to keep up with the growth of the financial services industry in India. There is now a new project underway by the Government of Gujarat to build a new finance city 12 kilometers north of the Ahmadabad International Airport.[15] The project is called Gujarat International Finance Tec-City (GIFT). It is being developed by a state-private joint venture called the Gujarat Finance City Development Company Ltd., which is owned equally by Gujarat Urban Development Company Ltd. (state owned) and Infrastructure Leasing and Financial Services Ltd.

The Chief Minister of Gujarat (equivalent to a state governor in the United States), Narendra Modi, said GIFT would make Ahmadabad the Chicago of

---

[12]*Delhi Eighth Most Expensive Office Space in the World*, in *Times of India*, November 22, 2007. *London, Mumbai Top List of World's Most Expensive Office Markets*, CB Richard Ellis, http://www.cbre.com/EN/Research/Research+by+Region/. The six most expensive office markets were: London's West End, Mumbai, the City of London, Moscow, Tokyo's Inner Central Five Wards, Tokyo's outer Central Five Wards.

[13]*Bharat* is a traditional name for India.

[14]Sandeep Joshi, *Diamond Bourse Coming Up in Mumbai*, The Hindu, October 9, 2007.

[15]Indrani Roy Mitra, *Modi's GIFT Can Rival Mumbai*, rediff.com, June 28, 2007, http://www.rediff.com/money/2007/jun/28gift.htm.

India. This second city reference was wisely deferential, because the central government had recently unveiled a plan a few months earlier to make Mumbai an international financial center (Mistry, 2007). In fact, Mumbai is already an important financial center, but doesn't really have the land to do what its northern neighbor plans to do and there is not too much risk that such iconic institutions as the National Stock Exchange or the Bombay Stock Exchange would move to Gujarat.

Gujarat's plan is impressive. Already approved as an SEZ by the central government, the plan calls for a first phase of 500 acres, 25 million sq ft of built-out space, mainly in high rises in order to preserve 65% of the land area as green space. One of the buildings will be 80 floors. The built-out space will be 60% office, 25% residence, 11% commercial and 4% services. In contrast to the terrible traffic congestion of Mumbai, many people will be able to walk to work in the new development. The developers are benchmarking financial center developments in London, Paris, Tokyo and Shanghai and are retaining a Chinese architectural firm that was involved in the development of the Shanghai financial center.

8.4.4 SLUM REDEVELOPMENT

India has a housing problem. Some 62 million urban dwellers, 21% of the urban population, live in slums and squatter settlements.[16] In some cities, like Mumbai, the concentration is much higher. About half the people living in Mumbai live in slums, the biggest of which is Dharavi.[17] As the largest slum in all of Asia, Dharavi is bigger in every dimension. It squeezes about a million people and 15,000 small factories in less than one square mile. The people live in quarters where many sleep on their sides because there is not enough floor space to do otherwise. When Dharavi is redeveloped, the inhabitants will have much more space in high rises that will be built for them. The factories won't fare as well. Hidden in Dharavi, the clothing, toy and pottery factories generally escape regulation and taxes. In 2006, a tannery in the slum exported 25,000 belts to Wal-Mart in the United States. While redevelopment plans will attempt to accommodate the industries in the slum, only nonpolluting industries will

---

[16]Jai Hind, *India to Face a 24 Million Units Housing Shortage in Urban Areas,* INR News, November 17, 2006, which quotes and contains the transcript of the address by Kumari Selja, Minister of State Housing and Urban Poverty Alleviation at the National Conference on Housing and Human Settlements.

[17]An Economist reporter wrote about his four days living in Dharavi, the people he met, the homes and factories he visited, and he showed it to be a wonderfully vibrant and terrible place that will be missed by at least some. *Urban Poverty in India: A flourishing slum,* Economist, December 19, 2007.

be allowed. This means the leather fabricators will have to move elsewhere and the potters fear the same.

In June 2007, the Maharashtra state government solicited expressions of interest in developing Dharavi from developers who met certain experience and net worth criteria. The idea is to take the 144 ha which is to be redeveloped initially (that's about 65% of the total 223 ha slum) and break it into five parcels, each of which will be auctioned off to a different developer. The final project will have 15% open space, 10% amenities (schools and hospitals) and then 30 million square feet of slum dweller relocation space, 20 million square feet of luxury housing, and 20 million square feet of other commercial space.

Given the slum's location between the Bandra Kurla Complex and South Mumbai, the project is incredibly valuable. When rumors circulated that a specific infrastructure development firm was getting the government's nod to redevelop Dharavi, its stock rose by the maximum limit allowed every day for just over a month, for a cumulative gain of 502%.[18] Even within Dharavi, there has been something of a property boom. In 1976, the State of Maharashtra gave slum dwellers the status of identified encroachers, a status which came with water, electric power and a promise that they would be compensated should their dwellings be razed. It also came with a cost—they had to start paying a tax, which is currently $2.50 a month. The result is that the tiny shanties of the slum are currently being exchanged for about $12,500 each.[19]

One of the first of several real estate developers who focus at least part of their attention on slum redevelopment is Akruti Nirman.[20] Brothers Hemat and Vyomesh Shah decided to get into property development, but found the market pretty locked up by two firms, Hiranandhani and Raheja. So they took the path of least resistance into a new area, slum redevelopment. They worked long days and held street meetings late at night with the slum residents. Back then slum development provided 80% of their revenue. Today Akruti is a diversified, successful, publically listed property developer and slum development accounts for less than 20% of its total revenue.

Working with government entities on slum projects, Akruti will come in and raze a slum and build on the now-vacant land a high rise to house the former slum dwellers. In addition, the developer has the right to build other profit-making ventures on the land, such as upscale residences or offices. Typically, a third of the land goes to the new buildings for the former slum dwellers (who

---

[18]Nesil Stanley, *Shares of Reliance Industrial Infrastructure Soar on No News*, Wall Street Journal, LiveMint.com.

[19]*Urban Poverty in India: A Flourishing Slum*, Economist, December 19, 2007.

[20]Conversations with Hemant Shah, Chairman, Akruti Nirman, and article on the firm, *Living the Dream*, Hindustan Times, December 7, 2007.

get a free one-room apartment), a third to commercial space and a third to utilities such as schools, hospitals, roads and gardens. The result appears to be win-win-win. The developer gets free land. The slum dwellers get free housing and decent sanitation. And the government gets rid of an eyesore and does something good for its lowest-income citizens.

Of course, the process is not always smooth. On December 27, 2007, for example, 3,500 slum dwellers and activists held a protest against large-scale slum demolitions in Mumbai.[21] The complaint was that land had not yet been set aside for displaced slum dwellers as promised by the government two years earlier, despite the fact that 600 homes had been bulldozed during the previous week. The slum dwellers also claimed that while they had been told that only those dwellings erected since 2000 would be razed, many who had built their homes prior to 1995 had lost them. In Dharavi, families of potters who moved to the area in the 1890s say they were given land and 999-year leases in 1933, although development proponents claim the leases were granted under colonial law which has since been repealed.[22]

8.4.5   MALLS

The development of malls has grown rapidly in India. Before 2004 most mall space was developed and then sold to the stores. Today, there is much more of a tendency for the developer to retain ownership and control and simply lease the space to the stores. There is also a shift away from fixed rents and toward arrangements where tenants give building owners a percentage of revenues. The potential for growth in this sector is huge. In the United States, 85% of retail sales derives from the organized portion of the industry. In India, only 3% of the retail industry is organized.

8.4.6   INFRASTRUCTURE—THE BANGALORE
INTERNATIONAL AIRPORT

When comparing India and China, it is common to note how far behind India is in infrastructure development. It is, however, trying to catch up. But one of the biggest gaps is in the airport sector. With welcome participation from the private sector, a number of competitive private airlines have been launched in the

---

[21] *Activists Protest Slum Demolition*, in *Times of India*, December 27, 2007.

[22] *Dharavi's Real Estate Threat*, in *Down to Earth: Science and the Environment Online*, Vol. 16, No. 13, November 29, 2007, http://www.downtoearth.org.in/fullprint.asp.

past few years, but the new passengers find themselves crowding into airports designed to handle far fewer fliers. Delhi Airport, for example, processed 37% more passengers than its official capacity allowed in 2007 and it will get worse before an expansion project is complete in 2010. So we have begun to see at least a partial privatization of the sector.

A case in point is the new Bangalore International Airport.[23] Twenty-six percent will be held by the government (half central, half state government), and 74% held by private entities, including Siemens of Germany (40%) and Zurich airport (17%). The 26% public ownership is not a random number. Since there are some important things that a company cannot do (like appoint new directors, issue new shares, or change auditors) without a 75% shareholder vote, the government maintains a veto on these important matters.

Some interesting features of the Bangalore airport deal set in July 2004 were copied in the Hyderabad airport deal inked only six months later:

- The Siemens-led private company is the concessionaire, which will develop, build, operate and maintain the airport for 30 years, renewable for another 30 years at its sole discretion.
- Of the 4,300 acres set aside, the concessionaire can set aside up to 300 acres for purely commercial, nonairport activities such as malls, country clubs, hotels, and even special economic zones.
- The Government of India (GOI) promises to support the project and not interfere, and to ensure that all bodies under the control of the GOI do likewise, including the prompt granting of all statutory compliances, unless it is for reasons of public safety, national emergency or violation of a law.
- The GOI has also agreed to protect the concessionaire from competition by prohibiting any new airport from setting up within 150 km of this project for 25 years and ensuring that no other airport in the country gains an unfair competitive advantage over the Bangalore airport.

The Bangalore and Hyderabad international airports are the first two green field airports to be started. Two brown field projects have begun at Mumbai and Delhi. Bids for another 6 green field and 35 brown field airports have either been solicited or will soon be. Whether some of the unique features of this first concession agreement, like the last two on support and competition, find their way into future agreements remains to be seen. The Government of India has

---

[23]This treatment heavily draws on a talk by Sumeet Kachwaha given in Beijing and reproduced in Sumeet Kachwaha, India: *Greenfield Airports in India: A Case Study of the Bangalore International Airport*, Kachwaha & Partners, September 19, 2007, http://www.mondaq.com/article.asp?articleid=50362.

discussed the creation of a Model Concession Agreement for such projects in the future, but nothing had happened as of the end of 2007.

8.5   INVESTORS

When one asks who is investing in Indian real estate, the answer is often "everybody." Real estate prices in many parts of India have risen rapidly and this has been accompanied by the usual flipping of flats by individuals. In many cases a development will sell units before the project is completed, and the purchasers will often resell to others before project completion. There have also been cases where developers have sold flats even before the land was acquired and permits were obtained for the project, a promotion that is called pre-launch. The developers promised that the deposits would be returned with interest if the project was not completed, and there have been lawsuits against developers who did not keep their promise. The government has also cracked down on this practice, but the market has been booming and offering such high returns that new entrants don't always abide by government guidelines.

There are several ways that one can invest in the Indian real estate market:

1. Buy existing property or property under construction. This is a route available to resident Indians, Non-Resident Indians (NRIs) and People of Indian Origin (PIOs), but not to foreigners. Foreigners are not allowed to purchase property in India.
2. Purchase equity in a publically traded property development company.
3. Purchase equity directly from the owners of a privately owned property developer.
4. Create a new property development company.

It is becoming easier to buy into publically traded real estate companies. By July 2007, CMIE included 47 such companies in its real estate index.[24] This was a third more than the number of companies in the index only a year earlier. One of the most recently added was DLF, which, as the biggest real estate company in India, caused the index to more than double in one month. But both DLF and Housing Development and Infrastructure IPOs of July 2007 had first day closes that were relatively small premiums (11 and 12% respectively) compared to their IPO prices. These paled in contrast to the 74 and 80% jumps experienced by Sobha Developers (which builds for Infosys in Hyderabad) and Parsvnath Developers the year before and may well be a sign that the market is beginning to soften or at least be less frothy.

---

[24]*Indian Industry, A Monthly Review*, Center for Monitoring the Indian Economy, August 2007. http://tinyurl.com/2a8xd2.

There are two other indexes of publically listed property companies, both narrower than the 47-company CMIE real estate index. One was created by the Bombay Stock Exchange (the same people who publish the Sensex) on July 9, 2007. The BSE Realty Index includes 11 companies, which the BSE claims captures 95% of the market cap of real estate companies in the BSE 500 index.[25] The index was 1000 in its base year of 2005.

The other is the CNX Realty Index published by India Index Services and Products Ltd. (IISL, the same who publish the S&P 500 CNX Nifty. IISL is a joint venture of the National Stock Exchange and the big Indian rating agency called CRISIL). The companies in the index represent 91% of market cap and 64% of turnover of all listed property companies. This index also uses 1000 as its base, but the base period is a little later: December 29, 2006.

There are a few Indian property companies listed overseas. For example, both Ishaan Real Estate Plc and Unitech Corporate Parks Plc were listed on the London Stock Exchange near the end of 2007.[26] As of the end of 2007, there were no active ADRs in Indian property companies traded in the United States.

Real Estate Investment Trusts (REITs) are likely to arrive some time in 2008, as SEBI released draft REIT regulations on December 28, 2007.[27] However, for some time there has been a pseudo-REIT available to local investors. Here's how it works. A real estate broker or some other agent will collect funds from a group of investors. The agent then approaches a developer just before the construction phase and offers to buy, say, 20% of the flats to be built at a slight discount off the asking price. There are two reasons for the developer to accept. First, this technique gives the developer capital toward the development of the property. Second, it's useful for marketing in that it allows the developer to say that the building is already 20% sold.

8.5.1 FOREIGN INSTITUTIONAL INVESTORS (FIIS)

It has gradually become easier for foreign capital to enter the Indian real estate market. Prior to February 2007, only big projects, i.e., townships in excess of 100 acres, could be 100% owned by foreign investors. Because that policy seemed to be keeping out needed foreign direct investment (FDI) in real estate, the township minimum was lowered to 25 acres and some other projects could

---

[25] The top three companies account for 82% of the market cap of all 11. These are DLF with 36%, Unitech with 32% and Indiabulls with 14%.

[26] Ishaan was listed November 24, 2006 and Unitech on December 20, 2006 on the London Stock Exchange.

[27] *SEBI Announces Guidelines for REITS*, The Hindu Business Line, December 29, 2007.

be as low as 8 acres. But to ensure foreign money is for development and not for quick speculation, there are some restrictions. Foreign investors cannot resell undeveloped land, cannot repatriate profits in less than three years and must complete projects within specific time frames. For foreign direct investment (FDI) in joint ventures with real estate companies, foreign individuals or institutions cannot own more than 74% of the joint venture. And the Reserve Bank of India must give permission for any such investment.

For example, in November 2007, a Merrill Lynch entity paid $370 million to DLF for a 49% stake in seven residential project special purpose vehicles in Chennai, Bangalore, Kochi and Indore. DLF claims to have a target of keeping about 350 million sq ft of residential property under development, but had let that drift up to about 480 million sq ft before the sale to Merrill.[28]

For portfolio investment, where the investment takes the form of shares in property related companies, FIIs cannot own more than 24% of the equity of such companies. Investors from Singapore and Dubai have been particularly active in the Indian property market.

There have been many international investments in the Indian property market. Here are a few:

- Goldman Sachs in March 2006 announced it would invest $1 billion in Indian private equity, real estate, private wealth management, and other businesses for its institutional clients.
- California public employees Retirement System (CaLPERS) invested $100 million in a $400 million real estate fund promoted by India's Infrastructure Leasing and Financial Services.
- Deyaar Development PSC, one of the fastest growing real estate companies in the United Arab Emirates, took a 40% stake in a joint venture with Delhi-based Ansal API to create a mega mixed-use township.
- JP Morgan Property Fund joined with Chennai-based Arihant Foundation to create a $100 million, 45-acre residential development in Chennai.

8.6   TITLE AND TRANSPARENCY IN INDIAN REAL ESTATE

International investors may want a sense of how easy it is to navigate the Indian real estate market. One of the big obstacles is certainty over title. In India, there is neither title insurance nor any government authentication of title, which leaves a lot of ambiguity during the purchase of property. Normally it is left to the buyer to research the validity of the title he is receiving and there are risks. As

[28]*DLF Sells 49% in Housing Projects to Merrill Arm*, Business Line, November 11, 2007.

this book goes to print there are very many state governments which are now, through GIS and satellite imagery, establishing a computer-based electronic database of ownership patterns in an attempt to reduce the ambiguity in property ownership issues.

Regarding market transparency, there is at least one way to compare the Indian market to real estate markets in other countries. Jones Lang LaSalle, a leading global real estate services and money management firm, publishes an index called the Real Estate Transparency Index.[29] The index is based on a survey of Jones Lang LaSalle employees regarding five factors in 56 different countries. The factors include the following:

- Availability of investment performance indexes
- Availability of market fundamentals data
- Listed vehicle financial disclosure and governance
- Regulatory and legal factors
- Professional and ethical standards

The most recent survey in 2006 ranked India 41st out of 56 countries. So, of those surveyed, 40 countries were more transparent and 15 countries less transparent than India. The good news is that India had experienced a significant improvement in transparency since the survey two years earlier. Within the 15 Asia Pacific countries surveyed, India ranked 11th. Australia, New Zealand, Hong Kong and Singapore were considered highly transparent and were at the top of the list. Vietnam was considered opaque and at the bottom of the list. China was just slightly less transparent than India.

8.7   THE SENSITIVE ISSUE OF CORRUPTION

Human nature being what it is, all countries have some degree of government agents accepting money for the facilitation of government approvals and permits. But there are huge differences across the world. India has a long tradition of very poorly paid government workers supplementing their income by accepting, or even soliciting, payments to bend rules or accelerate the approval process. It is a tradition that extends to the highest levels of both state and central governments. The cost of making these payments in the property market are typically many times the level of the actual government fees themselves. The largest real estate player in India, Mr. K.P. Singh, Chairman of DLF Ltd, the country's largest real estate group, complained about corrupt

[29] *Real Estate Transparency Index*, Jones Lang LaSalle Research, 2006. http://www.us.am. joneslanglasalle.com/en-US.

practices in India's real estate market.[30] Another very knowledgeable participant in a major firm told us that about half the value of large real estate deals disappears into the pockets of politicians.

There are two ways in which public officials obtain compensation in the real estate sector. One is the normal everyday bribery, where payments are made to either obtain approvals that would not otherwise be given or to simply speed up the process for something that would be given but would normally take more time. The other is where the politicians insert themselves into the transaction and actually purchase the land they know is required for a project, then resell it to the developers at a marked-up price. One of the reasons they can sell to the developer at a higher price is that the politician purchases the land before it has been reclassified from agricultural to residential or commercial land.[31] Of course, the politician never has his name on the title to the land and never directly receives the money. A bagman is required to act as intermediary to handle all of this. We bring this up because most insiders to whom we spoke mentioned it. Some spoke of the value added by the politician or government official. A modest bribe can save a lot of time and money when it results in an applicant being moved up in the queue. Even more important is the case where a developer is buying multiple parcels for a big project. The local politician knows all of the families involved and will know whether all the relevant players in each family have been consulted on the transaction, to avoid later lawsuits by disgruntled family members who felt they were not properly consulted.

To get an outsider view on the extent of bribery in the Indian market, we turn to Transparency International, an organization that publishes two indexes of corruption.[32] The newest of these is the Bribe Payers Index which measures the extent to which the firms of the world's top 30 exporting countries are likely to pay bribes when operating abroad. Of these 30 countries, India ranked dead last in 2007. Its firms were the most likely to pay bribes. This simply points out that bribery is a two-way street and that firms will offer bribes in order to get special treatment.

[30] Interview, Realty Plus, Vol. 4, Issue 2, November 2007.

[31] Much land used for new township developments is agricultural land and can be owned only by agriculturalists. This means that the land must be held in the names of those considered agriculturalists until the land use change has been officially granted, often by the politician involved in the scam being described here.

[32] Transparency International was founded in 1993 to promote a shift toward a world free of corruption. They argue that the biggest victims of corruption are the poor and they work to raise awareness of and diminish apathy and complacency toward corruption. The organization has 90 chapters around the world that work on practical solutions to the problem (http://www.transparency.org/).

The other index published annually by Transparency International is its Corruption Perception Index, which is a measure of how business people and country analysts view the degree of corruption within 180 different countries (pretty good coverage since there are about 200 countries in the world). A score of 10 is extremely clean, while a score of 1 is extremely corrupt. Corruption is the extent to which public officials and politicians accept bribes. No country was perfect. No country got a 10. The highest ranking countries in 2007 were Denmark, Finland and New Zealand with a score of 9.4. The most corrupt countries were Myanmar and Somalia with a score of 1.4. The United States was number 20, with a score of 7.2. India, along with a group of six other countries (Brazil, China, Mexico, Morocco, Peru and Suriname) was ranked number 72 with a score of 3.5. So 40% of all countries were less corrupt than India (and the six others), while 60% of all countries were more corrupt. This is a substantial improvement over the 1991 survey in which 78% of the 91 countries surveyed were less corrupt than India.

While it is unfortunate that honest government officials and politicians are blemished by the activities of their less-than-honest peers, bribes are extremely common in India and this is especially so in the real estate market. And while the international investor may not directly be caught up in the various payments that must be made to politicians in the case of real estate transactions, those payments are generally required and are being made by their partners or agents.

8.8   CONCLUSION

The Indian property market is long-term bullish, being driven by both population and strong economic growth. Like real estate markets elsewhere, there will be good and bad times to invest depending upon short-term over- or under-expansion. The market is diverse, offering many different property types and forms of investment. In general, the country is growing more open to foreign investment. The caveats are that in addition to the usual real estate cycle-driven price risk, there is also some degree of both regulatory risk and corruption risk.

CHAPTER 9

The Rupee

9.1 MARKET DESCRIPTION

The Indian rupee is not an international currency, owing to capital controls. However, as in most countries, the currency market is one of the biggest financial markets of the country. In April 2007, turnover on the spot and forward markets (put together) amounted to $12 billion a day.

9.1.1 THE SPOT MARKET

Rupee settlement can only be done in India, and RBI permission is required for setting up a currency trading system. There are three currency trading systems which have been approved by RBI: Reuters, FX-Clear (run by the Clearing Corporation of India, CCIL), and IBS. These are interbank systems. Almost all trading takes place in the first two. The rupee-dollar is the most traded currency pair.

The Reuters dealing system offers a negotiation mode, in which dealers have conversations with each other, and a computerized order matching system. There are roughly $7 billion a day of transactions in negotiation mode and roughly $1 billion a day through order matching. CCIL's FX-Clear does roughly $300 million a day, which is all through order matching.

As an example, on May 16, 2007, the bid-offer spread on the Reuters system was Rs.0.01 (0.025%) for a depth of $1 million on each side. At the identical moment, FX-Clear was offering quotes of 40.8825/40.9000, i.e., a spread of 0.043%, with a depth of $0.5 million on each side. As with the equities trading system, FX-Clear shows a market by price (MBP) display where the top five prices on both buy and side are displayed in real-time. The Reuters system shows only a bid and offer with the best prices. The mean transaction size in the overall currency market in April 2007 was $4.06 million.

End-customers of the currency market, such as institutional investors, access the currency market by talking with banks. Some of them are assisted in their dealings with banks by brokers. Brokers become particularly important in times of market volatility, when their services of identifying best-price counter-parties are more useful. Their charges are roughly Rs.500 per million dollar transaction on the spot market or Rs.700 per million dollar swap transaction. Roughly 5–10% of the spot market and 20–25% of the swap market involve brokers.

In India, the equity market sets the benchmark for transparency of financial transactions. There is pre-trade transparency (order books are visible in real-time) and post-trade transparency (exact transaction information is put out in real-time). In addition, equity market intermediaries separately reveal (a) the price at which a transaction was executed on the market as opposed to (b) the brokerage fees charged by the intermediary.

In contrast, the Indian currency market fares poorly on all three counts. It is highly nontransparent from the viewpoint of customers, lacking post-trade and pre-trade transparency. This makes it difficult for customers to ensure that they are getting best-price execution. Banks do not unbundle the price on the currency market as opposed to their intermediation fees.

Owing to the deficiencies of the market design, currency trading is extremely profitable for banks. Customers pay high prices for buying and get low prices when selling. If a bank gets a buy and a sell order which it is able to serve internally, it earns the full spread (that is shown to customers). Only the net imbalance at a bank reaches the interbank market.

The excessive intermediation charges imposed by banks on the currency market reach all the way to retail transactions. A traveller who seeks to buy or sell on the rupee-dollar market faces a bid/offer spread of roughly Rs.1.50 (3.67%). As a consequence, an extensive black market has sprung up all over the country. This involves a network of dealers who run a book on the rupee-dollar. They offer a bid/offer spread of roughly Rs.0.15 (0.37%). The rupee is convertible on the current account, hence this black market is only focused on undercutting the intermediation charges of banks, and on avoiding the constraints which prevent competing trading systems from emerging.

Foreign investors getting involved with India would do well to be cautious in how they access the currency market. One strategy that could be used by any significant-size customer is to run an auction where ten banks are told to send in an email with a price for a transaction of the desired size at exactly 10 A.M. All the bidders should be told that the best price would be chosen out of this auction at 10:01 A.M. Bidders would be able to look at conditions on the interbank market at 9:59 and send in an aggressive bid. If selected as the best bid, a trade can be put on the interbank market at 10:01.[1]

As explained above, there are three elements to the currency spot market: negotiation on the Reuters system, order matching on Reuters, and CCIL. In a remarkable Indian innovation, all three streams of transactions come to CCIL for settlement (CCIL is a clearing corporation which induces netting efficiencies, and eliminates credit risk). Hence, authoritative data on the overall currency market is available from CCIL. This data shows that foreign banks account for 61%, public sector banks for 27% and private banks for 13% of the turnover.

Spot market transactions fall into three categories: cash (T + 0 settlement), tom (T + 1 settlement) and spot (T + 2 settlement). In 2006–2007, turnover under these three headings was $233 billion of cash, $316 billion of tom and $885 billion of spot.

9.1.2   THE FORWARD MARKET

The rupee-dollar forward market is a bilaterally negotiated market: there is no pre-trade or post-trade transparency. In 2006–2007, 85,106 forward transactions came to CCIL for settlement, with notional value of $342 billion. In late 2006, forward market turnover was nudging $2 billion a day. Foreign institutional investors are able to do transactions on the currency derivatives market, but only "hedging" of the currency risk exposure on their Indian investment is permitted.

There are three remarkable features about the Indian currency forward market:

- Even though trading is negotiated off-exchange, there is netting by novation at CCIL, so that credit risk is eliminated.
- Even though it is an OTC market, it trades standardized contracts that expire on the last business day of each month.
- Ordinarily, currency forward markets have pricing that is controlled by covered interest parity (CIP). However, the system of capital controls involves considerable barriers on CIP arbitrage. Hence, it is often the case that the forward price strays away from fair value.

In addition to the onshore rupee-dollar forward market, there is active trading for cash-settled rupee-dollar forwards in Hong Kong, Singapore, Dubai and London on what are termed nondeliverable forwards (NDF). The NDF market

---

[1]This auction is analogous to the prevailing market practice for large deposits placed by corporations with banks, where an auction is used to select the bank(s) offering the highest rates.

is a response of the market to capital controls which inhibit participation in the onshore currency forward market. In addition, there is a currency futures product at DGCX in Dubai, which has not yet achieved significant liquidity.

NDF turnover is estimated at $0.5 billion to $0.75 billion a day, compared with $1.5 billion to $2 billion a day for the onshore INR/USD forward market. The typical quote depth on both markets is $5 million. The spread on the onshore market is roughly 0.5 to 1 paisa, while the NDF market has a spread between 0.5 to 2 paisa. The NDF market is interesting to entities who are prevented from doing transactions on the onshore market owing to capital controls or the requirements that transactions on the onshore market must only be for the purpose of hedging.

9.2   GOING UNDER THE HOOD

From 1993 onward, the Indian rupee has been a market determined exchange rate. However, this market determined exchange rate has often not reflected the supply and demand of private market participants. The central bank, RBI, has often traded extensively on the market in attempts to shift the market exchange rate away from supply/demand conditions on the market. The transactions of RBI (Figure 9.1) are substantial. RBI makes no announcements about currency targets or about what it is doing on the currency market. Data about RBI trading on the currency market is released with a lag of two months. On a day to day basis, the trading by RBI on the currency market is a key factor which affects exchange rates; however, this data is not disclosed.

Currency risk is important to every foreign investor, and also to many Indian firms and households. Therefore, it is important to apply economic reasoning

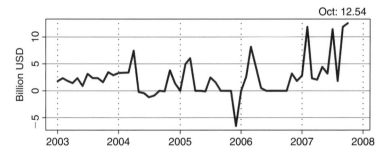

FIGURE 9.1   Net Purchase of Foreign Exchange by RBI on Currency Market (billion USD per month)

to try to understand the nature of the currency regime, particularly given the lack of official statements from RBI about what the currency regime is.

9.3   A *DE FACTO* PEGGED EXCHANGE RATE TO THE US DOLLAR

One extreme possibility is a rupee-dollar rate which is fixed by RBI. In this case, the rupee-euro rate, or the rupee-yen rate, would mechanically follow the dollar-euro and the dollar-yen rates respectively. Since the dollar-euro and dollar-yen exchange rates are floating rates, a fixed rupee-dollar fixed exchange rate would imply high volatility of the rupee-euro and rupee-yen rates, reflecting the fact that the dollar-euro and dollar-yen rates are floating rates with high volatility.

The empirical evidence shows that while this extreme case does not hold, it is a suggestive approximation. Table 9.1 reports the standard deviation of weekly percentage changes in exchange rates, in annualized form. The relationships seen in this table are:

- The lowest volatility in the table is the INR/USD exchange rate with a low volatility of 4.22% per year.
- The volatility of rupee exchange rates with respect to currencies other than the USD are much like the volatilities of all the floating exchange rates in the table.
- The volatility of the INR/EUR rate—9.86% a year—is a lot like the volatility of the EUR/USD rate—9.71% a year.
- The volatility of the INR/JPY rate—11.78% a year—is a lot like the volatility of the JPY/USD rate—11.55% a year.
- The volatility of the INR/GBP rate—8.72% a year—is a lot like the volatility of the GBP/USD rate—8.02% a year.

These facts suggest that the INR/USD exchange rate is a *de facto* pegged exchange rate (Patnaik, 2007).

TABLE 9.1   Cross-Currency Annualized Volatilities: 1993–2007

	EUR	JPY	GBP	INR
USD	9.71	11.55	8.02	4.22
EUR		10.92	6.89	9.86
JPY			12.14	11.78
GBP				8.72

9.4   DIFFICULTIES OF IMPLEMENTING THE PEGGED EXCHANGE RATE

The impossible trinity of open economy macroeconomics suggests that a country can only have two out of three of: (a) a fixed exchange rate, (b) an open capital account and (c) an autonomous monetary policy. If there is an open capital account, then attempts to fix the exchange rate lead to a loss of monetary policy autonomy. This suggests that the implementation of the pegged exchange rate should run into conflicts with the needs of domestic monetary policy as India opened up to capital flows.

9.4.1   SHIFT TOWARD *DE FACTO* CAPITAL ACCOUNT CONVERTIBILITY

Prior to the 1990s, India had a closed capital account and a small trade account. Under these conditions, India was able to have a fixed exchange rate without loss of monetary policy autonomy. In impossible trinity parlance, India was at a consistent solution involving a closed capital account, pegged exchange rate, and autonomous monetary policy. Over the years, there has been a remarkable opening up of the capital account. For foreign institutional investors, for foreign FDI investors, and for domestic corporations, there is convertibility to a substantial extent. Equally important has been the growth of the current account. As an example, Figure 9.2 shows that gross flows on the current account grew from roughly $20 billion a quarter in 2002 to $60 billion a quarter in 2007—a tripling in five years. Firms involved in

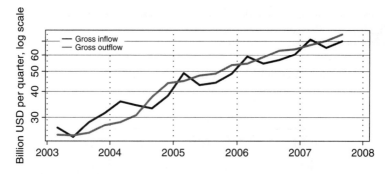

FIGURE 9.2   Gross Flows on the Current Account (billion USD per quarter)

international trade can shift capital across the boundary through overinvoicing or underinvoicing. When there are gross flows on the current account of $500 billion a year, an average 10% misinvoicing can shift $50 billion or 5% of GDP across the boundary. This would constitute a very large capital flow.

A complex system of capital controls remains in place; India does not have *de jure* capital account convertibility. However, the flexibility that the private sector has to shift capital on the capital account and on the current account adds up to a substantial degree of *de facto* capital account convertibility.

In 1992, nominal GDP was $240 billion. Gross flows across the boundary, summing across the current account and the capital account, were $97 billion. By 2007, both values were in the range of a trillion dollars a year. While GDP grew by roughly four times in nominal terms over 15 years, transactions on the current account and the capital account grew by roughly 10 times (Shah and Patnaik, 2007a). This dramatic globalization over the 1992–2007 period has far-reaching implications for the implementation of the pegged exchange rate.

9.4.2   IMPLICATIONS FOR CURRENCY REGIME

This growing openness has meant that currency policy has run into conflicts with monetary policy (Patnaik, 2005). The major elements of this story have been as follows:

- In the early 1990s, there was a surge of capital flows. RBI prevented the rupee from appreciating above Rs.31.37 per USD. These purchases of foreign currency led to a high expansion of domestic money supply and are believed to have helped ignite inflation.
- In January 1998, in the aftermath of the Asian Crisis, there were concerns about a large depreciation of the rupee. RBI engaged in an interest rate defense, raising the short-term interest rate by 200 basis points to help attract capital flows and prop up the rupee. This tightening of monetary policy was arguably poorly timed when juxtaposed against domestic business conditions.
- From 2001 onward, RBI tried to resist currency appreciation. This led to an enormous reserves accumulation (Figure 9.3). This led to a hectic pace of money growth, and helped ignite high inflation. This led to criticism of RBI policy and events where RBI backed away from currency trading, giving sharp appreciation in these periods.

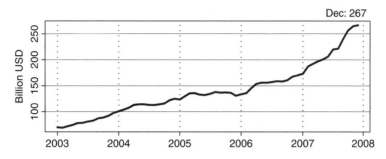

FIGURE 9.3   Foreign Currency Reserves

9.5   FOUR PHASES IN INR/USD VOLATILITY

As with many other emerging markets, the picture of the Indian rupee is one of a shifting currency regime. In some periods, RBI has been able to run a quasi-fixed exchange rate. At other times, the distortions of domestic monetary policy that are caused by exchange rate pegging are so large that rupee-dollar volatility comes about.

Figure 9.4 shows three events of structural change which isolate four phases of India's currency regime. The three dates of structural change work out to February 17, 1995, August 21, 1998 and March 19, 2004. The upper graph shows the rupee-dollar exchange rate. The lower graph shows squared weekly percentage changes, which measures currency flexibility. The four phases have clearly different levels of currency flexibility.

Table 9.2 shows the characteristics of the rupee-dollar rate across these four periods. As seen in Table 9.1, the overall volatility of the rupee-dollar rate over 1993–2007 works out to 4.22% per year. However, this has exhibited sharp differences across the four periods, going from 1.17% in Period 1, to a high of 6.69% in Period 2, dropping again sharply to 2.02% in Period 3 and then rising to 4.56% in Period 4.

The largest and smallest values of weekly percentage changes are also revealing. For the full period, the one-week percentage change in the rupee-dollar rate has been between −4.74% and +4.96%. As an example, in Period 3, when currency flexibility fell sharply, these values narrowed to −0.97% and 1.10%.

As argued in Section 9.3, a key feature of a *de facto* pegged exchange rate between the rupee and the dollar is when the rupee-euro volatility is the same as the euro-dollar volatility. Figure 9.5 juxtaposes moving window estimates of three volatilities: the rupee-dollar, the dollar-euro and the euro-rupee. It shows that in recent months, the three lines have diverged considerably, suggesting an upsurge in rupee flexibility that is independent of the dollar.

TABLE 9.2   Features of Weekly Changes in Rupee-Dollar across Four Periods (figures in %)

Period	Volatility (annualized)	Largest depreciation	Largest appreciation
Period 1	1.17	−0.92	0.90
Period 2	6.69	−4.74	4.96
Period 3	2.02	−0.97	1.10
Period 4	4.56	−2.21	2.02
Overall	4.22	−4.74	4.96

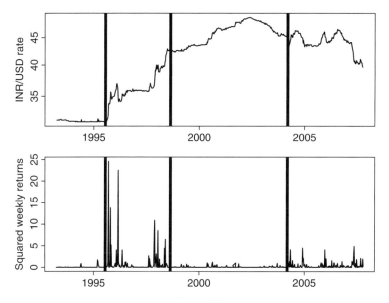

FIGURE 9.4   Four Phases of the Currency Regime

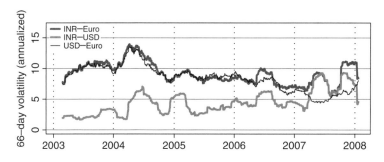

FIGURE 9.5   Moving Window Cross-Currency Volatility

There is an excessive focus on the rupee-dollar rate in discussions about India and currency movements. Figure 9.6 juxtaposes the rupee-dollar, the rupee-yen and the rupee-euro rates over the last five years. All three time-series have been rescaled so as to start at the numerical value of the starting point of the rupee-dollar series. This graph shows that while there has been a small appreciation of the rupee when compared with the dollar, it has depreciated significantly against the euro, reflecting the depreciation of the dollar.

The real effective exchange rate (REER) puts together fluctuations in exchange rates and inflation across a large number of trade partners. RBI produces a trade-weighted REER series using data for 36 countries. This is shown in Figure 9.7. It shows that, broadly speaking, the combined effect of currency fluctuations and inflation differentials has been to hold the REER within a ±10% band.

In understanding the relationship between currency fluctuations and Indian imports or exports, the REER is not particularly useful. As an example, over 2002–2007, there were small REER changes. At the same time, total receipts on the current account, which roughly corresponds to exports of goods and services put together, tripled. Merchandise exports doubled. This was not done

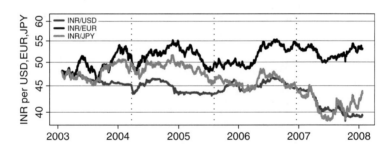

FIGURE 9.6   Movement of Three Exchange Rates, Forced to the Same Starting Point

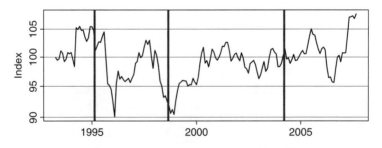

FIGURE 9.7   Real Effective Exchange Rate (REER)

by ceding profitability; over these five years, profitability of the corporate sector consistently rose.

It is unusual to see such large gains in manufacturing exports or total exports at a time when there was apparently no large change in the REER. However, there are many ongoing changes which affect exports, and inflation + exchange rates is only one element of the story. Customs duties were cut, so raw material prices in India dropped, thus improving competitiveness of production. Capital controls came down, enabling both inbound FDI and outbound FDI. The bulk of global trade now takes place within MNCs with globally dispersed production chains, so this FDI is the foundation of exports. Transport and communications infrastructure improved. This induced reduced charges immediately, coupled with far-reaching gains by enabling new locations for production. When international telecom links became cheap, many nontradeable services became tradeable.

REER calculations fail to capture this wealth of changes, which are of prime importance in understanding the fast-changing and dynamic Indian economy. Hence, REER fluctuations are of little relevance in understanding the impact of exchange rate fluctuations on imports and exports.

9.6   CONCLUSION

India's *de facto* openness on the capital account deepens every year. Regardless of whether India announced *de jure* capital account convertibility or not, the complexities of macroeconomic policy making in an open economy are present in India. Over the years, increasing openness has accentuated these tensions. In the past, RBI has been able to deliver a *de facto* pegged exchange rate with an extremely low volatility averaging 4.22% per year. This was an attractive umbrella of free public-sector currency risk management being given to the private sector by the RBI.

It is likely that in coming years, the execution of this currency policy will become progressively more difficult. The conflicts between currency policy and monetary policy will become accentuated. In these conflicts, it is likely that the needs of autonomous domestic monetary policy will take precedence. Hence, higher rupee-dollar currency volatility may be expected in the years to come.

CHAPTER 10

Financial Firms

An essential part of any financial system is the array of *financial firms* that form its foundation. In this chapter, we turn from products and markets to the firms that ultimately facilitate the aggregation, transformation and allocation of capital.

10.1   A BIRD'S EYE VIEW

Figure 10.1 gives us a useful way of thinking about the financial firms which inhabit Indian finance. We will first briefly discuss the diagram at an abstract level, and then dive deeper into some (though not all) groups of firms. Financial firms are usefully composed of three groups: those that run money, those that are focused on transactions, and the infrastructure providers who are the lifeblood of finance. This infrastructure is made up of exchanges, clearing corporations, depositories, and the elements of the payments system.

The transaction-oriented firms are the firms that primarily earn revenues from achieving transactions (large or small). These include investment banks and securities firms. The Indian term *primary dealers* is listed here, because in India, a primary dealership is not a mere characteristic of a large multi-product financial firm, but a name given to a certain small group of firms. The Indian term *merchant bank* also appears here, denoting a class of firms who participate in primary securities issuance in various ways. Finally, the Indian term *nonbank finance company* (NBFC) is listed here, even though we recognize that this is a somewhat uneasy classification.

Fund-based activities are logically broken up into two groups. Banks and insurance companies generally make promises about the returns that a customer will get at a future date. They are hence termed defined benefit fund managers. Mutual funds, pension funds, private equity funds and hedge funds

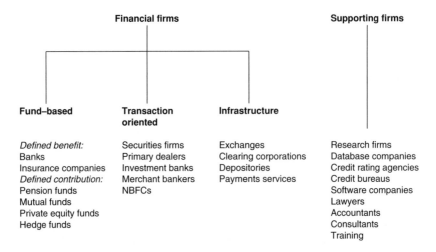

FIGURE 10.1   Financial Firms and Their Ecosystem

are classified as defined contribution fund managers, in that the risks of the portfolio are passed on to the customer.[1]

These three groups of financial firms are surrounded by an ecosystem of supporting firms, including research, information, software, legal, accounting, etc. While these are an essential feature of the ecosystem of finance, this chapter does not describe them.

10.2   THE NATURE OF THE FINANCIAL FIRM IN INDIA

In India, financial sector policy has traditionally forced a silo model. Unit Trust of India (UTI) was a pure (government-owned) mutual fund. Life Insurance Corporation (LIC) was a pure (government-owned) insurance company. State Bank of India (SBI) was a pure (government-owned) bank. Each firm did only one business. In addition, each firm faced only one regulator. The silo model is in force even today. Thus, even though NSE has the capability to support all financial trading, it is prohibited from trading currencies, bonds and commodities because these fall under other regulators and belong in different silos.

---

[1] There are no defined benefit pension funds in India, other than programs offered directly by the government.

TABLE 10.1 ICICI—A Large Complex Financial Institution

Firm	Area	Business
ICICI Bank	Banking	Personal banking; corporate banking
ICICI Prudential	Life insurance	Insurance for individuals
ICICI Lombard	General insurance	Insurance
ICICI Venture	Venture capital and private equity	
ICICI Securities	Investment banking and securities	Corporate finance, fixed income trading, equities trading, equity brokerage for retail and institutional
Prudential ICICI	Asset management	Mutual funds, portfolio management services

This silo approach has adverse effects on cost. In the United States, a primary dealership is an attribute of a large financial firm. In India, a primary dealer is a free-standing firm which does only the business of a primary dealer. The effort of the government has been to reorganize the financial sector into pieces which fit conveniently into the structure of government agencies.

Financial firms have sought to grow into large complex financial institutions (LCFIs) despite this silo architecture. The two biggest financial firms—HDFC and ICICI—are *de facto* LCFIs (see Table 10.1). This is achieved through a network of subsidiaries which inhabit each of the silos. The largest and most sophisticated firms follow in the footsteps of these pioneers, and grow out of the silo mindset into complex multi-product firms.

The classification scheme and organization of this chapter represents a tension between the silo structure—with watertight compartments between classes of firms—and an evolution toward complex multi-product firms. The truth lies somewhere in between the two polar cases with a steady evolution away from the silo structure.

10.3 INFRASTRUCTURE

The critical infrastructure of the financial system involves exchanges and the payments system. It also involves a maze of acronyms, summarized in Table 10.2. (See also an extensive list of acronyms in Appendix B.)

There are three groups of exchanges:

- SEBI regulates NSE and BSE, which primarily trade equities and equity derivatives.

TABLE 10.2   Acronyms in Exchange Infrastructure

BSE	Bombay Stock Exchange
CCIL	Clearing Corporation of India Ltd.
CDSL	Central Depository Services Ltd.
FMC	Forward Markets Commission
MCX	Multi Commodity Exchange
NCDEX	National Commodity Derivatives Exchange
NDS	Negotiated Dealing System
NSCCL	National Securities Clearing Corporation Ltd.
NSDL	National Securities Depository Ltd.
NSE	National Stock Exchange
RBI	Reserve Bank of India, the central bank
SEBI	Securities and Exchanges Board of India
SGL	Subsidiary General Ledger

- RBI regulates CCIL which trades some interest rate and currency products. RBI owns and operates NDS, which is a trading system for government bonds.
- FMC regulates NCDEX, MCX, and other commodity futures exchanges.

As is typical of the silo structure of Indian finance, these three groups are held apart by government. They are unable to compete with each other. It is essentially impossible to start a new exchange in RBI's space. FMC has an ambivalent approach to competition; in practice it is difficult to start a new exchange. SEBI has the most open approach on entry into the exchange business.

Surrounding the exchanges are the infrastructure of clearing corporations and depositories. NSE does clearing through its subsidiary, NSCCL. CCIL is itself a clearing corporation and does clearing for OTC transactions on the fixed-income and currency markets, and for the transactions that takes place on its exchange platform. BSE, NCDEX and MCX do their own clearing.

In terms of depositories, NSDL and CDSL are two depositories dealing primarily with equity holdings. They also have dematerialized holdings of government bonds, corporate bonds and mutual fund paper. SGL is a depository for government bonds and is owned by RBI. While NSDL and CDSL compete with each other, they are prohibited from competing with SGL.

In the exchange industry—comparing exchanges, clearing corporations and depositories—India has evolved a unique silo structure, where there are three parallel industries. The industrial organization of the industry has been reshaped to suit the convenience of the regulatory structure. There is competition within the silo in two cases (SEBI's silo and FMC's silo), but there are no competitive forces running across silos. Weak firms in all the silos lobby to uphold the silo structure when they are fearful of competitive pressure from firms from other silos.

10.4   TRANSACTION-ORIENTED FIRMS

10.4.1   THE FIRMS

For all practical purposes, there are six exchanges that matter in India: two equity exchanges (NSE, BSE), two commodity exchanges (NCDEX, MCX) and two fixed income exchanges (NDS, CCIL). Each securities firm in India tends to have memberships in more than two of these six exchanges.

The regulatory framework attempts to enforce vertical silos where commodities, equities and fixed income markets are walled off from each other. All large financial firms try to overcome these constraints, in order to create multi-product financial firms, through various kinds of corporate structures with varying degrees of success. These mechanisms constitute financial engineering seeking to get around the silo structure that has been built by the government.

Table 10.3 shows estimates for the daily notional turnover (measured in billion rupees) on all elements of the securities markets, as prevalent in December 2007. The summation works out to Rs.2.7 trillion a day.

At a practical level, there are roughly 1,000 securities firms in the country. These firms are primarily engaged in three kinds of activities: proprietary trading, agency business and investment banking. While there are roughly

TABLE 10.3   Organized Financial Trading in India (end 2007)

Market	Daily turnover (Rs. billion)
NSE equity derivatives	680
CBLO	400
Currency spot	350
Repo	200
NSE equity spot	190
Interest rate derivatives	150
Call money market	150
Currency forwards	150
MCX commodity futures	150
CLS (cross-currency pairs)	100
BSE equity spot	85
GOI bond spot	60
NCDEX commodity futures	25
BSE equity derivatives	10
Corporate bonds spot	4
Total	2704

1,000 significant firms in the country, a few large firms inevitably matter more. There is a core of roughly 400 firms which do over Rs.10 billion of equity derivatives turnover a month. The biggest 25 firms might account for roughly 40% of the overall business.

Proprietary trading consists of active management of funds, belonging either to the owners of the firm, or near friends and family. In Indian parlance, financial firms with exchange memberships are called brokerage firms. They have high speed connectivity to the exchanges, are able to trade with full confidentiality, and are able to set up algorithmic trading systems. Some brokerage firms are almost exclusively focused on proprietary trading—for all practical purposes, they are hedge funds. Other brokerage firms take pride in saying that they do no proprietary trading and are completely focused on the agency business of trading on behalf of customers.

The second activity which these firms are engaged in is the agency business, where trades are placed for customers. Customers are typically offered trading services on many exchanges. The smallest firms of this nature have one or two locations and perform family broker functions for a few dozen families. The biggest firms have hundreds of locations and offer Internet-based trading to a very large client base across the country.

The entry barriers into this business are low. Anyone with a few million dollars of capital can set up exchange memberships and an office. This is the only element in Indian finance where a few firms die every year. This adds up to an environment of fierce competition with genuine contestability: this is the part of Indian finance where the competitive pressure is the highest. Profit margins of these firms have been high in recent years, but in a downturn a tremendous margin compression is likely.

Table 10.4 shows the financial characteristics of the aggregate of brokerage firms observed in the CMIE database. Two years are chosen: 2001–2002, a year of a difficult business cycle downturn, and 2006–2007, the most recent

TABLE 10.4   Financial Characteristics of
Brokerage Firms

	2001–2002	2006–2007
Growth (%)		
Revenues	−25	57
Net profit	−5	56
Net profit margin (%)		
To net worth	13.41	21.09
To total assets	4.85	8.49

information which also happens to reflect buoyant business cycle conditions. It shows that these firms—as a group—suffered a 25% decline in revenues and a 5% decline in profits in the bad year (2001–2002), and a 57% rise in revenues and a 56% rise in profits in the good year (2006–2007). The numerical values for profit margins in the table give a sense of the range of possibilities for this industry.

Among the firms observed in the CMIE database for 2005–2006, the revenues of the top five were: DSP Merrill Lynch (Rs.17 billion), Indiabulls Financial Services (Rs.11 billion), Motilal Oswal (Rs.5 billion), India Infoline (Rs.3 billion) and Geojit Financial Services (Rs.2 billion).

In late 2007, as a rule of thumb, the large securities firms had one employee per Rs.0.8 billion of transactions annually. As a rough estimate, the entire universe of NSE, BSE, NCDEX and MCX turnovers works out to Rs.1 trillion a day or Rs.250 trillion a year. This yields an estimate that this industry employs approximately 300,000 people.

10.4.2 PRICES PAID BY CUSTOMERS

Internationally, customers of transactional services, such as the purchase of shares or futures on an exchange, generally pay a flat price per transaction (e.g., $10 a trade). In India, generally the price paid by the customer is a percentage of the notional value of the transaction, implying that a bigger trade (in rupee terms) pays more than a smaller one.

As an example, the website of ICICI Direct, a large brokerage firm, says that their tariff *ranges from 0.1% to 0.15% for margin trades, 0.2% to 0.425% for squared off trades and 0.4% to 0.85% on delivery based trades.* A squared off trade is a transaction on the spot market which is netted off on the same day—e.g., buying 100 shares at 11 A.M. followed by selling them off at 11:30 A.M. A delivery based trade is a position which is held to the end of the day, which results in a delivery on T + 2.

These tariffs appear enormous by international standards. However, the typical transaction size on the spot market ranges between $1,000 and $2,500, so an ad valorem charge of roughly 0.5% corresponds to between $5 and $12.5, which appears less extreme. Further, ICICI Direct is one of the most expensive firms in this business. Much cheaper alternatives exist; prices drop sharply for frequent flyers, and the tariffs are much lower on the derivatives market.

Mistry (2007) shows some calculations[2] in which tariffs suffered by a customer doing an index futures transaction in India of the size of one S&P e-mini contract are tabulated. For a retail customer, the tariff in Chicago of Rs.374

[2]Box 2.8, page 29.

compares against Rs.3,343 in India. For a high-volume customer, the tariff in Chicago of Rs.109 compares against Rs.1,235 in India. For proprietary trading, the cost of Rs.31 in Chicago compares against Rs.789 in India.

The source of these numbers lies in the burden of taxation on transactions in India. The securities firm has to pay 0.01 basis points into an SEBI-mandated investor protection fund; 0.2 basis points of a stamp duty; a service tax which is 12.24% of the brokerage fee and a securities transaction tax of 1.7 basis points (charged to the seller only). External levies work out to 2 basis points while the fees paid to the exchange work out to a tenth of this. This suggests that the essence of reducing transactions costs in India lies in removing the 2 basis point charge that is caused by the investor protection fund, stamp duty, and the securities transaction tax.

10.4.3   COSTS AND CHARGES AT NSDL

Tables 10.5 and 10.6 focus on the expenses incurred, and tariffs applied, by the National Securities Depository Ltd. (NSDL), which is the largest stock depository in the country. This is an interesting measure both because settlement services are an integral requirement for doing market transactions, and because these numbers are undistorted by transaction taxes.

Table 10.5 shows the rising number of transactions per year at NSDL. This helps induce economies of scale. In addition, over the years, there are improvements in efficiency and gains from harnessing reduced costs of computer hardware and telecommunications. As a consequence, the total expenditure of NSDL expressed per transaction has dropped from Rs.21.33 per transaction in 2000–2001 to Rs.3.67 in the first 9 months of 2007–2008.

TABLE 10.5   Internal Cost of Production of Transactions at NSDL

Year	Number of transactions (million)	Expenditure per transaction (rupees)
2000–2001	25.6	21.33
2001–2002	35.3	13.98
2002–2003	41.9	10.50
2003–2004	79.1	5.53
2004–2005	96.6	5.23
2005–2006	127.8	4.73
2006–2007	135.2	5.08
2007–2008 (9 months only)	142.4	3.67

TABLE 10.6   Tariff Charged
by NSDL to Securities Firms

Period	Tariff
May 2002–Dec 2003	10
Jan 2004–Sep 2005	8
Oct 2005–Dec 2007	6
Jan 2008–	5

While NSDL is a for-profit corporation, it has a unique ownership and governance structure which emphasizes working as a public utility, in spirit. As a consequence, the tariffs applied by NSDL, per transaction, have also dropped sharply from Rs.10 per transaction to Rs.5 per transaction between 2002 and 2008.[3]

In other IT-intensive fields also, where the burden of taxation has not been present, Indian firms have achieved production at world-beating prices. Examples of these include mobile telephony, where Indian telecom firms have driven down the internal production cost of an SMS to Rs.0.01. India is unique in that telecom companies are highly profitable, earning an average revenue of $5 per customer per month. Similarly, the lowest cost of production of a transaction by a customer of a bank ATM is now found in India. These examples emphasize the opportunity for obtaining extremely low prices for transactional services in India.

10.5   BANKS

There is a very large number of banks in India, particularly when regional rural banks (RRBs) and cooperative banks are taken into account. However, the bulk of these entities, by number, are economically insignificant. For all practical purposes, there are roughly 100 significant banks in the country.

---

[3]A comparison of tariffs applied by NSDL against those applied by other depositories worldwide is not directly meaningful because of some key differences in the nature of the service offering. India is unique in that the stock depository maintains records at a *client* level, and tracks all transactions down to the ultimate beneficiary. This is in contrast with depositories worldwide, who track ownership of shares at the level of the depository participant (typically a large securities firm) which then maintains internal databases pertaining to individual customers.

10.5.1   BROAD FINANCIAL CHARACTERISTICS

Table 10.7 shows the financial characteristics of the aggregate of banks observed in the CMIE database. Two years are chosen: 2001–2002, a year of a difficult business cycle downturn, and 2005–2006, the most recent information which also happens to reflect buoyant business cycle conditions. Over this four-year period, the rupee values for total assets, net profit and net worth more than doubled, reflecting the recovery from a downturn. While the bad year—2001–2002—involved revenue growth of 6.35% and a net profit which was 0.73% of assets, the good year—2005–2006—involved revenue growth of 16.01% and a net profit which was 0.96% of assets.

10.5.2   THREE OWNERSHIP GROUPS

Ownership is a major factor influencing the personality of a bank in India.[4] There are three groups of banks. Roughly three-quarters of bank deposits are with 28 banks owned by the government. In India, they are called public sector unit (PSU) banks. The second group is the private banks, and the third group is the foreign banks.

Table 10.8 shows the market share of the three groups of banks by a few different measures. In each row, the three numbers shown are the market share

TABLE 10.7   Financial Characteristics of Banks

	2001–2002	2005–2006
Nominal values (billion rupees)		
Revenues	1532	2320
Net profit	107	251
Net worth	797	1877
Total assets	12,989	28,225
Growth over previous year (percent)		
Revenues	6.35	16.01
Net profit	53.83	15.34
Net profit margin		
To net worth	14.51	12.31
To total assets	0.73	0.96

---

[4]For a contrary view on this, see Sarkar et al. (1998).

TABLE 10.8 Market Share of Three Groups of
Banks (2006)

Measure	Public sector	Private	Foreign
Branches	88	12	0
Loans	75	20	5
Deposits	73	19	8
Bank guarantees	68	20	12
Debit cards	62	36	3
ATMs	55	41	4
Credit card spend	42	41	18
Cash management	32	43	25
Forward positions	20	18	62
POS terminals	11	77	12

Each line shows the market share of each of the three groups of banks. As an
example, public sector banks have 75% market share in loans; private banks
have 20% and foreign banks have 5%.
Source: Axis Bank.

of the three groups of banks. The rows in the table are sorted by public sector
market share.

- The public sector is very strong in branches (88%), loans and deposits
  (roughly 75%).
- The public sector is present in some new fields like debit cards (62%),
  ATMs (55%) and credit cards (42%).
- The public sector is weakest in cash management (32%), forward posi-
  tions (20%) and POS terminals (11%).

A good metric of the operational efficiency of a bank is the operating expenses expressed as percent of assets. By this measure, foreign banks are at
2.68%, public sector banks are at 1.82% and private banks are at 1.65%. The
stock market has a gloomy outlook on public sector banks. While private banks
have a price to book ratio of 2.96, public sector banks stand at 1.11. While
private banks have a P/E of 25.19, public sector banks stand very low at 6.85%.
This suggests that the outlook for dividends and dividends growth is poor,
and that the true assets of PSU banks may not be as strong as those claimed
in accounting disclosures.

Table 10.9 shows how the stock market sees the ten biggest banks (by market
capitalization).[5] It shows a striking gulf between private and public banks. Only

[5]The source for this table is the banking report in *Indian Industry: A Monthly Review* by CMIE,
January 2008.

TABLE 10.9   How the Stock Market Sees Large Banks (January 2008)

Rank	Name	Market capitalization (Rs. billion)	P/E	Beta
1	ICICI Bank*	1378	39.2	0.83
2	State Bank of India	1248	22.3	1.02
3	HDFC Bank*	612	46.1	0.61
4	Kotak Mahindra Bank*	446	216.9	1.01
5	Axis Bank*	347	43.4	1.04
6	Punjab National Bank	210	11.6	1.20
7	Bank of India	178	12.4	1.46
8	Bank of Baroda	167	13.6	1.39
9	Canara Bank	136	9.0	1.21
10	IDBI	120	18.4	1.44
	CMIE Cospi Banking Index	**6243**	**21.5**	**1.02**

*A private bank.

one public sector bank—State Bank of India (SBI)—has a P/E that matches the overall P/E of the banking sector. For the rest, there is a sharp gulf with private banks having high P/E ratios and high market capitalizations. There is a remarkable gulf between the picture seen in Table 10.9 and the fact that roughly three-quarters of Indian bank deposits or loans are with public sector banks.

Another interesting feature of this table is the high beta of public sector banks. This partly reflects their higher leverage; other things being equal, when a business has greater leverage, the stock beta is higher. It may also reflect greater macroeconomic vulnerability of these entities in the eyes of the market. It may reflect a sense that in a downturn, the credit quality of their portfolios would be under greater stress.

10.5.3   THE STASIS IN BANKING

Most industries in India are highly dynamic, with a vigorous process of creative destruction, whereby some firms die and some new entrants come into the business every year, and where the players are globally competitive and constantly innovating and competing. The dominant feature of banking in India is the policy-induced stasis, which comes in at five levels:

1. The top managers of public sector banks have little operational flexibility, dramatically inadequate compensation structures, and no incentive to run the organization with creativity and vigor.

2. Entry by private banks takes place at a very low pace—roughly one new bank is permitted every five years.

3. Foreign banks are walled off from participation by having a rule which specifies that all foreign banks (put together) cannot open more than 18 branches a year in the whole country.

4. An elaborate system of regulation and supervision involves micro-management of banks, prohibition of a large swathe of products and processes routinely found with banks worldwide, and an attempt at preventing progress.[6] One element of this is pre-emption in the asset portfolio, where banks are forced to place roughly two-thirds of their portfolio in government bonds and other areas deemed meritorious by the government.

5. This falls in the larger context of the silo system of public policy in Indian finance, where government defines silos such as banking. Firms in the silo are prevented from competing in the broader financial services space; and firms within the silo are protected from competition from outside the silo. The pressure that banks elsewhere in the world feel owing to money market mutual funds that have access to the payments system, and electronic innovations in payments (such as eBay or payments made from mobile phones) have been blocked in India on the grounds that only banks can engage in any payments-related activities.

Some of these difficulties, such as the silo system, afflict all of Indian finance. But there is no component of Indian finance where all five elements—public sector domination, entry barriers against private and foreign firms, micro-management coupled with prevention of progress, and the silo system—come together to foster inefficiency and stasis as effectively as in banking.

Table 10.10 shows the top 10 banks, ranked by assets, in a recent bad year (2001–2002) and the latest available data (2005–2006), which also happens to be a time of buoyant business cycle conditions. At about Rs.40 a dollar, a bank with assets of $1 trillion would have assets of Rs.40 trillion. The first outstanding fact seen in the table is that the big banks of India are small by world standards.

The second outstanding fact lies in the domination of the public sector. Barring ICICI Bank, which appears twice in the table, and HDFC Bank, which appears once, all the other names are public sector banks. This vividly illustrates the domination of the government in the banking industry.

The third outstanding fact lies in how little the ranks have changed between the two time points. This points to the lack of competition in banking. In almost

---

[6]As an example, see http://ajayshahblog.blogspot.com/2006/12/regulatory-anomalies-rbi-edition.html.

TABLE 10.10   The Biggest 10 Banks

2001–2002			2005–2006		
Rank	Bank	Total assets (Rs. trillion)	Rank	Bank	Total assets (Rs. trillion)
1	State Bank	3.48	1	State Bank	4.94
2	ICICI Bank*	1.05	2	ICICI Bank*	2.52
3	Punjab National	0.73	3	Punjab National	1.45
4	Canara	0.72	4	Canara	1.33
5	Bank of Baroda	0.71	5	Bank of Baroda	1.13
6	Bank of India	0.70	6	Bank of India	1.12
7	Central Bank of India	0.53	7	Union Bank of India	0.89
8	Union Bank of India	0.44	8	IDBI	0.89
9	Indian Overseas Bank	0.35	9	Central Bank	0.75
10	Oriental Bank	0.32	10	HDFC Bank*	0.74

*A private bank

any other industry in India, the names of the top ten firms would jostle around much across this four-year period, reflecting a strong process of creative destruction. But banking is an area afflicted by a public policy framework that is focused on preserving stasis, rather than encouraging competition.[7]

A small group of private banks are now at the vanguard of progress in banking. This group includes ICICI Bank, HDFC Bank, Axis Bank, Kotak Mahindra Bank, Centurion Bank of Punjab, and Yes Bank. These banks have set new standards for the use of technology, sound human resource management, customer service, risk management, and looking beyond the banking silo to the larger role of banks in finance. These banks have gained market share, particularly in activities involving customer service and information technology. These banks are highly profitable, given the lax competition in Indian banking. However, there are too few such sophisticated private banks. Roughly 75% of bank deposits continue to be with public sector banks, and the pace of change is only glacial.

A more rapid transformation of banking could come about through privatization of public sector banks. However, bank privatization requires an amendment to the Bank Nationalization Act, which (in turn) requires support of 51% of members of Parliament. This degree of support has, as yet, not come together in Indian politics.

---

[7] This creative destruction perspective on banking is found in Mistry (2007) and Thomas (2006a).

TABLE 10.11   Cost of Intermediation in Banking

Country	Spread
Singapore	2.4
USA	2.9
China	3.4
Thailand	4.0
India	5.1

TABLE 10.12   Leverage of Various Groups of Firms (2006–2007)

Group	Leverage (times)
PSU banks	19.5
Non-PSU banks	13.2
All banks	16.8

Table 10.11 shows how some countries compare on a key measure of the efficiency of a banking system: the difference between the typical lending rate and the typical deposit rate. It shows that by international standards, India has fairly high values for the spread between the price paid when borrowing and the price earned when lending. This highlights the restrictive rules about assets, low competition, and other infirmities of Indian banking. If anything, given low wages in India, the spread in India should be *lower* than that seen among peers.

10.5.4   LEVERAGE AND ITS CONSEQUENCES

By and large, Indian banking does not have a traditional credit quality crisis: nonperforming assets at small levels of 1%. To some extent, these numbers are understated given that they show the situation after five years of buoyant business cycle conditions and a rapidly growing banking system.

As Table 10.12 shows, banks in India are highly leveraged. Banks as a whole have total assets which are 16.8 times bigger than equity capital. In the case of PSU banks, leverage is even larger at 19.5 times. Under such conditions, banking is a high-wire act; Indian banks have more leverage than most hedge funds. Losses of just a few percent would suffice in destabilizing a bank. The highest sophistication of risk management is required to run a portfolio with such high levels of leverage.

The environment of low competition and innovation, banning of sophisticated products and markets, and a regulatory climate of micro-management have served to stifle the development of risk management capabilities of Indian banks. This combination of high leverage coupled with poor risk management suggests that acute difficulties will arise.

10.5.5   IMPLICATIONS FOR THE ECONOMY

The weaknesses of Indian banking, juxtaposed against the sophisticated equity market, has helped encourage the early transformation of India from a bank-dominated financial system to an equity-market dominated financial system. Firms and households are increasingly finding other ways to achieve tasks that, in many other countries, would involve banks.

The liabilities of all nonfinancial firms in the CMIE database sum up to Rs.29 trillion in 2006–2007. Of this, bank borrowing accounted for just Rs.3.8 trillion or 13%. Banks play an even smaller role in many dynamic sectors: e.g., in 2006–2007, all software companies (put together) had liabilities of Rs.944 billion, of which just Rs.27 billion was from banks.

As emphasized in Section 2.3, Indian firms have evolved into a financial structure where the equity market dominates. For this reason, the economic significance of the difficulties of banking are limited. India's economy is not being held back by the highly unsatisfactory banking system. It has found other ways to connect the savings of households with the needs of firms. This is in contrast with the financial sector of most East Asian countries, where banks are much more important.

10.6   INSURANCE COMPANIES

The Life Insurance Corporation (LIC) used to be a government-owned monopoly, and it was the last element of Indian finance in which private competition was brought in against a public sector incumbent. A new regulator—the Insurance Regulation and Development Agency (IRDA)—was created. However, while this reform was being undertaken, political constraints led to a limit on FDI of 26% on the ownership of insurance companies. This has limited competition. Because of this reform, the life insurance market has grown rapidly, with premiums growing from $7.4 billion in 2001–2002 to $35.2 billion in 2006–2007. LIC has retained a very strong presence. The new entrants had built up a market share of 29% in new business premiums by 2005–2006.

Two key features of the insurance industry are (a) generous tax treatment and (b) a distributor-led sales model. The generous tax treatment has generated incentives for the industry to create fund management products which are disguised by a small actuarial component. These compete in the larger space of fund management products, but have a more favorable tax treatment. These unit-linked products make up roughly half of the business. The distributor-led sales model has generated a toxic environment, with a race to the bottom where insurance companies compete with each other in offering bigger fees to distributors who are perceived to control the customer.

Health insurance is another area with very high growth. The Indian middle class is evolving into the US-style health system, featuring expensive health services coupled with health insurance purchased by each family. McKinsey estimates that the premium flow for health insurance in 2010 would work out to be $3.2 billion.

In some countries, insurance companies have come to play an important role in the field of pensions. In India, the mandatory pension system for private firms run by the Employees Provident Fund Organization (EPFO) does not involve companies. The mandatory pension system for civil servants recruited after 2004—the New Pension System (NPS)—involves defined contribution fund management by a new cadre of pension fund managers with a new regulator (the Pension Fund Regulation and Development Agency (PFRDA)). It involves purchase of annuities from insurance companies upon retirement. This would generate a substantial flow of customers of annuities for insurance companies from roughly 2035 onward.

Insurance companies have been making inroads—based on the tax advantages and the distributor model described above—in terms of selling pension products to individuals directly. These products involve substantial fees and expenses.

10.7 PENSIONS

The Indian pension system (Shah, 2006; Dave, 2006) is composed of three elements.

10.7.1 UNFUNDED CIVIL SERVANTS PENSION

In most parts of the government, employees recruited prior to about 2004 were entitled to an unfunded defined-benefit pension of 50% of the terminal wage. This pension system is a purely fiscal endeavor: government pays out pensions every year out of general tax revenues. There is no prefunding, no pension assets, and no pension fund managers.

10.7.2 Mandatory System for Private Firms with over 20 Employees

The Ministry of Labour runs an agency called the Employee Provident Fund Organization (EPFO) which runs a defined contribution and defined-benefit pension system which is mandatory for many employees of most private firms with over 20 employees. The defined contribution part is called the Employee Provident Fund (EPF), and was created in the 1950s. Through generous rules about premature withdrawal coupled with poor fund management, the buildup of assets with EPF has been remarkably small: roughly Rs.1.5 trillion in 2007. The defined benefits part is called the Employee Pension Scheme (EPS). This was created in 1995 and, lacking generous rules about withdrawal, it has had a faster buildup of assets: roughly Rs.0.8 trillion in 2007.

The EPFO's fund management is outsourced to State Bank of India (SBI). However, the trustees of EPFO have very detailed rules about what can be done in fund management, so that (for all practical purposes) this fund management is merely a clerical function. The predominant fraction of assets are deployed into government bonds. Investment into corporate bonds and equities is absent.

EPFO is controlled by the Ministry of Labour. The legislation that led to the creation of EPFO has given considerable importance to trade union leaders in shaping the policies of the organization. As a consequence, the evolution of EPFO into anything resembling modern pension fund management is unlikely in the near future. EPFO reforms will require rewriting the underlying legislation.

10.7.3 The New Pension System

From 2004 onward, most fresh recruits into the government were placed in the New Pension System (NPS). The NPS is a defined contribution system with a few standardized investment profiles and multiple competing fund managers. Auction-based procurement is used to drive down the cost of fund management. A Central Recordkeeping Agency (CRA) aggregates assets of individuals and maintains records, thus requiring only bulk fund management by the fund managers. These features have helped ensure that NPS has very low fees and expenses compared to all other mechanisms of fund management in the country. Oversight of NPS is done by a new agency, the Pension Fund Regulatory and Development Agency (PFRDA).

In 2007, PFRDA awarded the contract for the execution of the Central Recordkeeping Agency (CRA) to the stock depository, NSDL. In addition, a competitive procurement process was employed to recruit pension fund managers (PFMs). Owing to political constraints, only public sector financial firms were permitted to bid. Three firms were chosen: Unit Trust of India (UTI), State Bank of India (SBI) and Life Insurance Corporation (LIC). The full NPS architecture is expected to start functioning in mid-2008.[8]

While NPS is an attractive and modern design of a pension system, it only began in 2004, and it only extends to civil servants. For one decade or so, the assets under management with NPS are unlikely to exceed 1% of GDP. If the NPS reform is carried forward into the unorganized sector, then there is a possibility of much sharper growth.

10.7.4   UNORGANIZED SECTOR

Policy discussions about pensions tend to focus on the EPFO and the NPS. However, these two systems account for only a small slice of the population. Most people in India have no formal pension provision. To a significant extent, the interactions of individuals with banks, insurance companies, mutual funds, and other financial firms reflect an expression of their need for financial planning for old age.

10.8   MUTUAL FUNDS

10.8.1   DESCRIPTION OF THE INDUSTRY

As with banking and insurance, mutual funds in India also started out with a history of domination by a public sector monopoly (UTI) from 1964 until 2000. However, this area is the best experience in terms of lowering entry barriers and the rapid evolution of the industry away from this heritage. Unlike the situation with banking, there is a steady pace of entry by new firms. Unlike the situation with banking and insurance, the barriers faced by foreign financial firms are low. When compared with most elements of Indian finance, the regulatory structure has been relatively sound, and the restrictions placed by the government on mutual funds in India look much like those seen elsewhere in the world.

The assets under management of the industry grew dramatically after 2003, to reach Rs.5.5 trillion or $139.6 billion in December 2007.

Table 10.13 shows all mutual fund houses with more than Rs.100 billion in assets under management. These 16 firms add up to $112 billion in assets under

---

[8]See http://ajayshahblog.blogspot.com/2007/11/new-pension-system-coming-to-life.html.

TABLE 10.13   The Largest Mutual Funds

Firm	Assets under management		Market share (%)
	Rs. billion	Billion USD	
Reliance	807	20.5	14.69
UTI	568	14.43	10.34
ICICI Prudential	567	14.41	10.32
HDFC	485	12.32	8.83
SBI	292	7.42	5.32
Tata	235	5.97	4.28
DSP Merrill Lynch	210	5.34	3.82
Kotak Mahindra	204	5.18	3.71
HSBC	158	4.03	2.88
LIC	138	3.52	2.52
Principal	138	3.51	2.51
Standard Chartered	130	3.32	2.38
JM Financial	125	3.19	2.28
Sundaram BNP Paribas	118	3.02	2.16
Deutsche	112	2.84	2.04
Fidelity	110	2.8	2
Sum of above	4,404	111.8	80.1
All 33 firms	5,499	139.6	100.0

management, or 80% of the industry. The overall industry has $139.6 billion of assets under management. The erstwhile monopoly public sector firm—UTI— is now in second place by market share, and has 10.3% market share. The only other public sector firm in the table is SBI, which has 5.3% market share. Summing across these two, roughly 15% of the mutual fund industry is now in the public sector; the remaining 85% is made up of domestic or foreign private firms. This transformation of the market structure of the industry constitutes an important accomplishment of economic reforms.

Of the Rs.5,499 billion in assets, Rs.1,148 billion are in closed-end schemes, with the remainder in open-end schemes. In the Indian experience, a substantial closed-end fund discount has been persistently observed. This is partly related to difficulties faced in doing closed-end fund arbitrage. As a consequence, open-end schemes have predominated.

From a regulatory perspective, mutual funds have fairly good flexibility in being able to hold assets across equity, debt and equity derivatives. This is one region where the financial repression that afflicts many other aspects of finance in India is not found. Mutual funds in India have a limited ability for international diversification. For all practical purposes, this diversification has not begun; mutual funds are afflicted with an extreme degree of home bias.

While money market mutual funds exist, they have been kept separate from the payments system in an effort by the RBI to protect banks. Hence, the developments seen internationally—where money market mutual funds have emerged as defined contribution alternatives to the traditional defined benefit checking accounts offered by banks—have not come about in India. When this barrier is broken down, a one-time jump in the size of mutual funds might come about.

10.8.2   THE PROBLEM OF DISTRIBUTION

A key difficulty of the mutual fund industry lies in the strategy for distribution. Distribution is primarily done through a set of individuals and firms termed distributors. Distributors are paid a fee for selling products. Distributors tend to own customers and have a disproportionate influence on the decison making of customers. This has given rise to many difficulties:

- Distributors have an incentive to encourage customers to churn (to switch in and out of various mutual fund schemes) since each entry earns them a fee. This results in higher turnover by mutual funds, higher revenues for distributors, and inferior performance for customers.
- SEBI regulations permit a bigger fee to be paid when a new mutual fund product is launched. This is termed a New Fund Offering (NFO) in India. Since a bigger fee is earned with NFOs, distributors emphasize NFOs to customers, which (in turn) has given the mutual fund industry a bias in favor of inventing more NFOs. This results in higher fees being paid out to distributors, lower returns to customers, and the lack of mutual fund products with a multi-decade history. The bias in favor of NFOs has, in turn, hindered the development of products with a large and growing size coupled with a long track record.
- Distributors will emphasize the products that pay the highest fees to them. This has generated a race to the bottom where mutual fund houses that are attracted to having a high rank (Table 10.13) are prone to pay very high fees to distributors.

10.8.3   OVERCOMING THE PROBLEM OF HIGH FEES OF DISTRIBUTORS BY MUTUAL FUNDS

There are three promising avenues for avoiding these problems within the mutual fund industry:

Exchange traded funds (ETFs): ETFs were pioneered in India by Benchmark Mutual Fund. There is now a small industry offering ETFs. The key benefit of ETFs lies in their harnessing the massive distribution network of the members of NSE and BSE. Customers of ETFs buy and sell these products on the exchange screens, and benefit from the rock-bottom prices charged by securities firms for trading on NSE and BSE. This avoids the charges of distributors.

In one rare breakdown of the silo system of Indian finance, Gold ETFs are also available in India, regulated by SEBI, even though gold is a commodity and gold futures are regulated by FMC.

As the Gold ETFs suggest, ETFs in India have started going beyond simple equity index funds. One particularly innovative and successful ETF is the Liquid BeES product of Benchmark Mutual Fund, which is an ETF that is a money market mutual fund.

Index funds: As with elsewhere in the world, index funds in India tend to have low costs. As yet, really large index funds, which deliver really low fees and expenses, have not come about. The overall industry had Rs.72 billion of assets under management in November 2007, which suggests that it can now be a significant part of the strategy of all households and most financial firms. The biggest 10 products are shown in Table 10.14.

The substantial assets under management with ETFs investing in bank indexes or PSU bank indexes, featured in this table, reflect a feature of capital controls. Foreign investors are able to own index fund paper which invests in firms where the quantitative restrictions on foreign ownership are binding. This has channeled foreign interest in owning Indian banks in general and Indian PSU banks in particular into ownership of ETFs.[9]

TABLE 10.14   The Biggest Index Funds (November 2007)

Product	Index	Assets under management (Rs. billion)
Bank BeES	CNX Bank	57.7
PSU Bank BeES	CNX PSU Bank BeES	4.0
Nifty BeES	Nifty	3.6
UTI Nifty Fund	Nifty	1.0
Franklin India Index Fund	Nifty	0.8
HDFC Index Fund	BSE Sensex	0.7
Junioer BeES	Nifty Junior	0.7
Kotak PSU Bank ETF	CNX PSU Bank BeES	0.5
LIC Index Fund	Nifty	0.5
LIC Index Fund Sensex Plan	BSE Sensex	0.4

[9]See http://ajayshahblog.blogspot.com/2006/01/capital-controls-in-operation-tales.html.

Direct distribution: Quantum Mutual Fund is the only mutual fund which has embarked on a distributor-free strategy. Customers purchase products over the Internet, and the payments to distributors are eliminated.

In 2007, SEBI announced that in order to help customers combat the frictions of distributors, it would force all mutual funds to offer customers the *choice* of direct distribution for all products. Mutual funds would have to set up a mechanism through which customers could, if they chose, bypass distributors and access products directly from the Internet.[10]

10.9 FOREIGN INSTITUTIONAL INVESTORS

The term foreign institutional investor (FII) used in India blurs the lines between global buy-side and sell-side financial firms. Some registered FIIs are buy-side natural-longs such as university endowments and pension funds. Some registered FIIs are securities firms such as the big Wall Street firms. In the functioning of global finance, it is clear that these are very different kinds of firms. However, in India, there is a single registration process which leads to them becoming FIIs and thus able to access the Indian market.

There are no entry barriers against foreign sell-side firms; there is a homogeneous competitive market involving both local and foreign sell-side firms. Roughly a dozen FIIs are active in the business of selling participatory notes, which are OTC derivatives, to foreign financial firms that desire access to the Indian market but are not registered FIIs.[11]

In January 2008, there were 1,255 FIIs. They had roughly 3,000 sub-accounts. A sub-account is a mechanism through which a buy-side customer can achieve transactions through the registered FII who is a sell-side firm. Transactions by FIIs made up roughly 10.4% of the overall equity turnover (summing across spot and derivatives markets). These transactions worked out to roughly Rs.10 trillion of buy orders and Rs.10 trillion of sell orders.

FII ownership of Indian equities has grown dramatically. Between March 2001 and March 2007, the market value of shares owned by FIIs went up from $9.7 billion to $124 billion. This large change requires an explanation.[12] In the analysis of firm level data on ownership patterns, the first issue that merits focus is nonpromoter shareholding. FIIs can only buy shares in the space that has been freed up by promoters. In recent years, promoters have increased their

---

[10]See http://ajayshahblog.blogspot.com/2008/01/combating-fees-and-expenses-in-fund.html.

[11]For recently introduced capital controls against participatory notes, see http://ajayshahblog.blogspot.com/2007/10/middle-muddle.html.

[12]For cross-country work on these issues, see Claessens and Schmukler (2006).

shares in many companies, which has actually reduced the space for FIIs. This suggests a focus on FII ownership as a percentage of nonpromoter ownership. Here, there is a two-part story. First, there appears to be a club of companies which have nonzero FII ownership. Firms which fail to make the grade on size, liquidity and corporate governance do not get into the FII club. Then, once club membership is secured, similar factors (size, liquidity, corporate governance) affect the proportion of nonpromoter holding that is bought by FIIs.

The most interesting result of this exploration (Shah and Patnaik, 2007b) lies in the extent to which it explains the dramatic change in foreign ownership of Indian equities from 2001 to 2007. The bulk of the change in foreign ownership (expressed as a proportion of nonpromoter shareholding) can be explained based on changes in size, liquidity and corporate governance.

The improvements in stock market liquidity are rooted in the successful reforms of the equity market which began in 1993 and particularly the build-up of derivatives trading. The improvement in profits of Indian firms is rooted in the strong performance of the macroeconomy. In a business cycle downturn, profits will go down, the firms will be smaller, and unchanged behavior on the part of FIIs will generate lower ownership of Indian firms.

10.10   PRIVATE EQUITY FUNDS

In 2007, it was estimated that there were 250 private equity firms operating in India. Almost all the capital in this field is raised abroad. Prominent domestic firms in the field include India Value Fund, ChrysCapital, IDFC Private Equity, UTI Ventures, etc. In addition, most large global firms, such as Kleiner Perkins or Blackstone, also operate in India.

Internationally, PE funds often tend to buy companies, focus on financial engineering, and emphasize returns through leverage. In India, PE investors have employed a different set of strategies. PE investments in India tend to have little leverage. The focus leans toward placing bets on firms before they become big, and on obtaining profit growth through business process engineering. While good data is hard to come by, the numbers are now significant. The gross investments of PE funds were estimated at $13 billion in 2006–2007 and $20 billion in 2007–2008. The PE industry may have investments in 1,500 companies, meaning it is now applying its professional incubation function upon a full 1,500 companies.

The investments in place today might generate 1,000 exits over the next four years. On average, the PE industry might produce one company per week-day. Some of these exits would be through an IPO; the others would involve sale to an existing listed company. In either event, this would give growth to the overall market capitalization of India and grow the modern sector of the economy. Rough estimates suggest that 20% of investments by PE funds are small stakes in listed companies. Another 20% involves substantial stakes in listed companies. The remaining 60% is invested in unlisted companies.

10.11   THE FUNDAMENTAL DIFFICULTIES OF FUND MANAGEMENT

In the best of times, it is difficult for a customer to know that a fund manager has added value. A fund manager earns returns as a compensation for systematic risk, a compensation for illiquidity, and payments for short option positions. The returns of the portfolio—over and above these three aspects—is the alpha of the portfolio, and is measured in basis points per year.

The customer does not know the true α of the fund manager. This can at best be estimated using historical data for the performance of the fund manager. As is well known, this is extremely difficult to discern. A mainstream example from an industrial country context[13] is as follows. Suppose a fund manager has an enormous α of 20 basis points a month or 240 basis points a year. In order to reject $H_0: \alpha = 0$ at a 95% level of significance, 32 years of data would be required.

There are four dimensions which make this task even more difficult in India:

1. Broad market volatility is higher: stocks, indexes and portfolios are more volatile. Until a sound framework of monetary policy and fiscal policy (Shah, 2008) falls into place, macroeconomic risk in India will be higher than that seen in mature market economies. This means that it is harder to pick up the signal of fund manager performance above the noise of market fluctuations.
2. The Indian fund industry is young, which generally induces short time-series.
3. The Indian institutional environment is particularly hostile to performance measurement:
   (a) SEBI's rules give mutual funds an incentive to come up with New Fund Offerings (NFOs); assets under management of older products tend to dwindle away. This worsens the problem of short series.
   (b) The behavior of foreign institutional investors has been continually reshaped by the rapidly evolving situation on capital controls and the characteristics of local investee firms.

---

[13] This is drawn from page 735 of the 1989 edition of *Investments* by Bodie, Kane, Marcus.

   (c) Insurance companies have poor disclosure. Hence, the measurement
      of their performance is difficult.

These aspects impede performance measurement.
4. In a young and fast-changing financial industry, staff turnover is acute.
   The history of fund performance might often reflect the risk preferences
   and skills of differing groups of individuals who managed the fund.

These problems imply that even if a fund manager genuinely had α, a customer in India requires even more than 32 years of data to discern this with confidence. Fund managers know that customers have little ability to discern performance. Hence, fund managers have incentives to do things which adversely affect the interests of the customer, knowing that the reduction in α would not be discernable to the customer.

The field of fund management in India is thus at a low-level equilibrium where a variety of factors have conspired to yield an intractable principal-agent problem. This low-level equilibrium involves fund managers who have poor incentives to deliver performance. Toxic sales strategies are used to round up funds from uninformed customers. It involves a race to the bottom where the most generous tax breaks and the most egregious sales incentives to distributors are the path to large assets under management.

These problems afflict insurance companies, mutual funds, FIIs, etc. This diagnosis constitutes the intellectual foundations of the design of the New Pension System (Section 10.7.3), which represents a public policy effort at overcoming these difficulties through auction-based procurement of index funds.

CHAPTER 11

Policy Issues

This chapter reviews the strengths and weaknesses of Indian finance and sketches the directions for reform.

11.1 THE STATE OF INDIAN FINANCE

The outstanding success story of Indian finance is the equity market, which has achieved a full ecosystem with high levels of liquidity and market efficiency. It has:

- Private equity investors;
- The IPO market;
- A fairly liquid secondary market, with electronic trading, competing exchanges, nationwide anonymous electronic trading, risk management at the clearing corporation;
- Derivatives trading;
- Mutual funds;
- Stock market indexes, index funds and index derivatives;
- Barring barriers faced by pension funds, few domestic participants are blocked from market access;
- Participation from overseas players through the FII framework, accentuated using participatory notes.

All these features have been described in various chapters of this book. While the government is involved in regulation and supervision of the equity market, it has no role in determining prices of equity securities.[1] In contrast, with the three other elements of finance, namely currencies, commodities and bonds,

---

[1] For a treatment of the policy debates and evolution of the equity market, see Shah and Thomas (2000) and Echeverri-Gent (2007).

speculative price discovery does not take place in India. The government is deeply involved in determining prices.

Figure 11.1, drawn from Mistry (2007), shows the Bond-Currency-Derivatives Nexus as it operates in a mature market economy. In an Indian setting, the BCD Nexus would involve the rupee riskless yield curve, with issuance and investment from all over the world of riskless rupee denominated government bonds. There would be rupee credit curves, also with issuance and investors from all over the world. The fixed-income markets would interface with global yield curves through the currency spot and derivatives markets. Alongside this would be the credit derivatives market, which would (in turn) be linked with the equity market through arbitrage.

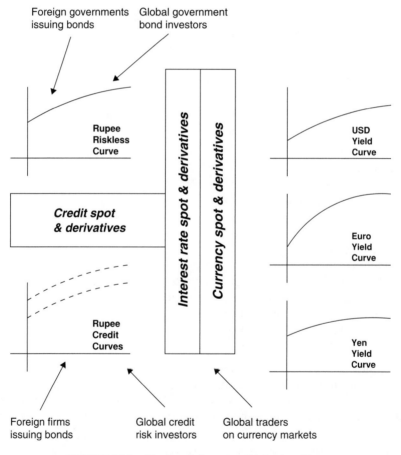

FIGURE 11.1   The Bond-Currency-Derivatives Nexus

None of this exists in India today. All elements of the BCD Nexus are riddled with bans on trading, restrictions on market access, rules that prevent player x from trading in market y, etc. In the absence of the BCD Nexus, Indian finance is lacking in many core functions of finance, ranging from fund-raising to information signals and risk management. This is a core failure of India's financial markets.[2]

Surrounding the financial markets are the financial firms. This is another area where India has major weaknesses. Financial firms are unable to organize themselves effectively, thanks to the silo structure of regulation that has come up. In addition, most regulated financial firms are forced to do a large array of inefficient things by regulators. This hinders their ability to engage in rational trading strategies on the markets. This, in turn, holds back the liquidity and market efficiency of the markets.

11.2   REFORM

11.2.1   THE REFORM PROCESS

Change in Indian economic policy takes place through a process that is reminiscent of that found in other democracies: through a combination of broad intellectual consensus tempered by hard-nosed political economy. Policy changes *follow* the broad intellectual consensus. It is rare in India for a great leader to articulate a direction and lead the flock to it.

The Indian policy discourse attaches considerable importance to the committee process. Periodically the government sets up a committee to ponder an important question. Committee members are typically a mix of practitioners, bureaucrats and intellectuals. A key feature of the best committees is that the drafting of the report is done by individuals who are not civil servants.[3] The committee process is an important mechanism through which the policy process is opened up to participation from individuals outside government.

Committees fall into two classes. Sometimes, a *decision* has already been taken to move on a certain question. In this case, the terms of reference of the committee are narrowly spelled out. The committee is tasked with working out the nuts and bolts of what needs to be done. These committees can be thought of

---

[2]See Thomas (2006a).

[3]In contrast, some government committees involve a group of civil servants who write a report, while the members of the committee play a passive role of reviewing the drafts written by civil servants. Such committees tend to reflect the interests of an existing bureaucracy, and they fail to harness the intellectual capabilities found outside government.

as doing staff work of a high quality that is not easily achieved by purely internal work done by civil servants. The committee process also ensures transparency of proposals and public discussion.

The second kind of committee is given a broad term of reference. Such committees have an opportunity to write what will be a widely read report. Such a committee is no more, and no less, than an opportunity for the members to be heard. The reports are widely read and discussed in government, the media, and among practitioners. In India, the think tanks are weak, and active discussions take place in opinion pages of newspapers. The recommendations of the committee have no intrinsic significance other than being a widely discussed set of policy proposals.[4]

If the report persuades, it shapes the broad consensus about where policy needs to change, and many of these ideas tend to be gradually implemented, while of course being modulated by political economy considerations. At its best, the big picture committee process fosters debates, puts new ideas on the table, legitimizes radical reform proposals and makes them mainstream. It takes many people forward from an inchoate discomfort with the status quo to a fully articulated program for change. The committee process can also give the government a way to shape the expectations of practitioners about future policy changes without making binding commitments.

In the recent period in financial sector policy, three important committees have been formed:

R.H. Patil committee on corporate bonds and securitization: There is a considerable consensus among policymakers that India needs an active market in corporate bonds and securitization paper. A committee was appointed, chaired by R.H. Patil, to work out the mechanics of how this should be done. The report was submitted in December 2005, and can be accessed at http://tinyurl.com/2ezsbl.

Percy Mistry committee on Mumbai as an international financial center: This is a committee with a broad term of reference tasked with thinking through the financial and macroeconomic policy efforts required so that Mumbai can become an international financial center over a 10- to 20-year horizon. The MIFC Report was submitted in February 2007. The report and associated materials can be accessed at http://tinyurl.com/2osms4.

Raghuram Rajan committee on financial sector reforms: This is a committee with a broad term of reference, focused on domestic financial sector

---

[4] Cynics will point to the third kind of committee, one that is intended to do nothing. A government that is faced with a question that it seeks to dodge often sets up a committee to ponder the question. Large, unwieldy committees signal an interest in delaying tactics. Sometimes supporters of existing bureaucracies are drafted into committees which go on to write reports that propose no reform. These reports quickly die a natural death; they are inconsequential in the reform process.

reforms required to support high GDP growth. Their report is expected to be completed in March 2008.

The R.H. Patil report is a nuts and bolts report that works out details about how an agreed-upon goal (creating a market for corporate bonds and securitization paper) can be achieved. The other two committees are big-picture efforts that modify the intellectual consensus on how financial sector policy should go in an important way. The three reports, put together, give a valuable sense of where the policy framework for Indian finance is likely to go in the coming years. Many of the ideas in this chapter have been shaped by these three reports.

11.2.2 ISSUES

There are seven areas for financial sector reform where there is a broad consensus:[5]

1. Mistakes in regulation of institutional investors
2. Flawed regulatory architecture
3. Flawed legal framework
4. Inadequacies of financial firms
5. Tax distortions
6. Capital controls
7. Outward orientation of financial firms

Regulation of Institutional Investors

In the regulation of institutional investors, there are three key difficulties:

1. Over-prescriptive and irrational rules.
2. Resource pre-emption by the government.
3. Entry barriers.

The first issue is that of over-prescriptive rules, which often intrude against rational behavior on the part of institutional investors.

Sometimes rules are constructed so as to effectively ban a financial market. As an example, under the guise of prudential regulation, RBI rules specify that banks must only have short positions on interest rate futures: long positions are prohibited. With banks being the largest holders of government bonds, this effectively ensures that exchange-traded interest rate futures do not exist. As a consequence, interest rate derivatives trading does not take place on exchange.

---

[5]On these issues, see Rajan and Shah (2005); Bhattacharya and Patel (2003).

Sometimes the rules inhibit participation, even if they do not achieve an outright ban on a market. As an example, RBI prohibits banks from trading on the equity derivatives market—even if it is for the purpose of riskless arbitrage positions. This diminishes the arbitrage capital available, and thus adversely affects the market efficiency of the equity derivatives market. However, alternative pools of capital are available, so the equity derivatives market has succeeded despite the RBI restriction on banks.

The next issue is that of resource pre-emption. With banks, insurance companies and pension funds, the existing framework of rules forces financial firms to hold government bonds to a considerable extent, much in excess of what prudence demands. Using powers amassed under the guise of prudential regulation, government is reducing the cost of funding its own deficit. This hinders the quality of risk-reward profiles that can be attained by these institutional investors. It results in an inferior allocation of capital for the economy as a whole. In addition, it inhibits the attractiveness of institutional investors in the eyes of customers; it encourages households to avoid banks, insurance companies and pension funds in their portfolio formation.

The most damaging feature of financial regulation lies in entry barriers. In the case of banking, branch opening is controlled, particularly by foreign banks. All foreign banks (put together) are permitted to open just 12 branches a year. Starting a bank is difficult; on average one new bank is started every few years. Foreign participation in banking, insurance and pensions is restricted, thus hurting entry by competent firms and adversely affecting competition.

Regulatory Architecture

India has an alphabet soup of regulatory agencies dealing with finance:

Reserve Bank of India, RBI: Central bank; investment banker to the government; banking regulator; owner and operator of payments system, depository and bond exchange; regulator and supervisor of currency and bond market.

Securities and Exchange Board of India, SEBI: Regulation and supervision of stock exchanges and mutual funds.

Insurance Regulatory and Development Agency, IRDA: Regulation and supervision of insurance.

Pension Fund Regulatory and Development Agency, PFRDA: Regulation and supervision of the New Pension System.

Employee's Provident Fund Organization, EPFO: Government agency that runs the (unregulated) mandatory pension system for large firms.

Forward Markets Commission, FMC: Regulation and supervision of commodity futures trading.

Department of Company Affairs, DCA: Regulation of limited liability companies (including unlisted firms).

Many elements of this regulatory architecture are rooted in decisions made many decades ago, when there was little knowledge of finance. As an example, the legislation underlying RBI and FMC date back to 1934 and 1952, respectively. SEBI, IRDA and PFRDA are modern agencies, created in the last 15 years. As a consequence, these three agencies have clarity and consistency in their role and function. The other agencies in this list are riddled with problems. Regardless of the history, once an agency comes about with a certain role and function, it engages in a tremendous effort to defend turf. There is a feudal notion of control, where a financial firm which comes under a given regulatory agency is sought to be completely controlled by the agency. Each regulatory agency is hence unwilling to tolerate activities by its regulated entities which involve other regulators. This has induced an excessively rigid silo structure in which each regulator deals with its own set of firms and activities, and activities spanning regulators do not take place. Instead of a single financial industry, with free-wheeling competition between various financial firms, India has set up a series of highly segmented sub-industries, where government prevents firms from engaging in activities outside of a narrow definition. This has greatly harmed competition, innovation and economies of scale and scope.

India urgently needs a transformation of this regulatory architecture. Fully unified regulation—as with the UK FSA—is viewed as a poor option in India, as it would involve concentrating too much power into one agency. The most credible reforms alternative, proposed by the MIFC Report, envisages four regulators:

1. An independent banking regulator (outside the central bank);
2. A securities regulator which deals with all organized financial trading (all underlyings, all markets);
3. An insurance regulator (the existing IRDA); and
4. A pensions regulator (an enlarged PFRDA).

Achieving this structure requires three moves:

1. Moving banking regulation out of RBI into a new agency, perhaps named Banking Regulation and Development Agency;
2. Folding all activities pertaining to organized financial trading that are presently at RBI and FMC into SEBI;
3. Placing all pension regulation and supervision with PFRDA.

Legal Framework

The difficulties of over-prescriptive rules, and the faulty definitions of financial regulators, are rooted in outdated law. India started out with a common law tradition, where the drafting of law is supposed to be flexible and the courts refine the interpretation of law under changing circumstances. However, in the post-independence period, India's experiment with socialism involved drafting laws which banned many activities, and writing down details about financial products and transactions into the law.

As an example, the Forward Contracts (Regulation) Act of 1952 defines the legal framework for regulation of commodity futures markets. The preamble of this Act reads: *An act to provide for the regulation of certain matters relating to forward contracts, the prohibition of options in goods and for matters connected therewith.* In addition to banning options trading, this Act also bans cash settlement for commodity futures.

A transformation of the regulatory architecture will undoubtedly require legislative activism: to place all organized financial trading at SEBI and to create a new independent banking regulator. This drafting needs to be accompanied by a shift of both banking and securities law toward broad principles, a removal of various bans, and the elimination of resource pre-emption by the government.

Financial Firms

Improvements in computer technology and financial economics are breaking down the walls which used to separate various kinds of financial firms. In the years to come, Indian financial firms have to compete by becoming multi-product firms that service the broad range of financial services that are consumed by their corporate or household customers. If India primarily does financial intermediation through securities markets, no financial firm can afford to not participate in the action. Broad-spectrum firms are likely to be safer by having diversified exposures in many markets. They are able to capture economies of scale and economies of scope. It is imprudent for a financial firm to insist it does only one thing (e.g., banking), for this will inevitably involve losing customers to competing firms which are able to offer a full spectrum of products.

In the traditional India silo model, UTI was a pure mutual fund, LIC was a pure insurance company, and SBI was a pure bank. Each firm did only one business and dealt with only one regulator. NSE has capabilities in all financial trading, but NSE is prohibited from trading currencies, bonds and commodities because these fall under other regulators. This silo mentality is a fundamental flaw underlying Indian finance. Global competitiveness and innovative firms cannot be achieved when the boundaries of a financial firm are thus circumscribed.

Making progress in Indian finance is critically about breaking these silos, about shifting toward a loose concept of a financial firm which thinks that all financial services are fair game. Government needs to change itself so that financial firms think in an innovative way, trying to dream up new products to deliver to existing customers or into pockets of perceived demand.

In the UK, this problem has been solved by unifying all financial regulators into the Financial Services Authority (FSA). Everything that a financial firm seeks to do is dealt with by one regulator. In India, the emerging consensus envisages four regulators: for securities, banking, insurance and pensions. How might financial firms be organized while there are four regulators? Sometimes, there is hope that there can be a large financial firm and each regulator can look at the activities of the firm that falls within its mandate. Unfortunately, in India, given the weak regulatory capacity and feudal mindset of regulators, this is often impractical. Further, the implications of firm failure are much greater in insurance and banking than in securities, so that government intervention is much more likely.

The Mumbai International Financial Centre (MIFC) report proposes a holding company which is the corporate headquarters. This would typically be a listed company. As an example, *SBI Holding Company* would be a listed company. This would be the owner of four subsidiaries—SBI Bank, SBI Securities, SBI Insurance and SBI Pensions. Each of these subsidiaries would deal with one regulator. Each subsidiary would be like a division of a large multi-product firm. The CEO and corporate headquarters would think like a complex multi-product financial firm, with the ability to launch any product and harness economies of scale by virtue of controlling four divisions covering all possible products. For these healthy features to hold, the holding company must not be regulated by any financial regulator; it must only obey company law and listing requirements. As an example, SBI Insurance being regulated by IRDA should give IRDA no power over, SBI Holding Company.

The MIFC report has pointed out five constraints which impede the transformation of Indian financial firms in this modern structure:

1. Rules about ownership that prevent 100% ownership of X Bank being with X Holding Company;
2. Consolidation of accounts for tax purposes is prohibited;
3. Tax inefficiency owing to double taxation of dividends;
4. Archaic restrictions in the Companies Act that impede leverage; and
5. Companies Act restrictions that impede intra-group transactions.

Tax Distortions

There are three key problems with the tax system in India:

Securities transaction tax: Securities trading in India suffers from an onerous set of taxes imposed by the government. As an example, trading at NSE involves a 0.2 basis points charge applied by NSE, which is competitive when compared with exchanges globally. However, layered on top of this are a host of taxes: a 0.01 basis point charge for an investor protection fund mandated by SEBI; a stamp duty of 0.2 basis points; a securities transaction of 1.7 basis points charged to the seller. There is a considerable consensus worldwide that taxing transactions inhibits market efficiency. The incidence of a transaction tax falls disproportionately upon business activities which involve more transactions (e.g., dynamic arbitrage).

Lack of pass-through treatment of fund management: A core principle of sound tax policy is that agency structures should not change tax treatment. Whether a person runs his own money or recruits a fund manager to run his money for him, the tax treatment should not change. This principle is not in place in India. As an example, domestic private equity funds are only granted tax pass-through status by the government if the investments of these funds are deemed meritorious in certain industries by the government. In other words, pass-through is not a fundamental principle of tax policy in India; it is a privilege granted by the government as part of industrial policy efforts.

Difficulties of taxation of corporations: All over the world, the taxation of corporations is a difficult problem. When income tax is paid once by the firm and again by the shareholder who earns dividends, this constitutes double taxation. India's partial solution to this involves full taxation of corporations, and a dividend tax of 15% (paid at the source by the corporation). This partially attenuates double taxation. However, there are myriad aspects where this concept has not been logically followed through. As an example, if a mutual fund earns income from coupons on bonds, and if the mutual fund pays out dividends, then the application of this dividend tax framework violates the pass-through principle for an individual who directly owns bonds and pays more tax than an individual who hires a mutual fund who owns bonds.

Removing Capital Controls

Competitive conditions in Indian finance would be enhanced by the removal of capital controls. At present, Indian households face monopolistic conditions where their needs can only be served by Indian financial firms. India has experienced the benefits that arise from the removal of trade barriers, whereby local customers are given a choice between local and foreign producers. These benefits are, as yet, not available to consumers of financial products.

Without capital controls in the picture, trading in shares of Indian firms at Singapore or Dubai could compete with trading in India. The trading in international commodity derivatives—such as gold or crude oil—that takes place onshore will come under severe competitive pressure from global derivatives exchanges once capital controls are removed.

Outward Orientation

Finally, Indian financial firms have evolved under decades of autarkic policies. Their outlook on financial services tends to be local. In the future, this will need to change to a global orientation, where Indian financial firms become producers of international financial services that compete in a global marketplace. This outward orientation is likely to flow inexorably out of (a) reduction in entry barriers in finance, (b) removal of capital controls and (c) removal of barriers to FDI. Once these three elements of policy are in place, financial firms will face the same pressures which drove Indian real sector firms to go from an inward orientation to an outward orientation.

11.3   THE AGENDA AT SEBI

Given the domination of the equity market in Indian finance, the most important financial regulator in the country is SEBI. Hence, in this section, we delve deeper into the tangible agenda for policy issues at SEBI.

SEBI is one of the most important new regulatory institutions created in the wake of the reforms of the early 1990s. India could not have succeeded in emerging as a trillion dollar economy without the critical role played by SEBI in enabling a trillion dollar equity market that has funded investment while fostering risk-taking and entrepreneurship.

The creation of SEBI was part of the new ethos of economic policy, where markets were respected, where government does not control prices and is not a player in financial markets, where financial prices were sought to be the outcomes of free market processes, and the role of the government is limited to ensuring that these markets function properly.

From its very inception, SEBI was different from the incumbent financial regulator, the RBI.[6] In socialist India, regulatory agencies (like RBI, DOT, EPFO, etc.) engaged in a class of activities in which the government was a monopoly provider. In modern India, it is now understood that the role of the State should be limited to the public goods of regulation while the actual service provision gets done in a competitive private industry. In socialist India, these regulatory agencies were directly involved in controlling prices either administratively or by manipulating markets using the unique market power that only government

---

[6]On the larger issues of establishment of new regulators in India, see Bhattacharya and Patel (2005).

can command. In modern India, it is now understood that the free market is a powerful mechanism for discovering prices, and that the role of the State should be limited to ensuring that there is no concentration of market power, and that there are high levels of competition, transparency and fairplay. SEBI is the first of the new-age regulators in India, created under the principles of modern regulation. The differences between the new (SEBI) and the old (RBI) regulators are summarized in Table 11.1.[7]

Traditionally, the task of building financial markets in India was viewed as a domestic problem. Here, the role of foreign financial firms was limited to bringing foreign capital into India. In recent years, the *Mumbai International Financial Centre* (MIFC) committee report, chaired by Percy Mistry, has brought a whole new perspective of international finance to this question. Indian firms are increasingly demanding *international financial services* (IFS), and India now has an opportunity to earn export revenues by producing and selling IFS to the global market. This marks a new development, where we go from a domestic-focused financial sector policy agenda to an export-oriented policy effort.

In this modern framework, the agenda for the role that SEBI can play in making markets function properly comprises three areas of work:

1. Policy framework that supports efficiency, competition, and innovation
2. Transparency and information disclosure
3. Ensuring the absence of market power

Each of these is dealt with in the following three sections.

TABLE 11.1   SEBI—The New Kid on the Block

RBI	SEBI
Owns and operates financial service businesses	Is a pure regulator—no financial services are produced within SEBI
Has an opinion about what interest rates and currencies ought to be	Has no opinion about what prices should be; is only concerned with ensuring free and fair prices
Trades on financial markets itself, and uses market power to distort market prices	Never trades on financial markets, enforces against players who have market power and distort prices
Is burdened with numerous other roles, which induce conflicts of interest	Has only one task: the fair and efficient functioning of organized financial trading
At the outset, faced a dominant public sector in banking	There was no public sector in the equity market barring UTI

[7] On the difficulties of RBI, see Khatkhate (2005); Chandavarkar (2005).

11.3.1   SUPPORTING EFFICIENCY, COMPETITION, AND INNOVATION

Domestic hedge funds: In India today, the most important form of organization of fund management is the mutual fund. Mutual funds involve capital garnered from small households, and consequentially involve a considerable burden of financial regulation which is focused on investor protection.

On an international scale, a valuable counterweight to the mutual fund is the hedge fund. In a hedge fund, the minimum capital invested by a single investor is set to a substantial number of roughly Rs.50 million. At this point, it is presumed that customers have the capability of protecting their own interests. In this case, the role for the government reduces to contract enforcement and fraud. The entire regulatory overhead of investor protection can then be dispensed with. This induces considerable improvements in the sophistication of trading strategies which hedge funds are able to undertake when compared with what mutual funds are able to do. Internationally, hedge funds have become a valuable source of risk capital doing intelligent things which make markets more efficient. These benefits would also accrue to India when a domestic hedge fund industry is allowed.

SEBI now needs to enable a domestic hedge fund industry, alongside the domestic mutual fund industry. The identical tax pass-through status needs to be applied to hedge funds as is done for all fund managers, where income tax is applied to the customer of the fund manager and not to the vehicle of fund management.

A three-tier system for organized financial trading: So far, the processes of organized financial trading in India have focused on exchanges. This was an appropriate strategy because large and liquid public exchanges are the foundation of modern finance. However, now that considerable success has been achieved with NSE and BSE, SEBI needs to take a larger view of the business of organized financial trading, which needs to evolve into a three-tier system:

1. *Exchanges patronized by the public.* This is the base of the pyramid of organized financial trading, which comprises large exchanges like NSE and BSE, where the minimum market lot for transactions is roughly Rs.100,000. These are markets accessed by the general public, which necessitates the burden of investor protection. These are also the core liquidity pools of the economy, with enormous order books available at all times.
2. *Professional exchanges.* In addition, SEBI now needs to create a concept of a *professional exchange* where the minimum market lot is set at

Rs.50 million. At this point, it is presumed that customers have the capability of protecting their own interests. In this case, the role for the government reduces to contract enforcement and fraud. The entire regulatory overhead of investor protection can then be dispensed with. Systemic risk concerns can be addressed by requiring novation at a clearing corporation for any product where the open interest exceeds Rs.10 billion.

Such exchanges can be a hotbed of innovation, where new ideas are developed and proven. A flow of ideas can then take place in the public exchanges.[8]

3. *OTC trading.* The third venue for organized financial trading is the OTC market, where there are bilateral negotiations between counter-parties. Once again, the requirement of a minimum market lot of Rs.50 million needs to be applied, so as to avoid the difficulties of investor protection. But once this is done, the OTC market plays a valuable role by permitted trading in nonstandard contracts.

So far, public policy in India has focused on the first case: the large liquidity pools which constitute the major exchanges, such as NSE and BSE. This focus has been an appropriate one, for this is the necessary first milestone in building financial markets. Now that India has achieved success with NSE and BSE, it is time to embark on the next two levels: of setting up professional exchanges and an OTC market, where the market lot is set to Rs.50 million, and a window of opportunity is created for innovation and for achieving transactions that are inconvenient on the mainstream public exchanges. Just as hedge funds constitute an unregulated alternative which will apply competitive pressure upon mutual funds, this three-tier system will induce greater competition for all three elements, as opposed to the present solution.

In the absence of an OTC equity derivatives market in India, a substantial market has sprung up in Hong Kong which serves these needs. The task now constitutes achieving a sophisticated onshore OTC equity derivatives business, which is able to bring some of this business back to India. SEBI needs to develop the legal and regulatory capabilities in order to go from the first tier (public exchanges) to the other two tiers.

Creation of the Wholesale Asset Management industry: The MIFC report has pointed out that banks, mutual funds, insurance companies, pension

---

[8]This is reminiscent of the efforts in the United States at the Commodity Futures Trading Commission, the CFTC, which is the regulator of derivatives exchanges. In the Commodity Futures Modernization Act (CFMA) of 2000, the CFTC created this demarcation between public exchanges and professional exchanges. The latter could be a website. This triggered off a flurry of entry and innovation in derivatives exchanges.

funds, etc., are all different front ends for garnering assets for management. All these resources can be concentrated into a single pool of factories for fund management, where economies of scale are achieved. This allows a decoupling of the front end (which is largely about product design, regulatory compliance and marketing) from the back end (which is where the actual fund management happens). For this to be done, SEBI needs to enable a new pool of Wholesale Asset Managers (WMAs). Banks, mutual funds, insurance companies, pension funds, FIIs, large corporations etc. should have the *choice* of outsourcing their fund management work to these Wholesale Asset Managers.

Decontrol of mechanisms of market access: The MIFC report has focused on algorithmic trading through Direct Market Access (DMA) as a profoundly important feature of modern finance. On an international scale, more than half the business of exchanges comes through DMA. DMA is a powerful ally for growing market liquidity, particularly for relatively illiquid products where it is not cost-efficient for financial firms to depute human traders. SEBI must be agnostic about how orders come into an exchange: whether an order is typed in by a human being or sent in by a computer program that works on behalf of a human being is irrelevant. This same issue applies for many other kinds of access to exchanges which are limited or banned by SEBI. They include:

- Internet trading
- Trading on mobile phones
- Trading through terminals placed outside India

SEBI must be silent about the *mechanism* through which a customer order reaches the exchange. As with all well-run securities regulators worldwide, it is perfectly possible for SEBI to achieve all its functions without getting involved in this technological detail.

The risk management system of the exchanges: The risk management system of the exchanges in India were designed about 10 years ago. At the time, confidence and comfort with risk management was limited. Numerous safety factors were layered on to achieve more safety. As a consequence, the risk management system suffers from acute over-margining. Exchanges hold much more capital than is required from a safety viewpoint. This is inefficient for India, for it constitutes a waste of precious capital. A fundamental review of the risk management system is now required, drawing upon the last decade of experiences and the state of the art in financial economics, in order to come up with a sensible system.

SEBI's role in risk management also needs to be modified. At present, SEBI designs a risk management system which is blindly implemented by exchanges. As a consequence, exchanges have stopped thinking about risk management. A more useful approach involves risk management systems designed by exchanges based on an ongoing R&D program on risk management. SEBI's role should be to do six-monthly reviews of the risk management system using a team of domestic and foreign experts in risk management. SEBI's task should be to review a system proposed by an exchange to verify its soundness. The design of a risk management system should not be the task of SEBI; it should be the task of a continuous R&D effort conducted by exchanges.

Such an effort involves a genuine risk of an exchange favored by SEBI and given support for requiring lower margins, thus gaining market share at the price of taking on greater risk. Hence, SEBI needs to ensure that the team of domestic and foreign experts, which reviews the risk management system of all exchanges, features top quality experts, and has transparent mechanisms of functioning.

Elimination of segments of exchanges: One archaic feature of NSE and BSE is that their activities are broken up into segments. As an example, a cash market, a derivatives market, and a debt market are separate markets whose distinctions have become meaningless and need to be abolished. There should be only three elements in the relationship: a clearing corporation, an exchange and a member. Once a firm is a member, it should be able to trade on all the products offered by an exchange. The full position of the member firm should be utilized for computing the margin requirements. This unification of information will help improve risk management. This desegmentation of exchanges will reduce overhead costs and improve market efficiency.

Delicensing of a wide variety of derivatives products: SEBI's role in permitting derivatives trading represents a case of regulatory excess. At present, every strike price, every maturity, every underlying needs to be cleared by SEBI. Issues like strike prices and maturities need to be delicensed, for there is no value added that SEBI plays in preventing exchanges from thinking freely on these subjects. On the question of underlyings, SEBI needs to establish large negative lists of cases where no permission is required. As a practical matter, exchanges should need to come to SEBI for only one in ten contract approvals. The scope of derivatives trading on individual stocks now needs to be extended to roughly 500 stocks in India, with substantially bigger position limits. This needs to be supported by a short selling capability for all stocks.

Process re-engineering for the primary market: The processes of the primary market have, unfortunately, not been revolutionized on the scale that has been observed for the secondary market. With contemporary computer technology, a primary market for either debt or equity issuance organized in the following steps is eminently feasible:

1. If a firm is already a listed company, then a barrage of disclosure is already in place. In that case, securities issuance should only require a two-page disclosure about the new securities being issued. All other information about the company is already in the public domain.

2. The sale of securities needs to be done through a pure auction, where the firm only announces how many securities are up for sale. The bids on screen—and the bids alone—would determine the price. This replicates the price discovery of the secondary market. A minimum participation by Qualified Institutional Buyers (QIBs) in the winning bids to an extent such as 50% would ensure that retail investors are not being defrauded. It is important to eliminate the retail quota in the primary market. The auction need only take an hour. While the auction is going on, full transparency needs to be given back to all market participants, where the full demand schedule and the notional market clearing price is displayed in real-time.

3. These auctions can take place on Fridays. Over the weekend, securities can be sent into the depository accounts of all successful bidders, so that on Monday morning, the secondary market will start functioning smoothly for these securities.

4. Every member of NSE and BSE should be able to bring customer order flow to the primary market auction.

This four-step process defines a low-cost, high-efficiency structure for the primary market that achieves sound price discovery. It is in the best interests of issuing firms and investors, but it is, unfortunately, not in the interests of investment bankers, who get dis-intermediated. The role of the investment banker drops down to that of organizing a few road shows; for the rest, the *price discovery* takes place on the screen. SEBI needs to understand the natural self-interest of investment bankers, and disregard their views on how primary market securities issuance can be done.

Primary issuance in India has lost ground considerably because of high costs when compared with offshore venues. The four-step process outlined above can harness India's strengths—the enormous distribution capability of NSE and BSE—to win back this market.

Transformation of the corporate bond market: The above principles for the primary market would yield a major payoff in enabling low cost issuance of corporate bonds. Desegmentation of exchanges would enable a close link between the shares and bonds issued by a firm. In a rational world, both prices must fluctuate in response to information about the firm. Through desegmentation, it would become possible to have a unified trading screen where the shares of ITC and the corporate bonds of ITC are viewed and traded on a single screen. SEBI would then need to apply rules for mutual funds and FIIs, forcing all orders to be exposed to the exchange screen, as a way to achieve transparency for the corporate bond market. IRDA and RBI need to do likewise for insurance companies and banks. At that point, the corporate bond market would be ripe for takeoff.

Move toward elimination of taxation of transactions: The MIFC report has pointed out that transactions at NSE are roughly ten times costlier for the end-user when compared with those at CME. About 90% of that cost difference is accounted for by taxes and levies. SEBI needs to eliminate the levies that it controls, and work with other government agencies to remove the levies that they control, so as to get to the destination of zero taxation of transactions. This is the recommendation of public finance experts, and the norm internationally.

Call auctions for open and close: At present, in India, trading starts at 9:55 A.M. with continuous order matching on the limit order book. In the morning, spreads are wide, and gradually market participants become comfortable and trading gets going. This is an inefficient strategy for overcoming the uncertainties associated with overnight news. The call auction—a single price double auction—is a superior mechanism for achieving this same task. Exchanges could start at 9:50 A.M. with a call auction for ten minutes, which yields a single price at which a large number of buyers and sellers are matched. Once this price is known, the continuous trading can commence in full force. The call auction is also convenient for customers who then gain a mechanism for obtaining a trade at exactly the official opening price of the exchange. This is the mechanism used at the start of trading at NYSE. The identical strategy can be used for the official closing price. Currently, this is the average price seen over 30 minutes of trading from 3 P.M. to 3:30 P.M. This can be replaced by a call auction from 3 P.M. to 3:30 P.M. This would, once again, yield a single sharp price based on the matching of a large number of orders. It would enable derivatives arbitrage by giving the arbitrageur a mechanism to obtain the exact closing price without uncertainty.

A securities lending mechanism: As the MIFC report has emphasized, SEBI needs to ensure there is a mechanism for borrowing all manner of securities, ranging across corporate equities, corporate bonds, government bonds, etc. This would support short selling, which should be a part of the ordinary rhythm for all traded products.

Political economy in the mechanisms for consultation and policy thinking: SEBI's policy process needs to be illuminated by a sound committee process to discuss contemporary policy issues, and to review all key documents before they are released. These committees need to have a diverse mix of practitioners and intellectuals. Many of the mistakes of SEBI in recent years could have been avoided through access to good quality expertise in committees.

One key challenge here is that of overcoming the natural self-interest of practitioners who would like to maximize their own profit rates. As an example, when the SEBI Primary Markets Advisory Committee is dominated by investment bankers, fundamental surgery of the primary market is unlikely to be recommended. SEBI needs to set up a quarterly process of benchmarking the costs and delays of a representative range of transactions in India against the situation found in Hong Kong, Singapore, Dubai and London, so as to constantly measure India's global competitiveness. These benchmarking studies need to be released to the public each quarter, so that there is a greater awareness of the gap that separates India and the world. This external pressure would help in overcoming domestic political economy. This is reminiscent of India's reforms of the real economy, where globalization was crucial for overcoming the barriers of domestic political economy.

11.3.2 Transparency and Information Disclosure

Fees of mutual fund agents: Many observers have voiced concerns about the sales practices of the mutual fund and insurance industries, where very large charges are paid to agents/distributors. SEBI cannot ban the payment of a fee to an agent by the customer. However, there is a legitimate role for SEBI to insist on transparency. On the stock market, when a customer buys shares through a broker, a contract note is given out to the customer clearly unbundling the amount of money that was invested and the intermediation fee of the stockbroker. In similar fashion, SEBI must insist that the mutual fund agent/distributor give the customer a clear bill that transparently reveals how much money went upstream to the mutual fund and how much money went to the agent.

On a similar note, the statements sent by mutual funds to their customers should clearly unbundle the fees and expenses charged by the mutual fund, as opposed to the core investment performance, in a standardized format. Once again, the goal is that of having informed consumers who know exactly what they are paying for fund management. In addition, SEBI's recent proposal, requiring mutual funds to create an Internet-based avenue through which customers have the *choice* of buying mutual fund units without going through the agent/distributor, is a sound one. Once there is transparency about the charges of agents/distributors, customers should have the *choice* of disintermediating them using the Internet.

These efforts need to be implemented at IRDA also, so that customers face the identical information-rich situation when buying fund management products from insurance companies.

High-quality quarterly disclosures: Quarterly release of information in India has been a big step forward in the ability of markets to process information about firms. This needs to be carried through to the destination of a quarterly release of the profit and loss statement and the balance sheet, both of which should be audited.

Treatment of bond cashflows: In India, at present, default on corporate bonds sometimes takes the form of brownouts, where politically influential bondholders are paid coupons on time while other bondholders are not. In addition, there is no public disclosure about default events. These problems can be solved by routing corporate bond cash flows through depositories. Each depository should know the full set of cash flows that are expected for all corporate bonds. Each depository knows how many corporate bonds it holds, in dematerialized form. Firms must be required to make a payment to each depository for the consolidated amount associated with the corporate bonds held with each depository. If there is a shortfall of even a rupee in the payment by a firm to the depository, then the depository should put out a press release announcing default on a corporate bond.

Mandatory release of high quality data by exchanges: SEBI needs to assist the development of sophistication in algorithmic trading based on Direct Market Access (DMA) by requiring that exchanges do more on the public goods of information disclosure. The three key steps are:

1. The computers at exchanges must be synchronized to atomic clocks through the Network Time Protocol (NTP), so that all time stamps are exact and comparable.
2. It should be possible to buy a high-speed telecommunications link to the exchange where, in real-time, the top 20 orders on the buy and sell side of all order books, along with traded prices and quantities, is given out in real-time.
3. Historical files with this information, for at least the last ten years, should be freely available from the exchange. This historical data would enable the statistical research required for constructing algorithmic trading systems.

11.3.3 ENFORCEMENT

High quality cases which are able to win at SAT: The first task of SEBI is to win high-visibility cases about market manipulation at the Securities Appellate Tribunal (SAT). In recent years, too often, SEBI enforcement actions have been overturned by SAT on the grounds that SEBI had not adequately proven the guilt of the accused, thus undermining the credibility of SEBI's enforcement work. There is a sense that the entities targeted by SEBI are often not the guilty ones, and the sense that SEBI lacks the competence to prove guilt beyond all reasonable doubt.

Achieving a reputation as a high-quality enforcement agency is a critical task for SEBI. As with all policing work, the bulk of the role of the government lies in achieving *deterrence*. If would-be miscreants believed there was a great chance of being caught, prosecuted and punished, then there would be less labor and capital invested into murky business plans.

Training for SEBI staff: This requires staff training at SEBI. The primary focus needs to be on conceptual clarity of the words speculation, arbitrage and manipulation. Too often, SEBI has mistaken the legitimate activities of arbitrage and speculation for the illegitimate activity of market manipulation. SEBI needs training by global financial regulators to learn the definition of manipulation and how it is proved in court.

One area where there is a direct link between staff quality and the needs of the economy is in the position limits for derivatives. When SEBI has low-quality staff, there is an incentive to avoid market manipulation by imposing small position limits through strategies such as a short squeeze. This imposes a cost on the economy by limiting the extent to which the derivatives can be used to achieve the goals of economic agents. When SEBI has better quality staff, enforcement against market manipulation will become more effective, enabling bigger position limits, and thus making derivatives more useful for the economy.

A dedicated three-member bench: SEBI suffers from overzealous punishments prescribed by investigating officers without giving the accused adequate opportunity to disagree with SEBI's findings. At a purely internal level, it would help if three of the SEBI members made up a bench. These members would be kept completely apart from the work of surveillance and investigation. A distinct team within SEBI would prepare a case file for a small hearing (within SEBI), where the prosecution makes a case and the accused gets an opportunity to defend himself. The bench would then choose whether guilt has been proved beyond all reasonable doubt, and would then award penalties.

This procedure would avoid the problem of overzealous SEBI investigators who get too easily convinced of the guilt of the person they are investigating. It exposes SEBI prosecution efforts to a first-level scrutiny before any case reaches SAT.

Case studies in enforcement: Financial firms are unclear about what SEBI does. It is not clear what manipulation means; it is not clear how SEBI works; it is not clear what SEBI will do in a given situation. In order to alleviate this situation, every month, SEBI must release one case study paper which gives full documentation about one enforcement case, showing all the steps about what SEBI did, with their full rationale.

11.4 CONCLUSION

Indian finance consists of one well-functioning element—the equity market—amidst a landscape of malperforming markets. The currency, fixed income, commodity and credit markets have basic deficiencies. While many of the apparent structures of markets are in place, the essence of a market—speculative trading by a wide variety of players without entry barriers—is lacking. There is a great deal of trading technology; many IOSCO checklists are satisfied. This gives the appearance of a sophisticated financial system to a casual observer. However, there is an absence of meaningful price discovery or liquidity in markets other than the equity market.

This sorry state of affairs is rooted in mistakes in the regulation of institutional investors, a flawed regulatory architecture, an obsolete set of laws, financial firms which are too small and too narrow in their outlook, distortions induced by flaws of taxation, capital controls, and a tradition of autarky. It is not hard to make a checklist of irrational rules that constitute the core of India's license-permit raj in finance. It is important to understand that these irrational rules are not based on ignorance, incompetence or oversight; they are the product of meticulous thought and care. When a market or a transaction is blocked by a rule, it is generally intended to be that way. From 1991 onward, a considerable effort at incremental progress has been attempted in all parts of finance. Yet, only one component of Indian finance has blossomed: the equity market.

There are deeper reasons that inhibit progress. These need to be understood and confronted. They involve reforms to the regulatory architecture, i.e., the role and function of the various regulatory agencies that deal with finance, and the macroeconomic policy framework.

CHAPTER 12

What Can Global Financial Firms Do with India?

As Figure 12.1 shows, there has been a dramatic upsurge of net capital flows into the country. Starting from values such as $5 billion a quarter roughly five years ago, the latest data shows that $33.9 billion came into India in the July through September 2007 quarter. However, the involvement of global financial firms in India is much bigger than suggested by this data.

Data on net capital flows hide the important *gross* capital flows that are taking place. As an example, while 2.34% of GDP came into the country in 2006–2007 by way of inbound FDI, 1% of GDP flowed out of the country by way of outbound FDI by Indian firms (Figure 12.2). This shows up as a net capital inflow into India on account of an FDI of 1.34% of GDP, but from the viewpoint of financial firms, the base of transactions that are customers for international financial services associated with cross-border FDI is 3.34% of GDP.

The demand for international financial services is, of course, driven by the integration of a country into the global economy, across both the current account and the capital account. Estimates offered in Mistry (2007) suggest that in 2005, roughly $13 billion was paid for the purchase of international financial services linked to India. This number is expected to quadruple by 2015. This suggests that India-related business is an important area of business for all global financial firms.

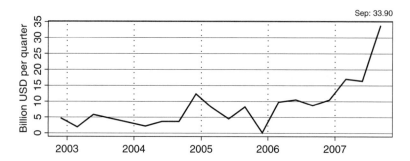

FIGURE 12.1 Net Capital Flows into India

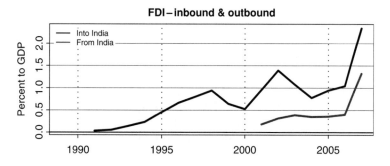

FIGURE 12.2 Inbound and Outbound FDI

12.1 PORTFOLIO INVESTMENT

Foreign institutional investors (FIIs) are permitted to operate in the Indian equity market, with some constraints. By default, the ownership of all FIIs put together in a firm is capped at 24%, but the firm can raise this to 98%. In practice, the constraint of 24% (or a larger constraint set by the firm) is rarely binding. Any one FII is blocked from owning more than 10% of any one firm.

FIIs have to register with SEBI, in order to have convertibility. They are able to bring capital in and out of the country, hedge currency exposures using the currency forward market, and trade on the equity derivatives market. Unlike the Chinese QFI framework, there are no quantitative restrictions or limitations on which global financial firms can participate in the Indian market (other than the two limits described above).

Thus the Indian policy framework gives FIIs an essentially open capital account, while requiring overhead costs of registration and reporting in India. There are two kinds of entities who do not trade in the Indian market through the FII framework: those that are ineligible (e.g., individuals) and those that find the overhead costs unacceptable. In order to overcome these constraints, an OTC derivatives market has sprung up for access products called participatory notes (PN). In this market, eligible FIIs sell OTC derivatives or linear exposures to others.

The PN mechanism creates value by reducing the burden of the Indian securities transaction tax. To the extent that an OTC dealer obtains offsetting trades in his PN book, hedging trades do not take place in India, and the transactions tax in India is avoided. In 2007, India placed some restrictions on this market,[1] thus encouraging more firms to step forward and become registered FIIs. This led to a certain growth in FII registration; in January 2008, there were 1,255 registered FIIs.

The FII framework is oriented toward equity spot and equity derivatives. Thus far, the adaptation of this framework for enabling global investments into the onshore, rupee-denominated bond market—either government or corporate bonds—has not taken place. Investment by all FIIs, put together, in government bonds is capped at $2.6 billion. Similarly, the investment by all FIIs, put together, in corporate bonds is capped at $1.5 billion.[2] With a large number of FIIs seeking to get invested in these markets, there is a particularly unfortunate bureaucratic process of allocation of these picayune limits between desirous firms. In this, what India has done is reminiscent of the Chinese QFI procedure.

12.2 PRIVATE EQUITY

Substantial PE transactions are taking place in India with almost all the assets under management being raised overseas. There are three distinct tracks involved. If a PE investment takes place in an unlisted firm, it falls under India's FDI rules. In other words, because India permits 100% FDI in, say, the manufacture of ball bearings, the foreign PE fund is able to obtain a substantial stake in a firm making ball bearings without difficulty.

A PE fund buying into listed companies for the purpose of Indian capital controls is an FII investment. In order to do such investments, the PE fund has to become a registered FII. Once this is done, there are two kinds of transactions: PIPEs (where the company sells shares directly to the PE fund) or ordinary secondary market transactions (where the PE fund buys shares on the secondary market). These two cases are not differentiated by capital controls.

---

[1] See http://ajayshahblog.blogspot.com/2007/10/middle-muddle.html.

[2] See http://ajayshahblog.blogspot.com/2006/04/doing-everything-wrong-on-debt-inflows.html.

12.3   FDI

In most parts of finance, foreign financial firms are able to establish operations in India, but there are many constraints. Foreign insurance companies cannot sell insurance products in India except by having an ownership stake in an insurance company regulated by IRDA. This ownership is restricted to 26%. Similarly, foreign banks cannot operate in India other than through FDI, and foreign ownership is restricted to 74%. In both areas, at a practical level, foreign firms have not achieved an important role.

The three areas where it is possible for foreign financial firms to set up operations in India with the least impediments, and where foreign firms have in fact built up a substantial presence, are securities firms, mutual funds and non-bank finance companies. In these three areas, as a practical matter, foreign firms are able to comfortably operate and have an important role in Indian finance.

12.4   THE MAURITIUS ROUTE

Foreign investment into India that comes from Mauritius has a preferential tax treatment: capital gains earned in India by a Mauritius-registered entity is exempt from the Indian capital gains tax. For this reason, many international firms prefer to establish a Mauritius entity which then invests in India. These practices are found with both FIIs and with private equity firms. For this same reason, roughly half the FDI coming into India apparently originates from Mauritius.

12.5   INDIA-RELATED FINANCIAL BUSINESS OUTSIDE INDIA

There are three major elements of India-related activities which take place outside the country. These are immune to Indian capital controls, and any global financial firm can easily participate in these areas. The first concerns offshore borrowing by Indian firms. While FII investment in the domestic debt market has been stifled and the domestic debt market is moribund, Indian firms have embarked on substantial offshore borrowing. Firms are allowed to borrow abroad through external commercial borrowing. This includes loans or bond issues abroad that are foreign currency denominated. Small transactions are processed by the government with automatic approval, and bigger transactions require permission. Under the present policy framework:

- External borrowing by firms must be of at least 3 years maturity for borrowing below $20 million, and at least 5 years maturity beyond.
- Borrowing up to $500 million by a firm for certain specified end-uses is allowed without requiring permission.

This debt, and credit default swaps on these firms, now constitutes a substantial market overseas.

The second area is a group of three OTC derivatives markets: derivatives on Indian equity (called participatory notes, sold by registered FIIs to others), derivatives on the Indian rupee and derivatives on rupee interest rates.[3] In particular, the nondeliverable forward (NDF) market on the Indian rupee has become an important market, particularly owing to the regulations that prohibit customers of participatory notes from trading on the onshore rupee-dollar forward market. In addition, some international bond issues have started using the rupee as the currency in which the bond is denominated.[4]

The third area consists of ADR/GDR issues. While the bulk of the market capitalization and trading takes place in India, particularly on the equity derivatives market at NSE, the ADR/GDR market continues to be important. A few products, such as the Infosys and ICICI paper listed in the United States, are remarkably liquid.

[3] See Box 4.2, page 56, in Mistry (2007).

[4] See http://ajayshahblog.blogspot.com/search?q=internationalisation.

Sources

This appendix is an annotated guide to source materials for learning and tracking the Indian economy and Indian financial markets.

National Stock Exchange (NSE) produces two outstanding books every year titled *Indian Securities Market Review* (ISMR) and *NSE Fact Book*. These serve as excellent materials on the equity market, and the other activities of NSE. They cover market design, regulations, traded products, NSE member firms, and liquidity. In addition, NSE produces a monthly newsletter about the derivatives market. All these materials are free downloads on the net.

NSE produces one CD every month ("NSE Release A CD") about the equity spot market, which is available to users at a nominal cost. It contains intraday trades and market index values, and offers four snapshots of the entire limit order book every day (at 11 A.M., 12 noon, 1 P.M. and 2 P.M.). These CDs are an invaluable resource for analyzing intraday data about the equity market. Comparable data on all other parts of Indian finance are not available.

Clearing Corporation of India (CCIL) is a key element of the currency and fixed income markets, making data captured at CCIL pertain to the overall market. CCIL produces a monthly magazine called *Rakshitra* which can be downloaded free on the net (http://www.ccilindia.com/newsletter.aspx).

Centre for Monitoring Indian Economy (CMIE) produces a report every year titled *Industry: Financial Aggregates and Ratios* which is the best source of summary statistics about the universe of firms. A strong set of databases about India by CMIE is available at http://www.business-beacon.com.

The NIPFP-DEA Research Program on Capital Flows and Consequences generates interesting research. This can be found at http://www.nipfp.org.in/nipfp-dea-program/index.html.

The four major business newspapers in India are *Economic Times*, *Business Standard*, *Financial Express* and *Livemint*. The bulk of the content on all four websites is free. Two interesting blogs on Indian finance are by Jayanth Varma and Ajay Shah.

Abbreviations

Abbreviations commonly used in Indian financial markets

ADR   American Depository Receipt
ARCIL   Asset Reconstruction Company of India Ltd.
BIFR   Board for Industrial and Financial Reconstruction
BIFR   Bureau of Industrial and Financial Reconstruction
BSE   Bombay Stock Exchange
CARE   Credit Analysis and REsearch Ltd.
CCIL   Clearing Corporation of India Ltd.
CDSL   Central Depository Services Ltd.
CIBIL   Credit Information Bureau of India
CLU   Change of Land Use
CMIE   Centre for Monitoring Indian Economy
CP   Commercial Paper
CRA   Credit Rating Agency
CRISIL   Credit Rating Information System of India Ltd.
DCA   Department of Company Affairs
DFI   Development Financial Institution
DMO   Debt Management Office
ECA   Essential Commodities Act of 1955
EPFO   Employees Provident Fund Organization
FCCB   Foreign Currency Convertible Bond
FCRA   Forward Contract Regulation Act of 1952
FDI   Foreign Direct Investment
FII   Foreign Institutional Investor
FMC   Forward Markets Commission
GDR   Global Depository Receipt
GIFT   Gujarat International Financial Tec-City
GOI   Government of India

IBFC   International Finance and Business Centre
ICICI   Industrial Credit and Investment Corporation of India
ICRA   Investment Information and Credit Rating Agency of India Ltd.
IDB   Industrial Development Bank of India
INR   Indian Rupee
IOD   Intimation of Disapproval
IRDA   Insurance Regulatory and Development Agency
ISIN   International Securities Identification Number
JNPT   Jawaharlal Nehru Port Trust
LCFI   Large Complex Financial Institution
LIC   Life Insurance Corporation of India
LSO   Loan Sell Off
MCX   Multi-Commodity Exchange
NBFC   Non-Bank Finance Company
NCAER   National Council of Applied Economic Research
NCDEX   National Commodity & Derivatives Exchange
NCMSL   National Collateral Management System Ltd.
NDA   National Democratic Alliance
NDF   Non-Deliverable Forward (in currency market)
NDS   Negotiated Dealing System (of RBI)
NFO   New Fund Offering
NHAI   National Highway Authority of India
NMCE   National Multi-Commodity Exchange of Ahmadabad
NREGA   National Rural Employment Guarantee Act
NRI   Non-Resident Indian
NSCCL   National Securities Clearing Corporation Ltd.
NSDL   National Securities Depository Ltd.
NSE   National Stock Exchange
PCM   Professional Clearing Members
PD   Primary Dealer
PE   Private Equity
PFRDA   Pension Fund Regulation and Development Agency
PIPE   Private Investment in Public Equity
PN   Participatory Note
PSE   Public Sector Entities
PSU   Public Sector Undertaking
PTC   Pass Through Certificate
QIP   Qualified Institutional Placements
RBI   Reserve Bank of India (the central bank)
SARFAESI   Securitization and Reconstruction of Financial Assets and
   Enforcement of Security Investment Act of 2002
SEBI   Securities and Exchange Board of India

SEZ Special Economic Zone
SGL Securities General Ledger
TCM Trading and Clearing Members
TM Trading Members
UPA United Progressive Alliance
UTI Unit Trust of India
WDM Wholesale Debt Market (on NSE)

Interpreting Those Strange Indian Numbers

As long as you get your information filtered through the *Economist* or *Financial Times* or *Wall Street Journal*, you will not need to know the following. But if you ever pick up an Indian newspaper, visit an Indian website or try to do a fundamental analysis on an Indian stock, take note.

Different countries format numbers differently and call large numbers by different names. Americans grew up with hundreds, thousands, millions, billions and, if they went far enough in school, trillions and some other big numbers. When numbers are written, commas are used to group them in sets of three numerals, starting from the right—e.g., the Earth is 93,000,000.5 miles from the sun. (We added the .5 for illustrative purposes.)

Europeans group numbers in the same way as Americans, but use commas where Americans use decimal points and decimal points where Americans use commas. Thus Europe is 93.000.000,5 miles from the sun.

Indians grew up with lakhs and crores. A lakh (rhymes with Yak) is 100,000 and a crore (rhymes with score) is 100 lakhs, or 10,000,000, though that placement of commas is American, not Indian style. In India, commas are used differently and this grows naturally out of the lakhs and crores. Going right to left, the first three numbers are grouped as in America or Europe, but after that, everything is in groups of two. The Earth, in India, is 9,30,00,000 miles or 9.3 crore miles from the sun.

In Indian financial markets, you will generally only deal with lakhs and crores, so there are only three things to remember: A lakh is 1,00,000 (Indian style) and 100,000 (American style). A crore is 100 lakhs, or 1,00,00,000 (Indian style) and 10,000,000 (American style).

Bibliography

Bhagwati, J. (1993). *India in Transition: Freeing the Economy*. Oxford University Press, 1st edition.

Bhattacharya, S., Patel, U. (2003). "Reform strategies in the Indian financial sector." *Technical report*, Conference on India's and China's experience with reforms and growth, IMF and NCAER, New Delhi, November 15–16, 2003.

Bhattacharya, S., Patel, U.R. (2005). "New regulatory institutions in India: White knights or Trojan horses?" In D. Kapur, P.B. Mehta (eds.), "Public institutions in India: Performance and design," chapter 10, pp. 406–456. Oxford University Press.

Bose, S., Coondoo, D. (2003). "A study of the Indian Corporate Bond Market," *Money & Finance*, Vol. 2, No. 12, January–March 2003.

Bubna, A., Prabhala, N.R. (2007). "When bookbuilding meets IPOs." *Technical report*, Indian School of Business. URL: http://ssrn.com/abstract=972757.

Chandavarkar, A. (2005). "Towards an independent federal Reserve Bank of India: A political economy agenda for reconstitution." *Economic and Political Weekly*. August 27, 2005.

Claessens, S., Schmukler, S. (2006). "International financial integration through equity markets: Which firms from which countries go global?" *Technical report*, World Bank.

Dave, S. (2006). "India's pension reforms: A case study in complex institutional change." In S. Narayan (ed.), "Documenting reforms: Case studies from India," pp. 149–170. Macmillan India, New Delhi. URL: http://www.mayin.org/ajayshah/A/Dave2006_saga.pdf.

Dossani, R., Desai, A. (2006a). "Accessing Early-Stage Risk Capital in India." *Technical report*, The South Asia Initiating Shorenstein APARC, and The Indus Entrepreneurs (TIE). URL: http://aparc.stanford.edu/publications/accessing_earlystage_risk_capital_in_india/.

Dossani, R., et al. (2006b). "Report of the Committee on Technology Innovation and Venture Capital." *Technical report*, Planning Commission, Govt. of India. URL: http://aparc.stanford.edu/publications/report_of_the_committee_on_technology_innovation_and_venture_captial/.

Echeverri-Gent, J. (2007). "Politics of market microstructure." In R. Mukherji (ed.), "India's Economic Transition: The Politics of Reform," chapter 11. Oxford University Press, New Delhi.

Gopalan, R., Gormley, T.A. (2007). "Stock market liberalisation and the going public decision." *Technical report*, University of Washington. URL: http://ssrn.com/abstract=1010116.

Gordon, J., Gupta, P. (2004). "Understanding India's services revolution." *Technical report*, IMF. URL: http://ideas.repec.org/p/imf/imfwpa/04-171.html.

Gorham, M.(2006). "Incredible India-Formidable Futures." Futures Industry, September/October 2006. URL: http://www.futuresindustry.org/fi-magazine-home.asp?a=1144.

Gorham, M., Thomas, S., Shah, A. (2005). "India: The Crouching Tiger." Futures Industry, May/June 2005. URL: http://www.futuresindustry.org/fi-magazine-home.asp?a=1039.

Green, C.J., Murinde, V., Suppakitjarak, J. (2002). "Corporate financial structures in India." *Technical Report 02/4*, Loughborough University.

Hanson, J. (2003). "Indian banking: Market liberalisation and the pressures for institutional and market framework reform." In A. Krueger, S.Z. Chinoy (eds.), "Reforming India's External, Financial and Fiscal Policies," Stanford Studies in International Economics and Development. Stanford University Press.

Kelkar, V. (2004a). "FRBM Implementation Task Force Report." *Committee report*, Ministry of Finance, Government of India. URL: http://finmin.nic.in/downloads/reports/frbm/start.htm.

Kelkar, V. (2004b). "India; On the growth turnpike." *Technical report*, Australian National University; K.R. Narayanan Memorial Lecture. URL: http://rspas.anu.edu.au/papers/narayanan/2004oration.pdf.

Kelkar, V. (2005). "India's economic future: Moving beyond State capitalism." *Technical report*, Gadgil Memorial Lecture. URL: http://www.medcindia.org/cgi-bin/index_files/middle_files/kelkar%20lecture.pdf.

Khatkhate, D. (2005). "Reserve Bank of India: A study in the separation and attrition of powers." In D. Kapur, P.B. Mehta (eds.), "Public institutions in India: Performance and design," chapter 8, pp. 320–350. Oxford University Press.

Kishore, A., Prasad, A. (2007). "Indian subnational finances: Recent performance." *Technical Report WP/07/205*, IMF.

Lahiri, A., Kannan, R. (2001). "India's fiscal deficits and their sustainability in perspective." *Technical report*, NIPFP.

Love, I., Peria, M.S.M. (2005). "Firm Financing in India: Recent Trends and Patterns." *Technical Report WPS 3476*, World Bank Working Paper Series 3476.

McGee, R.W. (2008). "Corporate governance in Asia: Eight case studies." *Technical report*, Florida International University.

Mistry, P. (2007). "Making Mumbai an International Financial Centre." *Committee report*, Sage Publishing and Ministry of Finance, Government of India. URL: http://finmin.nic.in/mifc.html.

Mitton, T. (2005). "Why Have Debt Ratios Increased for Firms in Emerging Markets?" *Technical report*, Brigham Young University. URL: http://www.darden. virginia.edu/em/PDFs/Mitton_Todd.pdf.

Mor, N., Chandrasekar, R. (2005). "Banking sector reform in India." *Technical report*, ICICI Bank. URL: http://scid.stanford.edu/events/India2005/Mor%205-18-05.pdf.

Panagariya, A. (2005). "India's trade reform: Progress, impact and future strategy." In S. Bery, B. Bosworth, A. Panagariya (eds.), "The India Policy Forum 2004," Brookings Institution Press and NCAER.

Patnaik, I. (2003). "India's policy stance on reserves and the currency." *Technical report*, ICRIER Working Paper No. 108. URL: http://www.icrier.org/pdf/wp108.pdf.

Patnaik, I. (2005). "India's experience with a pegged exchange rate." In S. Bery, B. Bosworth, A. Panagariya (eds.), "The India Policy Forum 2004," pp. 189–226. Brookings Institution Press and NCAER. URL: http://openlib.org/home/ila/PDFDOCS/Patnaik2004_implementation.pdf.

Patnaik, I. (2007). "India's currency regime and its consequences." *Economic and Political Weekly*. URL: http://openlib.org/home/ila/PDFDOCS/11182.pdf.

Patnaik, I., Shah, A. (2004). "Interest rate volatility and risk in Indian banking." *Technical Report WP/04/17*, IMF. URL: http://www.imf.org/external/pubs/cat/longres.cfm?sk=17095.0.

Patnaik, I., Vasudevan, D. (2000). "Trade Misinvoicing and Capital Flight from India." *Journal of International Economic Studies*, **14**, 99–108.

Pradhan, B.K., Saluja, M.R., Roy, P.K., Shetty, S.L. (2003). "Household savings and investment behaviour in India." *Technical report*, EPWRF and NCAER.

Raghunathan, V., Varma, J.R. (1992). "CRISIL Rating: When Does AAA Mean B?" *Vikalpa*, **17**(2), 35–42.

Rajan, R., Shah, A. (2005)."New directions in Indian financial sector policy." In P. Basu (ed.), "India's financial sector: Recent reforms, future challenges," chapter 4, pp. 54–87. Macmillan.

Rajan, R., Zingales, L. (1995). "What do we know about capital structure? Some evidence from international data." *Journal of Finance*, **50**, 1421–1460.

Sarkar, J., Sarkar, S. (2000). "Large shareholder activism in corporate governance in developing countries: Evidence from India." *International Review of Finance*, **1**(3).

Sarkar, S., Sarkar, J., Bhaumik, S. (1998). "Does Ownership Always Matter? – Evidence from the Indian Banking Industry." *Journal of Comparative Economics*, **26**(2).

Shah, A. (2006). "Indian pension reform: A sustainable and scalable approach." In D.A. Kelly, R.S. Rajan, G.H.L. Goh (eds.), "Managing globalisation: Lessons from China and India," chapter 7. World Scientific. URL: http://www.mayin.org/ajayshah/PDFDOCS/Shah2005_sustainable_pension_reform.pdf.

Shah, A. (2008). "New issues in Indian macro policy." In T.N. Ninan (ed.), "Business Standard India." Business Standard Books. URL: http://www. mayin.org/ajayshah/PDFDOCS/Shah2008_whatchanged.pdf.

Shah, A., Patnaik, I. (2007a). "India's experience with capital flows: The elusive quest for a sustainable current account deficit." In S. Edwards (ed.), "Capital controls and capital flows in emerging economies: Policies, practices and consequences," chapter 13, pp. 609–643. The University of Chicago Press. URL: http://www.nber.org/papers/w11387.

Shah, A., Patnaik, I. (2007b). "What makes home bias abate? The evolution of foreign ownership of Indian firms." *Technical report*, NIPFP.

Shah, A., Thomas, S. (2000). "David and Goliath: Displacing a primary market." *Journal of Global Financial Markets*, 1(1), 14–21.

Sheng, A. (2006). "The art of reform." *Finance and Development*, 43(2).

Shirai, S. (2004). "Assessing the impact of financial and capital market reforms on firms corporate financing pattersn in India." *South Asia Economic Journal*, 4(2).

Thomas, S. (2003). "The jaggery futures market at Muzaffarnagar: Status and policy recommendations." In S. Thomas (ed.), "Derivatives markets in India 2003," chapter 6, pp. 123–142. Tata McGraw-Hill.

Thomas, S. (2005). "Agricultural commodity markets in India: Policy issues for growth." In P. Basu (ed.), "India's financial sector: Recent reforms, future challenges," chapter 8, pp. 176–196. Macmillan.

Thomas, S. (2006a). "How the financial sector in India was reformed." In S. Narayan (ed.), "Documenting reforms: Case studies from India," pp. 171–210. Macmillan India, New Delhi. URL: http://www.igidr.ac.in/ ~susant/PDFDOCS/Thomas2005_financialsectorreforms.pdf.

Thomas, S. (2006b). "Resilience of liquidity in Indian securities markets." *Economic and Political Weekly*, **XLI**(32), 3452–3454.

Topalova, P. (2004). "Overview of the Indian corporate sector: 1989–2002." *Technical Report WP/04/64*, IMF.

Index

A

ABS. *See* Asset-backed securities
ADR. *See* American Depository Receipt
Agency business, 169, 170
Agricultural contracts
  chana, 118
  guar, 118
  jeera, 117
  rapeseed-mustard (R/M) seed, 118
American Depository Receipt (ADR), 52, 147, 217
Anglo-Saxon framework, 10, 11
ARCIL. *See* Asset Reconstruction Company of
  India, Ltd.
Asian Corporate Governance Association, 14
Asset-backed securities (ABS), 99
Asset prices, correlation with global prices, 26
Asset Reconstruction Company of India, Ltd.
  (ARCIL), 111
Assets
  banks ranked by, 178t
  of nonfinancial firms, 37
  fixed, 37–39
  structure of, 37t
Assets under management (AUM), 70, 105, 107,
  190, 215
  of mutual funds industry, 183, 184
Auctions, 87, 107, 155n, 208
AUM. *See* Assets under management
Axis Bank, 178

B

Bangalore international airport
  features of, 145
  infrastructure, 144–146
Banking
  cost of intermediation in, 179t
  policy-induced stasis in, 176–179
  problems, 10
Bank Nationalization Act, 178
Banks, 173
  big, 177, 178t
  deposits, international data for, 10
  financial characteristics of, 174t
  foreign, 174, 177, 196
  implications for economy, 180
  leverage of, 179
  market share of, 175t
  micro-management of, 177
  ownership groups of, 174, 175
  private, 174
  privatization of, 178

public sector unit (PSU), 95, 174, 176
  ranked by assets, 178t
Basket trades, 60
Benchmark Asset Management Company, 118
Benchmark mutual fund, 185, 186
Benefit fund managers, 165
Bhagwati, J., 4
Bhattacharya, S., 195n, 201n
BIFR. *See* Bureau of Industrial and Financial
  Reconstruction
Black money, 135
Bombay Stock Exchange (BSE), 11, 29, 53, 109,
  147, 168, 186, 204
  in CDSL, 56
  crisis at, 29
  features, 55, 206
Bond-Currency-Derivatives Nexus, 192, 192f, 193
Bond market, 11, 40
  key feature, 94
  trading venues, 92
Bonds
  central government, 96
  corporate, 95
  coupon bearing, 82
  issued by private firms, 98
  liquidity of, 86, 87, 94
  long-dated, 82
  municipal, 97
  pattern of issue maturity for, 83, 84
  prices of, 87
  PSU, 97
  state government. *See* State government bonds
  subnational, 95
  treasury, 82
Book-building process, 53
Borrowing and lending, 82
Bose, S., 105
British Banker's Association, 123
Broad market, 13, 189
Brokerage firms, 56, 125, 126, 170, 171. *See also*
  ICICI Direct
  financial characteristics of, 170t
BSE. *See* Bombay Stock Exchange
BSE Realty Index, 147
BSE Sensex
  calculation, 59
  market indexes, 59, 60
Bubna, A., 54
Buoyant business cycle conditions, 25, 171, 174,
  177, 179
Bureau of Industrial and Financial Reconstruction
  (BIFR), 101

ORLAND PARK
PUBLIC LIBRARY
A Natural Connection

**14921 Ravinia Avenue
Orland Park, IL 60462**

**708-428-5100
orlandparklibrary.org**